National Finance

Yunxian Chen
National Finance
A Chinese Perspective

Translated by
Heming Yong

Yunxian Chen
Advisory Council of Guangdong Province
Guangzhou, China

Translated by
Heming Yong
Guangdong University of Finance
Guangzhou, China

Jing Peng, Dinggang Chen, and Zemin Chen

ISBN 978-981-33-6091-4   ISBN 978-981-33-6092-1 (eBook)
https://doi.org/10.1007/978-981-33-6092-1

© The Editor(s) (if applicable) and The Author(s), under exclusive licence to Springer Nature Singapore Pte Ltd. 2021
This work is subject to copyright. All rights are solely and exclusively licensed by the Publisher, whether the whole or part of the material is concerned, specifically the rights of translation, reprinting, reuse of illustrations, recitation, broadcasting, reproduction on microfilms or in any other physical way, and transmission or information storage and retrieval, electronic adaptation, computer software, or by similar or dissimilar methodology now known or hereafter developed.
The use of general descriptive names, registered names, trademarks, service marks, etc. in this publication does not imply, even in the absence of a specific statement, that such names are exempt from the relevant protective laws and regulations and therefore free for general use.
The publisher, the authors and the editors are safe to assume that the advice and information in this book are believed to be true and accurate at the date of publication. Neither the publisher nor the authors or the editors give a warranty, expressed or implied, with respect to the material contained herein or for any errors or omissions that may have been made. The publisher remains neutral with regard to jurisdictional claims in published maps and institutional affiliations.

This Palgrave Macmillan imprint is published by the registered company Springer Nature Singapore Pte Ltd.
The registered company address is: 152 Beach Road, #21-01/04 Gateway East, Singapore 189721, Singapore

Preface

National finance is a new subject, and *National Finance—A Chinese Perspective* is a new work that deals with, from a Chinese perspective, the most essential, immediate, and intricate issues in national financial development with focus on the "hard nuts" that have to be cracked on both central and regional levels and on the fronts of both offshore and onshore finance. It attempts to discuss several formidable challenges that a country, particularly its top government officials, must meet in developing finance: How should national finance develop and overtake in the face of rising financial industries? How should it respond to the influx of AI+blockchain technologies? How does a country guard against and cope with systematic or regional financial risks with security, fluidity, and profitability serving as its cornerstones? How can it build up and promote the new international financial system and governance amid international financial powers around the world?

In order to address these issues, the author unambiguously proposes the top-level design of national finance from the perspectives of financial notions, approaches, institutions, and structuring, despite the obvious contradictions between the much publicized theories of laissez-faire economy and the unsparing abuse of financial means on the national level in the Western world. It is imperative for the state to provide a clear choice of directions and positions among controversies concerning whether its finance is to be oriented toward the bank-leading type or the capital market-dominating type, and in terms of the configuration of the modern financial system, the state should build up under the unified framework the market system, the organizational system, legislative system, the supervisory system, the environment system, and the infrastructure of modern finance. Under the broad vision of "big finance," the selection and adoption of objectives and instruments for monetary policies should vary and interact with national industrial policies, fiscal policies, foreign exchange policies, and regulatory policies once the "anchor" is fixed for national monetary policies. In considering national policies for finance, the state government should make a clear analysis of the advantages and disadvantages of a strong currency over the short, medium, and long range and make the best use of the most opportune timing to implement them. The crux of all this resides in an administrative authority on the national level in charge of state finance that can make major decisions concerning national finance and determine its future development.

Globally speaking, the existing financial regulatory systems fall roughly into three categories—single, multiple, and twin peak. A contrastive analysis demonstrates their advantages and disadvantages and a preference for the twin-peak regulatory system, which identifies functional regulation from behavioral regulation, integrates macro-prudential regulation and micro-prudential regulation and sets up a committee of financial policies or of stable development of finance on the basis of the existing currency policy committee of the central bank so as to effectively coordinate affairs regarding national financial regulation and development. What is of primary importance here is that the committee of stable development of finance should be able to implement what comes down from the top level of national finance with clear-cut rights and responsibilities, define the corresponding relations between the committee of stable development of finance, functional regulation office and behavioral regulation office in terms of rights and responsibilities, and specify relations of rights and responsibilities, interaction, and coordination between macro-prudential regulation and micro-prudential regulation and between functional regulation and behavioral regulation.

The vertical development of state financial regulation requires a division of power and responsibilities between the central and local levels. On the one hand, financial "liberalization" may directly bring about instability in national economic and financial development, and "financial suppression" may lead to stagnancy in local economic and financial development. It is important to take into account the level of national development and the actual situation of economic, financial, technological, and industrial development and give full play to the active role of the central and local government while making clear specifications of their respective financial authorities and responsibilities and avoiding the consequences of financial "liberalization" and "suppression." All this requires the central government to formulate rules for its financial agencies to function and specify their relations to local financial authorities in coordinating mechanisms, contents, and measures so as to enhance financial development while exercising rigid control over financial risks.

The vertical development of state financial regulation demands an interactive connection between offshore and onshore finance. In the early 1980s, the United States Federal Reserve Board opened an IBFs (i.e. International Banking Facilities) account, which granted preferential rights to domestic and foreign financial institutions, thus solving the fluctuation conundrum of the US dollar. In 1986, Japan set up the JOM (i.e., Japan Offshore Market) special account and designated an onshore transaction settlement center for the offshore market, thereby settling the Japanese yen coastal dilemma. It is of special significance for the globalization of a national currency by shifting from a currency of payment and settlement to a reserve currency and then to an anchor currency to put into effect policies, measures, and legislations for offshore and onshore interconnections. The globalization of Chinese currency into an international reserve currency will be expedited with the establishment of special accounts for offshore and onshore interconnection and with Hong Kong acting as an intermediary for Chinese Renminbi offshore transactions and its useful connections with Singapore and London.

Looking back upon past experiences, national finance needs resources and capabilities to overtake. It must utilize bulk commodity and energy trading while seizing competitive advantages to contend with global financial superpowers. The British economy rose in the eighteenth and nineteenth centuries because coal trading was bound with the British pound for settlement, which enabled it to gain an upper hand over the then dominating Dutch guilder and become one of the major world currencies. After World War II, the US dollar took the place of the British pound via the settlement of petroleum trade with the US dollar, which has so far become the reigning currency for international transaction settlement and reserve.

China is one of the largest carbon emitters in the world, and its carbon emission will reach its peak between 2020 and 2030. It is time that China should launch its standardized carbon trading market, make better improvement upon carbon spot market, develop carbon futures market, and accelerate the connection of carbon credit trading with Renminbi. By so doing, a new bulk energy trading system, subsequent to the "coal" pound and the "dollar" petroleum, will come into shape, engage the whole of Asia, and blanket the world. That will eventually make it an optimal choice for China to "overtake" in its internationalization of Renminbi and turn into reality Robert Mundell's conception of the Three Islands of Monetary Stability, a global monetary network of US dollars, Euros, and Renminbi.

The US dollar occupies a dominating position in the world monetary system. According to the statistics of the first quarter of 2019, the Chinese Renminbi assets amounted to a total of 217.6 billion US dollars, accounting for 1.95% of the allocated international reserve currency. The prospect of a global monetary system dominated by the US dollar is contingent upon the future development and strengths of the dollar, Euro, and Renminbi. The international monetary system is inclined toward three prospects—a single super-sovereign currency, a common international SDR currency, and a new international standard digital currency that takes the place of sovereign currency as super-sovereign currency. For lack of effective promotion by the "world government", the first option is hardly possible, and only limited possibility exists for the second option, as it involves huge interests of individual sovereign currency countries. A statutory digital currency that comes out of the rapid development of AI-block chain technology is highly likely to develop into a new global standard digital currency that will replace the sovereign currency. The development of Internet finance requires the establishment of an effective Internet financial settlement system, legislative system and risk preventing and controlling system, the protection of intellectual property rights of internet finance, and its standardized development, as well as the facilitation of the application and promotion of the statutory digital currency propelled by AI-block chain technology.

Countries around the world constantly grapple with the daunting task of preventing, mitigating, and handling financial risks. Some lessons should be learned from America's ways of handling financial risks and crises by means of monetary and fiscal policies, supervisory and regulatory policies, laws and legislation, and a combined package of industrial revitalization policies and stimulation measures. The trend of global economic integration and the internationalization of financial market call for a more sophisticated financial system and a more orderly international financial world. The challenges China will inevitably confront include how to internationalize its financial markets, financial instruments, financial participation, financial rules, financial risk prevention, and so on.

National Finance—A Chinese Perspective focuses on the regulation and development of a country's finance, its coordination between central and local governments and between offshore and onshore transactions, the opportunities and challenges in its overtaking and in the influx of high-tech impacts, its prevention of risks on national and international levels, the establishment of an international financial system, the reform and innovation in the international financial order, and so on. By strengthening the top-level financial design, governments around the world should pay more attention to the present and future of the financial industry.

Yunxian Chen

Contents

1 The Concept of "Big Finance" and the National Policy of a Strong RMB—A Policy Study of the Top-Level Design and Layout of Chinese Finance   1

2 The "Twin-Peak" Model for Financial Regulation—A Review of Financial Regulatory and Coordinating Measures in China   33

3 Local Economic Development and Financial Support—A Study of Chinese Financial Hierarchy   59

4 The Establishment of an Onshore Transaction Clearing Center for RMB Offshore Business—Explorations in the Interactive Model for Internal and External Finance   89

5 The Settlement of "Carbon Emissions Trading" in RMB—Explorations in China's Pathway of "Overtaking on the Curve" in Finance   131

6 The Present and Future of China's Internet Finance—The Trend of FinTech Innovation in China   175

Contents

7 The Prevention and Diffusion of Systematic or Regional Financial Risks—The Methodology for China to Resolve Financial Crises   217

8 Innovation and Improvement of the International Financial Architecture—China's Plan for Engagement in International Finance   265

References   319

List of Figures

Fig. 1.1	Independent monetary policy	17
Fig. 2.1	American financial regulation regime—depository institutions (before the 2008 international financial crisis)	36
Fig. 2.2	American financial regulation regime—securities, futures, and insurance (before the 2008 international financial crisis)	37
Fig. 2.3	American financial regulation system (after 2010)	38
Fig. 2.4	UK financial regulation systems—pre-crisis-tripartite model	42
Fig. 2.5	UK financial regulation system—twin-peak model (2012)	43
Fig. 2.6	EU financial regulation scheme: EA	45
Fig. 2.7	Canada financial regulation system—twin-peak model. (Source: Rotman School of Management, University of Toronto, Canada)	53
Fig. 2.8	Australian financial regulation system—twin-peak model. (Source: Rotman School of Management, University of Toronto, Canada)	54

List of Tables

Table 1.1	Classification of modern financial systems	3
Table 1.2	The six components of modern financial system	13
Table 2.1	Historical stages of British financial regulation	44
Table 4.1	Distribution of global offshore financial markets by 2019	97
Table 4.2	Comparison of the scale of deposits and loans in major world offshore financial centers (US$ 1 billion)	99
Table 4.3	Modes of international offshore financial markets	109
Table 5.1	Levels of carbon markets	146
Table 5.2	An institutional comparison of carbon markets in five designated regions	154
Table 5.3	Design of China's carbon futures contract	170
Table 6.1	Ten major virtual currencies (as of March 24, 2018)	184
Table 7.1	An overview of major TARP programs (unit: US$ 100 million)	247

1

The Concept of "Big Finance" and the National Policy of a Strong RMB—A Policy Study of the Top-Level Design and Layout of Chinese Finance

The top-level design of Chinese finance serves the purposes of financial planning and guidance, financial abidance and participation, and financial layout and implementation. Such top-level layouts for national finance have existed in developed Western countries for a long time. For developing countries, economic exchanges often begin from "merchandise trade" to "general service trade" and then to "high-end service trade." Their economic opening is often driven from "current accounts" to "capital accounts." Even the Free Trade Zone (FTZ) that many countries attempt to set up follows the steps of going from trade facilitation to investment and financing facilitation and to capital account convertibility. Consequently, the top-level design for a country's finance becomes an imperative.

Now the question is how the top-level design for Chinese finance should be structured. We believe that the overall layout should be implemented over a spectrum of understanding, structure, policies, and measures.

1.1 The Positioning of the Modern Financial System

1.1.1 An Overview of the Modern Financial System

The modern financial system is a basic framework where funds or assets flow and trade under the restraints of specialized systems, mechanisms, and standards in an economy. It is a complex labyrinth composed of financial elements such as fund flow tools (financial assets), market participants (intermediaries), and transaction modes (market). The economist Jordi Canals, for the first time in history, classified the financial system of industrialized countries into two types: bank-based and capital market-based. A financial system is defined as a bank-based financial system if banks and other financial intermediaries dominate financing, which means that the mode of indirect funding has been the primary source of external enterprise funds. Germany, Japan, and France are typical examples of countries that follow the bank-based system. A market-based financial system means that enterprises obtain funds directly from the market through issuance of shares and bonds. In this system, enterprises primarily gain external funds by direct financing. The United States is the chief representative of this practice. In terms of quantitative distribution, financial systems are either bank-based or hybrids in most mainstream countries except for the United States, whose system prominently manifests itself as being market-based (Table 1.1).

1.1.2 The Two Types of World Financial Systems

A marked distinction between the financial systems of developed countries resides in the importance of capital markets and financial intermediaries. Two obvious extremes exist here, one being represented by the United States, where the capital market plays a major role in the financial market, and the other being represented by Germany, where several large banks play a dominant role, with the capital market playing a minor role in the background. Other countries fall somewhere in between these two extremes. In Japan and France, for example, the bank-based system has

Table 1.1 Classification of modern financial systems

Type of financial system	Market-based	Bank-based
Financial market	Large scale, high fluidity	Small scale, low fluidity
Shares of listed companies on stock exchanges	Abundant	Scarce
Shared risks	Markets: inter-departmental	Banks: inter-period
Ownership and control	Decentralized	Centralized
Mode of influence	Withdrawal	Disclosure
Market controlled by companies	Frequent hostile takeovers	Rare hostile takeovers
Conflicts between major agents	Shareholders and management	Control and minority shareholders
Role of banks in external financing	Limited	Enormous
Debt-stock ratios	Low	High

traditionally played a major role, but their capital markets are undergoing a rapid growth and are playing an increasingly important role. In Canada and Great Britain, capital markets are better developed than in Germany, but the concentration of banks in the banking sector is relatively higher than that of the United States.

1.1.2.1 The American Capital Market-Based Financial System

The United States is the representative of the market-based financial system. In this system, direct financing is the primary mode for enterprises, and the capital market plays a significant role in providing financial services for the real economy. In the United States, the formation of a market-based financial system is closely related to the liberal economic policies that it pursues. On the market level, the US government encourages competition among commercial entities and plays a limited role in deciding the mode of interaction between capital and labor. The decision-making rights for capital accumulation are typically vested in private companies where they can pursue short-term profit objectives to the maximum possible extent. This also allows for the acquisition of capital through the financial market. American enterprises have engaged in free development through the "survival of the fittest" mentality and a quest for profits. These factors, along with fierce market competition and equity capital aimed at profit maximization, have formed a flexible market complete with a strong labor force and competitive products. Government intervention in economy traditionally manifests itself through indirect regulation and market control to prevent enterprise monopoly from causing distorted market prices. These regulations also ensure that the market can fully function.

It is precisely due to the liberal economic policies pursued by the United States on the market level that enterprises must expand their scale of operations through multi-channel financing to maintain their competitiveness and predominance in such a fierce market competition. In 1933, the Glass-Steagall Act was enforced to prohibit commercial banks from investment banking. Meanwhile, strict restrictions were imposed on trans-regional operations and deposit rates of banks. This law, combined with the liberal economic model in place, boosted the rapid development of the capital market and, unfortunately, posed challenges and caused crises to banking institutions. In 1999, the United States promulgated the *Financial Service Modernization Act*, and the financial industry returned to its mixed operation mode. Regrettably, the market-based financial system had already taken shape, and a bond market with rich varieties and a multi-level stock market had constituted the capital market system of the United States. This type of diversified capital market also provided variety for investment institutions, including citizens, most of whom held company shares and bonds. In comparison, the primary business of American commercial banks was to provide short-term loans for industrial and commercial enterprises, housing loans, agricultural loans, and inter-bank borrowing with relatively minor economic effects.

1.1.2.2 The German Bank-Based Financial System

Germany is the representative of a bank-based financial system. In this system, bank loans absorb a large portion of a company's liabilities and are the essential financing means of German companies. In particular, the three largest universal banks of Germany, including Deutsche Bank, Commerzbank, and Dresdner Bank, occupy a pivotal position in the banking system. Compared with the banking market, the German capital market features a smaller scale with low fluidity in market. Specifically, the German banking system is based on universal banks and supplemented by specialized banks. Universal banks include commercial banks, savings banks, and cooperative banks. Commercial banks are the core, and they can take part in all types of financial activities, including the absorption of deposits, issuance of loans, underwriting of securities, and the direct investments in various securities including shares. As multifunctional and all-around banks, they cannot only engage in the business of both traditional commercial banks and investment banks but also exploit various methods to exert a further impact on listed companies. This may include obtaining a seat on the board of supervisors of an enterprise by voting on behalf of shareholders. However, the financial services provided by German specialized banks are more limited than those offered by universal banks, such as those that specialize in mortgage loans, agricultural credit, or the credit for small- and medium-sized enterprises. The German stock market is not as relatively important and even though the German bond market is in a reasonable development period, its participants, in most cases, are the government and banks. General industrial and commercial enterprises rarely issue bonds, but they typically depend on bank loans for their external financing with a low degree of loan security.

The formation and evolution of the German financial system are closely related to its industrialization and the economic development environment Germany has been faced with. Germany became industrialized after the Great Britain and the United States, and therefore, it must leverage the hypervelocity development of its industry to win space for its development. To this end, Germany has adopted the mode of a market economy under national regulation. The government has taken direct and indirect intervention measures, including control of price formation and participation in enterprise investments, to regulate problems in its economic operations. Germany has been sticking to an economic path that focuses more on answering the appeals for employment, relies more on a real industry, and implements a favorable labor market and welfare policy. Correspondingly, its bank-based financial system is much simpler when compared with the market-based system. Its requirements for a legal system are relatively lower, and universal banks can adequately protect the interests of small and medium investors, which marks a striking difference from the situation in the United States, where the interests of small and medium investors are protected by a sound legal system. Furthermore, German banks go all out to develop their relationships with enterprises. They provide enterprises not only with long-term funds but also with additional support. From the historical perspective, a bank-based financial system has made significant contributions to Germany in developing its economy to catch up with the Great Britain and the United States.

As can be seen, a country's selection of a financial system that better suits itself or the evolution of the inner structure of its financial system is inseparable from its historical development path, its industrial economic foundation, and its actual national conditions. The standard is often judged as to whether the balance between "efficiency" and "stability" can be achieved under time and space conditions. In creating a mechanism for efficiency, for example, information disclosure, corporate governance, and transparency requirements, there must be perfect transmission and realization mechanisms. In creating a tool for stability, for example, deposit insurance, risk management, and bankruptcy mechanism, there should be similar modes of realization between different units within the financial system so that the financial system can form multi-level and multi-dimensional resistance capabilities. Furthermore, the building of excellent social credit culture and a social credit system are also indispensable components of a modern financial system.

1.1.2.3 Bank-Based Financial Systems Remain the Mainstream for Financial Development World Wide

On the market level, despite increasingly louder voices for developing capital market-based financial systems, what cannot be ignored is that global financial crises that took place in the past 100 years all originated in or had significant direct relations with capital markets. This forced countries to take a serious look at the pros and cons of bank-based versus capital market-based financial systems with regards to the top-level layout of finance. It has not been by chance that bank-based financial systems are regarded as the leading mode of contemporary financial systems in the world. Indeed, specific internal reasons and rationalities are identifiable for this conclusion.

First, the inherent law of the evolution of the financial system reveals that banks have dominated the financial policies of the past for a quite long time. According to the Yale University economist Raymond W. Goldsmith regarding the laws of financial development, the growth of modern finance originates from the development of the banking system and goes through three phases. In the initial phase, the ratio of financial correlation in a country or region is rather low and its financial instruments are rather singular. Its debt vouchers far exceed equity certificates, and the role of commercial banks in financial institutions is prominent. During the second phase, the creditor's assets of these countries and regions still take most of total financial assets. Banks still play a dominant role in financial institutions, and many large joint-stock companies appear. Once a financial system gets to the third stage, the proportion of creditor's assets in total financial assets continuously increases, and the trend of financial institutions toward diversified development becomes much more apparent. Banks will typically see a drop-in market position, but they will still account for a large part of the market against the backdrop of a gradually rising market position of non-banking institutions, to include securities and insurance companies.

Second, bank-based financial systems facilitate the accelerated development of industrialization. Due to its marked effect of scale economy, bank-based financial systems easily solve the problem of information asymmetry encountered during investment. Meanwhile, the existing long-term cooperation and mutual trust relationships between banks and enterprises often provide healthy and sustainable monetary support for industrial development, especially during rapid industrialization. When industrialization is taken into account, the large-scale industrial development of countries, such as Germany and Japan, is generally ascribable to the primary role of the banking sector in the financial system. The enormous funds for industrial development were mainly funded by the banking system and the capital market played an auxiliary role. For countries like Brazil and Indonesia, though their capital market has developed rapidly and the proportion of their direct financing has reached 70% over recent years, their industrialization has remained stagnant. Even today, they are still unable to bail their economies out of the morass.

Third, compared with their capital market-based counterparts, bank-based financial systems are better equipped to facilitate risk management and financial stability. In a capital market-based financial system, the cause of market unrest comes from the violent fluctuation of asset prices. Market crises originate in the deviation of asset prices from the basic situation and sustained asset bubbles. In the United States, the sparks that set off the stock disaster in 1987, the Internet calamity in 2000, and the financial crisis in 2008, were without exception asset price bubbles. Countries with market-based financial systems, for example, Thailand and Mexico, suffered more during these financial crises than those countries that had bank-based financial systems. It should be noted that under the capital market-based financial system, the boundary between financial services is vague. In addition, financial institutions of different types form links in the financial risk chain. These risks are brought to the capital market by lever manipulation and overreaching. They are easily transferred and dispersed into the banking market. They then often evolve into significant risks for the entire financial system.

Driven by financial innovation and IT revolution, the international financial market has become more integrated. As the scope and influence of the market expansion, financial risks have been steadily accumulating, transferring and dispersing. For example, the issues that arose on the subprime loan market in 2008 quickly spread to the entire housing mortgage loan market. These issues further impacted the intermediaries (investment banks and mortgage loan guarantee institutions). Next in the crosshairs to be affected were the financial institutions holding the securitized products of mortgage loans (commercial banks, insurance companies, and mutual funds). These combined blows finally engulfed the financial system in a full-scale financial crisis. In a bank-based financial system, the banking sector bears significant business risks, which can be seen through the central expression that the risk of default by many enterprises brought about by an economic slump can lead to a rapid increase in the bad debts of banks in a concise period. If they can receive a timely injection of funds, a much higher risk can be avoided. For example, immediately after the Subprime Loan Crisis took place, Germany set up a financial stability fund of 500 billion euros. This was designed to provide an insurance guarantee for the lending abilities of the financial industry, fortify banks assets, and help them dispose of their non-performing assets ("NPA"). In this way, the fluidity crisis of large banks was effectively alleviated and protected while greatly defusing financial risk.

To sum up, for purposes of the top-level layout of Chinese finance, careful considerations should be given. First, given the inherent risks of the financial market, the capital market-based financial system faces much higher requirements for risk control which may also bring greater systematic crises. Since a perfect capital market is impossible to develop overnight, bank-based financial systems will still occupy a dominant position for the foreseeable future. Second, when deciding which financial system to set up, we should consider the actual conditions, including the level of economic development, depth of the financial market, risk control capability, supervision, and management capacity. In this way, China will be able to select a financial system that better meets its national conditions. Third, the self-reform and timely evolution of our financial system are highly necessary. For both bank-based and capital market-based financial systems, a regulatory regime with clear targets, effective means, and enough accurate information is indispensable. It is important to adjust the mechanisms of financial regulation, operations, and risk management.

1.2 The Structure of the Modern Financial System

1.2.1 The Financial Market System

A financial market is a generic term for the transaction activities whereby the fund supply and demand sides leverage all kinds of financial instruments to actualize money lending-borrowing and financing. A financial market includes the money market and capital market. Money markets consist of the financial inter-bank borrowing market, repurchase agreement market, commercial bill market, bank acceptance bill market, short-term government bond market, and the market of a large-denomination negotiable certificate of deposits. A capital market includes medium- and long-term credit markets and the securities market. A security market is the market in which financing is enabled through the issuance and trading of securities. These securities include the bond market, stock market, fund market, and futures market. Whichever market it may be, the flow and dispersion of risks, as well as the wealth-sharing mechanism that goes along with economic growth, are the motive power for profound vitality and strong competitiveness of the financial market. Furthermore, the sound, stable, and orderly development of the foreign exchange market will play a much more critical role in the national financial market system.

1.2.2 The Financial Organization System

A financial organization is the cell of the whole modern financial system. Its system includes commercial organizations, management organizations (central bank and related financial regulatory organizations), and policy-related organizations (policy banks). The commercial financial organizations that fall under national regulations include traditional financial institutions, such as national commercial banks, securities companies, fund companies, and insurance companies. Large-scale conventional financial institutions with massive funds are often unable to satisfy consumers' diversified financial needs. This condition leads to the birth of local financial institutions that complement traditional financial institutions and new business formats. They may take the form of petty loan companies, financing guaranty companies, and P2P financing platforms. These local financial institutions and new organizations function more like capillary vessels because they can trickle into the demographics that are typically out of reach of traditional financial institutions. These institutions are represented by those such as the "San Nong" (agriculture, rural areas, and farmers), micro and small enterprises, and private enterprises. Local financial institutions are crucial, as a sound financial organizational system should start by meeting diversified financial needs to improve the business formats of the economic organization with different functions. It must also provide consumers with more innovative products and services.

1.2.3 The Financial Legal System

A market economy is an economy that exists under the rule of law. As the core of a modern market economy, finance must always adhere to the law as if it were a cornerstone and continuously improve the current financial rule of law system. These laws include a variety of aspects, such as financial legislation, financial law enforcement, financial judicature, and financial education. This is especially true of the propulsion of law-based regulations to ensure the justice and efficiency of the commercial market. In a broad sense, the financial rule of law also covers general provisions, practices, and the order of the financial market and financial activities. For China, financial mechanisms tested and implemented in the reform and innovation, such as the FTZ, are an important stimulus to the national advancement in the financial legal system.

1.2.4 The Financial Regulation System

A sound financial supervision system is the necessary condition for dispersing financial risks and maintaining financial stability. This system should include the supervision of the establishment of financial institutions, the control of the asset and liability business of financial institutions, the supervision of the implementation of monetary policies, laws, and regulations, the supervision of separate financial operations, and the supervision of the commercial market. This system should also include market access, market financing, market interest rates, and market rules. According to the powers of office, the function of financial supervision belongs to the central and local governments respectively. The primary purpose of a local government is to maintain the stability of regional finance and hold fast to the baseline of zero systematic and regional financial risks.

1.2.5 The Financial Environment System

An effective modern financial system must include a financial ecosystem. The financial environmental system is the software that allows the system to function, and it includes features such as the economic foundation, current property right system, social credit system, and modern corporate governance structure. It generally requires the following to build an excellent financial environmental system: (a) a solid foundation of the real economy, without which finance capital will dry up and is bound to cause bubbles in financial development, thereby triggering economic crisis; (b) a sound social credit system, which builds a good external ecological environment for the development of the financial industry and spurs its continuous upgrading and evolution; (c) a perfect corporate governance structure, which serves to straighten out government-enterprise relationships to better achieve the market-oriented development of modern financial system.

1.2.6 The Financial Infrastructure

Financial infrastructure is the underlying condition for the modern financial system to play an active role in the financial market, which includes hardware components, such as a stable payment settlement system, a safe scientific and technological information system, and a convenient financial service network, as well as matching facilities and technologies, such as online functional terminals, POS machines, and ATMs. With the rapid development of Internet technology, such as remote payments, account opening via facial recognition, and mobile transactions, these technologies have greatly enhanced and expanded the financial functions and means while advancing the revolutionary progress in financial infrastructure hardware construction. Financial infrastructure also includes software components, such as the establishment, determination, and implementation of the laws, accounting, audit, evaluation, credit, rules, procedures, and standards of the financial industry that correspond to hardware components. It is also an essential part of economic infrastructure, which signifies a significant direction for the

Table 1.2 The six components of modern financial system

(1) The financial market system, which consists of the monetary market, capital market, and foreign exchange market;
(2) The financial organization system, which covers management organizations (e.g., PBC, CBIRC, and CSRC of China), commercial organizations (financial institutions), and policy-related organizations (policy banks);
(3) The financial legal system, which covers financial legislation, financial law enforcement, financial judicature, and education in the financial legal system;
(4) The financial supervision system, which provides the supervision of institutions, businesses, markets, and the implementation of policies, laws, and regulations;
(5) The financial environmental system, which includes the foundation of the real economy, social credit system, and corporate governance structure;
(6) The economic infrastructure, which consists of the payment settlement system, scientific and technological information system, financial service network, and matching equipment and technologies, as well as the corresponding financial laws, accounting, audit, evaluation, credit, rules, procedures, and standards

construction of the modern financial system by integrating the networked, virtualized, and intelligent financial infrastructure facilities.

Therefore, in its top-level design and layout of finance, China should gain an all-around grasp of the structure of the modern financial system. That is to say, it should implement a new design and layout from at least six different aspects to promote the formation and perfection of the modern financial system (Table 1.2).

1.3 Policies for the Modern Financial System

1.3.1 Financial Policies

Here a mention must be made of the concept of "big finance," which I strongly advocate. The implementation of economic strategies primarily involves fiscal policies and a selection of whether to adopt proactive, tight, or neutral fiscal policies. The interaction between fiscal policies and monetary policies is shown in at least two aspects: (a) The sequence of proactive or tight fiscal policies, fiscal deficits, treasury bonds (inclusive of government bonds for construction and deficit government bonds), and interest rates generated from treasury bonds forms the interaction between interest rates of treasury bonds and floating spreads of monetary benchmark interest rates, thereby directly influencing and regulating everyday economic activities. Finance makes up deficits in three ways: increasing taxes, issuing treasury bonds, and changing base currency, thus giving rise to the second aspect reflecting the interaction between financial policies and monetary policies: (b) Finance plays a leading role in the formation of currency supply mechanisms, that is, the change of base currency and seigniorage taxes will directly affect money supply, and secondly, financial means will play a significant role as a stabilizer in addressing financial crises. The top-level design of finance in China should take into consideration monetary policies and create mechanisms for them to interact.

1.3.2 The Monetary Policy

The monetary policy involves three aspects: objectives, tools, and effects. The objectives can be single, that is, stabilizing commodity prices and controlling inflation. They can be dual, that is, developing economy and stabilizing commodity prices. They can be multiple, that is, creating full employment, advancing economic growth, stabilizing commodity prices, and balancing worldwide income and expenditure. For tools of the monetary policy, in selecting and utilizing the tools, China should first decide upon its guidelines, that is, where should the "anchor" of the monetary policy be? Three types of "anchors" have been created in the financial development. The first is the aggregation of a country's currency (or its change rate) to be used as target guidelines, which enables the exchange rate and price level to meet the money supply. The second is a certain price level to be used as the target guideline, that is, inflation or deflation levels, which enables the exchange rate and financial supply to accommodate the price level. The third is the exchange rate to be used as the target guideline, which enables the money supply and price level to meet the exchange rate target.

The monetary policy contains three major components—the supply of money, interest rates, and exchange rates. The priority for China's selection of monetary policy tools lies in determining the most appropriate "anchor" for its monetary policy through comparing, analyzing, and selecting the three components in the light of the objective reality of the national economic and financial development and in selecting its relevant tools by means of the "anchor." Where should the "anchor" of China's monetary policy be placed? The United States, for example, firmly pegs itself to the inflation rate as its currency guideline and leverages interest rates to effectively regulate and stabilize its economy. The Federal Reserve has also set the market benchmark interest rate for its base currency and achieved economic stability and growth by determining the "anchor" of the monetary policy under the guidance of its single objective of stabilizing commodity prices and controlling inflation, treating interest rates as a major consideration, and capitalizing more effectively on such adjustment tools of "interest rates" as "open market operations," "discount and re-discount," and "reserve requirement ratios." This approach does not hinder the diversity of the objectives of Chinese monetary policy, as long as it fits in with the economic development level, market maturity degree, and the status of open markets to the outside world and makes an effective selection of the "anchor" for its monetary policy. Consequently, its selection of the three components can be compounded and overlapped, which is largely contingent upon the effects of its monetary policy.

The money supply has remained to be a major consideration in many countries. Due to the differences in the degrees of economic development, market maturity, and market openness to the outside world, the central banks in many nations have regarded the total money supply as their top priority or treated the supply of money as the "anchor" of the monetary policy and its objective guideline. Traditionally, three factors influence the supply of money, that is, base currency, RRR (reserve requirement ratio), and the deposit currency ratio of commercial banks. There are four channels for issuing base currency, that is, purchasing treasury bonds on the secondary market, which is often used by the United States, issuing re-loans to financial institutions (including re-discount and borrow funds from the financial market), purchasing gold to increase gold reserves, and utilizing external surplus to create outstanding funds for foreign exchange. When regulating the total supply of money, the central banks should control currency at levels of M_0, M_1, M_2, and M_3 and give full consideration to how they affect each other. The regulation of total money supply involves the base currency and the currency multiplier. That means that among the three tools of the money policy, multiplier effects vary with the use of currency issuance or saving deposits to purchase and sell bonds. Therefore, in addition to the three primary tools, China can use other selection tools depending on actual conditions, which typically include consumer credit control, securities market credit control, firm property credit control, the directional reduction of RRR, and prepayment of import deposits.

Due attention should be paid to the time lag of the monetary policy. The implementation of monetary policy tools may entail "internal lag" (i.e., time to initiate the policy) and "external lag" (i.e., time for the policy to work on the economy). The former includes "recognition lag" (i.e., the time for problem identification), "decision lag" (i.e., the time it takes to analyze the problem before acting), and "action lag" (i.e., the time it takes to undertake the action), and the latter refers to the time lag created mainly by environmental factors. Therefore, the "automatic" initiation countermeasures in China are critical. This is especially true of the measures of "inverse period regulation" in the monetary policy.

1.3.3 The Exchange Rate Policy

Let's take the top-level design or selection of exchange rate policies for emerging market countries for example. Figure 1.1 shows Krugman's Impossible Trinity or "Trilemma."

Its logical conclusion is that it is unlikely for fixed exchange rates, free capital movement, and independent monetary policies to realize simultaneously. Therefore, central banks generally have three policy combinations to choose from—the combination of fixed exchange rates and free capital movement (i.e., abandoning independent monetary policies), the combination of separate monetary policies and free capital movement (i.e., abandoning fixed exchange rates), and the combination of fixed exchange rates and independent monetary policies (i.e., abandoning free

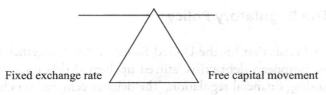

Fig. 1.1 Independent monetary policy

capital movement). Top-level financial designs worldwide require the selection of policy combinations.

As a country that has not yet fully opened its capital accounts, China would be well advised to select the third policy combination, that is, the combination of fixed exchange rates and independent monetary policies. From the perspective of my analysis, such "fixed exchange rates" are not purely "fixed." Preferably, China should select "fixed exchange rates" with space for upper and lower floating in the light of its national conditions and the gradual process of opening its capital accounts, which means adopting an "exchange rate of floating management" between fixed exchange rates and floating exchange rates. The size of the space for upper and lower floating should be based on the requirements for the top-level layout of national finance and the process of the continuous opening of China's capital accounts. In its internationalization, Chinese currency also needs the ongoing enhancement and improvement of its internal financial market and financial system. Given the various ways of the macroeconomic development and financial stability of a country responding to the policy for capital inflow in opening financial markets and the difficulty in internationally coordinating its monetary system and macro-prudential policy, it becomes imperative, in applying, balancing, and connecting the macro-prudential policy (MPP) and capital flow management (CFM) tools, to select from the options of MPP, CFM, and FX-related prudential measures, which should be treated differently according to the currency in the capital flow and applied to financial institutions under supervision and in particular banks. Judging from the practices in China, it is wise to utilize FX-related prudential measures more often at this stage.

1.3.4 The Regulatory Policy

The financial crisis that hit the United States in 2008, together with the subsequent European debt crisis, stirred up heated debates around the world regarding financial regulation. The debates centered on challenges to financial stability, highlighted by the "lean" versus "clean" debate. The crucial issues were which types of macro-prudential financial policy were required, what matching policy tools were needed, how the relations between these tools could be balanced, and who would manage them and be accountable for them. Those who held the "lean" viewpoint believed that the relationship between monetary stability and financial stability was closer than earlier imagined, with price stabilization as a prerequisite condition. However, the stabilization of prices must be supported by a robust and prudential macro-regulation framework to influence the implementation of the monetary policy. If the prudential macro tools are insufficient to achieve financial stability, it would be hardly possible for there to be a choice between flexibility and credibility within the monetary market.

Now let us have a look at how the issues were handled in the United States and European Union. The United States implemented the stress testing. Faced with the demand for financial crisis management subsequent to the 2008 crisis, the Federal Reserve selected America's 19 largest financial enterprises in early 2009 for a universal analysis and review of capital. They conducted the first stress test between the end of 2010 and the beginning of 2011. It included a stress scenario variable composed of 29 items, an analytical framework, a pricing model, a macro scenario versus market scenario, capital plan rules, coherent stress testing, reverse stress testing, and so on. The stress test filled in the information absent from the "value at risk" (VaR) management, consequently adding new elements to financial risk management. In 2014, the *Dodd-Frank Act Pressure Testing 2014: Supervisory Stress Testing and Results* and *Comprehensive Capital Analysis and Review 2014: Assessment Framework and Results* played a role in the supervisory capital assessment and financial crisis management of the Federal Reserve.

In the European Union, *Basel Accord III and Basel IV: Implications for Risk Management* strengthened the effect of risk management. In contrast to *Basel II*, Pillar 1 of *Basel III* intensified the minimum requirements for capital and fluidity, Pillar 2 reinforced the process of supervision and review, which was done to enable company-wide risk management and capital planning. Pillar 3 strengthened risk disclosure and market discipline. *Basel III* posed higher capital requirements and raised the capital ratio by introducing a new fluidity and leverage ratio. It also intensified the supervisory restraint mechanism directed at the credit and market risks of the counter-parties of the transaction book combination. *Basel IV* attempted to make extensive improvements on the market risk framework. After its finalization at the end of 2015, the supervisory concepts and measures were taking shape, and its influence within the industry reached a new height.

After deciding on macro-financial objectives, what countries needed to do is classify typical macro risk shocks into four types: domestic "internal" versus foreign "external" risks and demand shocks versus supply shocks. Then a cross-combination analysis of them was made, one by one. Five tools for macro-financial risk management were put forward: monetary policy, exchange rate policy, stability (tight) fiscal policy, facilitation (proactive) fiscal policy, and supervisory control (i.e., supervisory system). They strengthened micro-prudential supervision from the perspective of single institutions and called for macro-prudential supervision from the perspective of the overall financial market. Although related and supplementary, macro-prudential and micro-prudential supervisions differ in three basic aspects:

(a) Objects of supervision: macro-prudential supervision mainly focuses on the overall financial market, while micro-prudential supervision primarily focuses on single financial institutions.
(b) Targets of supervision: macro-prudential supervision pays high attention to systematic financial risks, while micro-prudential supervision concentrates on the prevention and disposal of individual risks.
(c) Mechanisms of supervision: macro-prudential supervision focuses on the asset prices of the market, total credit, and the leverage ratio of institutions, while micro-prudential supervision focuses on the capi-

tal adequacy ratio, fluidity and non-performing loan ratios of financial enterprises, concurrently utilizing and strengthening such measures as capital retention buffer, and counter-cyclical capital buffer. Macro-prudential supervision and micro-prudential supervisions are combined to become an effective means of enhancing financial regulation on the top level of finance.

Let us take another look at the financial regulatory framework of Canada in its present iteration. Canada implements a parallel financial regulation system on the federal and the provincial levels. At the federal level, the economic regulation of the banking sector mainly concentrates on the financial risk system, and at the provincial level, financial management focuses primarily on the financial service system. At the federal level, five departments make up the regulatory framework, that is, the Department of Finance (DOF), the central bank (Bank of Canada, BOC), the Canadian Deposit Insurance Corporation (CDIC), the Office of the Superintendents of Financial Institutions (OSFI), and the Financial Consumer Agency of Canada (FCAC). They report directly to the second Chief of the Cabinet and Minister of Finance. Their efficient and strong regulatory initiatives depend, to a great extent, on an architecture composed of three financial regulatory committees set up between the five departments. The first is the Senior Advisory Committee (SAC), which is chaired by the executive undersecretary of finance and focuses on matters like the formulation of financial strategies and legislation. The second is the Financial Institution Supervisory Committee (FISC), which is chaired by OSFI, which focuses on macro-prudential financial regulations. The third is the Heads of Agents (HOA). It was set up after the crisis in 2008 to meet the development of the capital market and derivative products. The HOA is chaired by the BOC and involves the participation of the OSFI in the four provinces. The target is on matters like the regulation of the macro-prudential capital market. Their operational mechanism of mutual independence, high coordination, clear duties, and adequate supervision has promoted the financial stability and development of Canada. Evidently, problems persist and need to be further addressed in Canada as well as the rest of the world.

Let's first consider the definition, development, and supervision of shadow banking. Is there a broad and narrow classification? Should its backstop include the two aspects of business promotion and risk prevention? How can its supervision and regulation be strengthened, and particularly how the backstop of shadow banking can be coordinated with the effective implementation of the Volcker Rule, if backstop is a fundamental requirement for its activities? Second, let's look at the determination of macro-prudential policies of the central bank and the effective selection of policy tools. Most developed Western countries have basically adopted a financial business format of mixed operations, mixed management, internal/external processes, and transnational management. The original macro-prudential policy that has traditional banking business as its main component, together with its tools and capital flow management, obviously has exhibited difficulties in achieving full coverage. Third, let's take the establishment of objectives for the financial development and regulatory mode for another example. Should economic development be based on the banking industry with most concurrent consideration given to the growth of the capital market, or should it be based on both? Alternatively, should it even be based more on the development of the capital market than on the development of the banking industry? Should the development of the financial group be based on domestic business with most concurrent consideration given to international trade? Should it be based more on international business than on the private financial industry for development? Should financial regulation be found on both national and local regulations to form an effective operation mechanism coordinated by the regulators, or should it be mainly based on governmental regulation? All these issues need to be further clarified and addressed in the top-level design or layout of Chinese finance.

1.4 The Development of a Modern Financial System

1.4.1 The Currency Area

Just as modern finance develops from one country to the rest of the world, so it is with the modern financial system. Robert A. Mundell, an international financial expert in America and the Nobel Prize laureate in economics, put forward the well-known proposition of creating a 3-in-1 currency area that covers the US dollar, euro, and RMB with a view to establishing a modern financial system, reforming the international currency system, and eventually forming a fixed exchange rate of 1:1.2 or 1:1.4 between the three currencies. Mundell introduced the concept of "monetary union area" that would consist of different countries and regions, use a single currency or several currencies that would maintain a permanently fixed exchange rate between them and a unified external floating function. The currency area is a sophisticated mode of manifesting currency integration. Currency integration is a trend toward currency cooperation between countries within a region or between regions.

According to the degree of collaboration in currency, it is divided into three levels: regional monetary cooperation, regional monetary union, and currency area. Currency area is a typical form of currency cooperation, characterized by the following attributes: (a) the nominal price parity between member currencies is relatively fixed; (b) one of the member currencies occupies a dominant position and serves as the common foundation for the exchange rate of the currencies in the region; (c) a dominant currency and member currencies can be converted freely, which can even be unified into a single currency. In the meantime, the form of the joint floating exchange rate can be adopted for other countries; (d) there should be an appropriate agency for coordination and management in this system, which will certainly weaken the sovereignty of member currencies. However, the proposition for a 3-in-1 currency area covering US dollar, euro, and RMB has made positive contributions to the development of a modern financial system and the reform of the international currency system.

1.4.2 The "National Policy" of a Strong US Dollar

A country's strong currency is characterized by its ability to keep the currency from devaluation, increase its permanency, and maintain a strong exchange rate. Two distinctive features are identifiable. The first is the sustained absorption of foreign capital, which not only reflects the domestic convenience in low-cost fundraising but promotes financial prosperity as well as supporting the development of the real economy. The second is the higher holding of the home currency by foreign investors, which will boost the substantive evolution for the home currency to become a primary international currency. Of course, a strong home currency will give rise to problems such as exporting difficulty and trade deficits. However, a comparison of the pros and cons brought about by a strong currency policy proves that the income received by the country should far exceed its cost.

The "Bretton Woods Conference" of July 1944, the "Marshall Plan" of April 1948, as well as a series of subsequent measures taken by the US government, pushed the US dollar to the status of a recognized world currency and is still controlling the international currency system today. The basic architecture of the existing international financial order remains to be an extension of the Bretton Woods System. The International Monetary Fund (IMF) and the World Bank (WB), which have been under American control, play a leading role and have an absolute say in the development of the modern financial system and the reform of the international currency system, and the United States holds absolute decision-making power in the operations of influential institutions such as the IMF and WB, as well as veto powers in deciding significant affairs.

In 1993, the United States introduced the "national policy" of a strong dollar, which facilitated the development of the modern financial system of the world, which was built on the foundation of the Bretton Woods Conference and the system dominated by the American dollar, and the reform of the international currency system. These helped to cover the natural "defects" in the modern financial system and the "flaws" in economic operation, under the guise of the trend of economic growth. That enabled the US dollar and its relevant institutions to dominate and maintain the financial order of the world.

1.4.3 The National Policy of a Strong RMB

Regarding the top-level design and layout of China's finance, serious thought must be given to the development trend, current situation, and future prospects of Chinese currency, as well as the position and role of Chinese currency in international economic affairs, once decisions are made and work done with regard to the positioning of the modern financial system, the comprehensive construction of the modern financial structure, the effective use of current economic policies, including fiscal policy, monetary policy, exchange rate policy, and regulatory policy, and the promotion of the sustainable development of Chinese economy. The trend is becoming clear. China should carefully weigh all options before choosing the best approach. Should it accelerate the internationalization of RMB or step into the "national policy" of a strong RMB?

Over the period of China's 13th Five-Year Plan, one of the formidable challenges and the bottleneck to being a greater economic power is how to deepen its financial reform and internationalize RMB. The World Bank announced four indicators for a great economy: total GDP accounting for 5% or more of the world's total, total trade of imports and exports for 5% or more of the world's total, Fortune 500 enterprises for 5% or more of the total of that country, and home currency, as an international reserve currency, for 5% or more of the world's total. China fulfilled the first three indicators long ago, but it has a huge gap in its proportion of RMB as an international reserve currency.

The reform and development of China's finance require strengthening top-level design, and its top priority is to accelerate the internationalization of RMB and work out feasible approaches for the "national policy" of a strong RMB. In addition, it needs to further promote the construction of a modern financial system; establish and improve the system for the coordinated and unified management of its fiscal policy, monetary policy, exchange rate policy, macro-prudential supervision policy; and reinforce and improve the administration of modern financial system and its related rules and regulations.

First, plans and measures should be put in place to study and advance the assumption proposed by Mundell regarding the creation of a 3-in-1 currency area, which covers the US dollar, euro, and RMB, and explore the advantages and disadvantages of the national policy of a strong RMB, so as for RMB to play its due role as an international currency that can be freely used. China must take advantage of the opportunity to gradually expedite the opening of capital accounts, develop a financial market with depth and fluidity, deregulate interest rates and exchange rates progressively, strengthen supervision, and improve the regulatory framework. In this way, it will align RMB with US dollar, euro, Japanese yen, and British pound and enable it to play its role as an international currency.

Second, the mechanism for the offshore and onshore interaction of RMB should be established along with the coastal transaction settlement center for overseas business RMB by leveraging the FTZ experimental plot. Specifically, the China International Banking Facilities (CIBF) needs to be in place. Measures must be taken to gradually promote the facilitation in trade, investment and financing, the convertibility of capital accounts, offline-online interaction, an exchange between local and foreign currencies, participation in domestic and international enterprises, and the deepened opening of current accounts toward capital accounts. The offshore RMB payment clearing system, which functions in the same way as the Chips system in the United States, should be established and ameliorated. Measures must be taken to gradually reform the current method of payment clearing that conducts foreign business of the RMB through agents and eventually makes it possible for the sound independent offshore RMB payment clearing system to play its role as a clearing and settlement system, a standard planning system, and a legal supervision system, which perform the linking function across multiple offshore regions and markets.

The national FTZ should strengthen its connection with the Hong Kong offshore center and jointly build a global RMB offshore financial market. It should gradually form an international management center for RMB foreign business, which holds the pricing rights of offshore RMB, conducts bidirectional investment and financing, joint interactive supervision, and orderly offshore and onshore outflow, and provides healthy backflow and external circulation. Advantage should be taken of international finance to develop new business formats and achieve bend overtaking in RMB internationalization. The development of online financing can be cited as an example, and the establishment of a standardized carbon spots and futures exchange that binds RMB as a settlement currency. Through the twenty-first century Maritime Silk Road, China will reach out to Southeast Asia and even the whole of Asia by leveraging carbon spot and futures and successfully achieve the bend overtaking in RMB internationalization, following the practice of binding coal to the British pound in the nineteenth century and oil to the US dollar in the twentieth century and consequently tying carbon emissions right trading to RMB in the twenty-first century for international settlement.

1.5 The Establishment of an Organization for the Top-Level Layout of China's Finance

In modern times, the United States relies on its military, IT, and financial development to dominate the international currency system and financial affairs. The underpinning power behind military strength and IT is the strong modern financial system.

Let us take a first look at China's tertiary industry, which accounted for 52.2% of its GDP in 2018, 57.3% during the first quarter of 2019, and 54% during the first three quarters of 2019, a distance of more than 20% for growth, compared with the world's average level of 55% to 60% and the advanced level of 70% in developed countries and regions. The development of the modern financial system is bound to play an essential role in its process. During its 40 years of reform and opening up, China designated the People's Bank of China as its central bank early in 1983, promulgated the *Law on Commercial Banks* in 1995, which established the regulatory system of finance in China and called for the implementation of separate operations and management. It completed its organization mode in 2003 for the independent supervision of banking, securities, and insurance. Currently, with the intensified transnational financial progress, the increasing number of tasks for promoting growth and for assisting transformation, China is faced with the crucial and urgent task of making top-level designs and layouts for its finance, due to its limited time span, the intensification of change, and the high speed of development. Now let us look at it from a global perspective. The third industrial revolution assumed the characteristics of individuation, dispersion, and intelligentization, service industry was deemed as a new growth point, and the innovative integration of modern financial sector and science and technology became the core of development. Therefore, China should consider establishing an organization for the top-level layout of national finance to effectively cope with domestic and international financial affairs and forming a leading, deliberating, and coordinating body that is responsible for top-level design of national finance, regulation of major financial issues, significant financial decision-making, and prevention of systematic financial risks to boost stable, healthy, and sustainable development of finance in China.

It goes without doubt that the organization for top-level design and layout of China's finance will be a consulting and decision-making body for the state in formulating major financial policies and economic initiatives. These policies will play an essential role in the macro control of domestic and international finance, the formulation of monetary policy, and responding to financial emergencies. The organization should be composed of about 15 people, including the state leader in charge of finance, leaders of the Ministry of Finance, the People's Bank of China, CBIRC, CSRC, other banks, securities, insurance and financial institutions, financial experts, and the officials responsible for finance in Beijing, Shanghai, and Guangdong, which are the leading economic regions in China. The state leader will act as chairman. Within the organization, a secretariat is set up as a permanent body and performs the duties of creating and adjusting major financial policies as well as formulating relevant objectives, tools, and initiatives of fiscal systems on the basis of a comprehensive analysis of the macro-financial situation at home and abroad with focus laid on the national targets for macro-financial design and adjustment. As a result, this body, which will lead, coordinate, and decide upon the top-level layout of national finance, the regulation of major financial affairs, the making of major financial decisions, and the prevention of significant business risks, will report directly to the central government.

The work procedures of such a body should go as follows: regular meetings should be held, and preferably in the first month of each quarter; at the motion of the chair or one-third of the body members, an unscheduled meeting may be called; the meeting is to be presided over by the chairman, or by the vice chairman if the chairman cannot attend for one reason or another; a bill which is filed by members will become a written proposal only when it is voted on and approved by two-thirds of the members present at the meeting; proposals and meeting minutes are to be attached as an appendix to the proposal to be submitted to the central government for examination and approval; once the central government approves a monetary policy and its matching measures, the body should be responsible for their immediate enforcement by financial entities through leading, organization, and coordination.

A good case in point is the direct effects of America's QE monetary policy upon China's vast reserve of American dollar and exporting conditions and, consequently, upon the stable and sustainable growth of Chinese economy. China needs not only to adjust and improve the structure of its national foreign exchange reserve but, more importantly, to speed up the establishment of its home currency as one of the major international currencies for settlement in the drive for the internationalization of RMB and secure its say and initiative in international financial affairs.

Another case is the question of whether China should continue adhering to its present independent financial policy of separate operation and management amid the disputes over the American financial crisis and the supervision of mixed operations. It is my belief that China should decide according to its actual situation and reality and continue implementing its supervision policies of separate operation and management in the foreseeable future. It has not been a long time since China completed its system of separate operation and management, and there is a great deal of room for promotion, enhancement, and improvement. When viewed from a professionalized perspective, commercial banks can conduct supervision by referring to the asset-liability ratio and capital adequacy ratio in the *Basel Accord*, while supervisory norms for the securities industry and its derivatives need to be improved. When viewed from the perspective of preventing financial risks, China's growing financial market needs effective firewalls for financial development. Therefore, for those existing financial groups of mixed operations, regulatory and technical measures must be taken for the supervision of separate operation and management. Quick decisions must be made to define the scope and nature of those newly emerging financial businesses that should be effectively incorporated into the development and supervisory framework of separate operation and management. The development path of finance in China should be promoting competition according to planning and seeking growth in stable development.

Whether PBC should expand, enhance, and improve its functions is another issue for discussion. As central bank, PBC should not only fulfill its duties of currency supply, fluidity adjustment, and foreign exchange affairs but intensify its functions of adjusting and supervising banks, securities, and insurance markets, including the incorporation of securities and insurance investment funds into the underlying factors for currency issuance and adjustment, the utilization of monetary market funds to effectively adjust securities and insurance markets, and the inclusion of investment and credit ratios of securities and insurance as a tool for monetary policies, as well as the extended regulation and supervision of overseas businesses Chinese financial institutions conduct. All these enhance the dominant and central position of PBC in the development of the modern financial system.

It is worth discussing whether the central bank of China should quickly set up the relevant auxiliary financial supervision institution to adequately improve the financial regulatory system. An example of this type is the China Deposit & Insurance Company, which protects the rights and interests of investors and consumers in the same way as the FDIC of the United States does. This also functions as a mutual fund on the monetary market under the control of the central bank of China. It effectively adjusts the stable development of the demands of banks, securities, insurance, and investments.

Additionally, some attention should be paid to whether China needs to focus more on the legal system building and organizational improvement and the creation of market-oriented mechanisms for bearing financial risks and making up for losses, including the harmonization, coordination, and consistency of relations between PBC functions and those of financial regulatory bodies in the implementation of monetary policy, financial stability, and financial regulation, the establishment of a counter-cyclical, macro-financial prudential management system with differential reserves, counter-cyclical capital requirements, and prospective provisioning requirements, and the formulation of stricter regulatory standards that contain provisions for additional capital and fluidity as well as the exposure of significant risks. By so doing, this mechanism will intensify the supervision of systematically important financial institutions.

Furthermore, there is the question of whether it is necessary to set up a sound organization and long-term mechanism, such as an institution like FDIC in the United States (apart from the Ministry of Finance and the central bank of the state). This institution will exercise effective supervision of financial institutions and perform its duty of orderly clearing the systematically important financial institutions. Its deposit insurance system of scientific design will become a platform of comprehensive disposal for the state to respond to the financial crisis while maintaining public confidence so that it may facilitate the overall stability of the financial system. Moreover, market-oriented disposal methods can also be an option for reducing the cost of handling financial risks and increasing disposal efficiency. It covers the establishment of a mechanism for the risks shareholders and creditors share. The loss will be shouldered by shareholders first and then creditors. This risk sharing mechanism will answer the need for senior management to be responsible for operation failures, formulating deposit insurance systems, reducing the reliance on public relief funds, and making plans for the restoration and disposal of systematically important financial institutions so as to set up and improve the mechanism for the orderly market-oriented resolution of financial risks. It is of the same importance to strengthen the monitoring, assessment, and early warning of financial risks and even dangers so as to genuinely and adequately protect the interests of small and medium investors while disposing of financial risks.

One more issue is to do with importing and exporting, which are among the major ways of China's more effective participation in international affairs. China should be not only a trade partner but an economic partner of low-carbon policies in such areas as traffic system and water resources administration and regional public resources administration. From a more profound and broader perspective, it is more of an issue of China's resolve in becoming a positive participant in international economic and financial affairs. Asia, for example, accounts for 60% of global fund reserves, and China should work out ways of getting involved in this field. Is it possible to set up an organization like the "Asian Monetary Fund" and consider it as a breakthrough point under the same framework as IMF? On the one hand, it will achieve the cyclic use of the huge foreign exchange reserve of Asia and the effective use of fund demand adjustments in the case of any fluctuations on the trade circulation market. On the other hand, it can also function as a platform for Asian economies to work together to stabilize their economy and pursue cooperation and joint development through mutual help and benefit so as for China and other Asian countries to strengthen their say in international financial affairs.

It is of essential significance and urgent necessity to reinforce top-level design of China's finance, explore more of the current situation and future development of modern financial system at home and abroad, and improve top-level layout of China's finance.

2

The "Twin-Peak" Model for Financial Regulation—A Review of Financial Regulatory and Coordinating Measures in China

Chinese financial regulation is rooted in two major theories—the theory of financial risk and the theory of investor interest protection. The first one stems from the following considerations: finance is an industry of high risks, such as risks of interest rate, exchange rate, fluidity, and credit; finance can spawn a chain reaction leading to payment crises; and finance directly influences the stability of the currency system and macroeconomy. The second considers asymmetry of market information and a fair and just environment for investment.

What are of relevant significance here are the improvement of financial regulatory policies and measures and the top-level design and selection of modes for financial supervision in China.

2.1 The Financial Regulation System in America

America is often cited for the complexity of its financial regulation system, which takes its financial supervision from segregated business management to mixed business management. In 1933, America passed the

Glass-Steagall Act, which set forth the following principles for financial regulation: (a) separating operation and management of both commercial banks and investment banks, (b) prohibiting banks from directly dealing with the underwriting and proprietary trading business of securities and treasury bonds, (c) prohibiting investment banks from carrying out any deposit absorption business, and (d) prohibiting affiliates of the Federal Reserve and its related banks from dealing in securities transaction. In addition, the Federal Deposit Insurance Corporation (FDIC) was established along with its relevant auxiliary organizations for financial regulation.

In 1999, after decades of debate, the *Gramm-Leach-Bliley Act* was passed. It formally repealed in the legal form the *Glass-Steagall Act* and lifted strict restrictions that the *Glass-Steagall Act* had placed on the financial industry. The provisions that separated the banking industry from the securities industry for operation and management were reversed. The new act allowed the establishment of subordinate financial holding companies (FHC) and their full participation in banking service, securities underwriting, proprietary businesses, and insurance transactions.

In 2010, America passed the *Dodd-Frank Wall Street Reform and Consumer Protection Act*, which called for the universal intensification of financial regulation that would cover the setup of government regulatory organs, the prevention of systematic risks, the promotion of financial segmentation, financial product and consumer protection, crisis management, and so on. This law became the most extensive in terms of regulation and range in America from the 1929–1933 Great Depression. A new federal regulatory body—the Financial Stability Oversight Council (FSOC)—was setup with rights to gather information from financial institutions and make proposals to the Federal Reserve and other regulators in relation to standards for prudential supervision. The scope of the Federal Reserve regulation was expanded so that rights were granted to formulate regulatory standards to maintain compliance with regulatory principles and supervise matters of payment, clearing, and settlement that pertained to securities products of financial institutions under its regulation. The "Volcker" rule was enforced to limit the scale of investments made by commercial banks through hedge funds and private equity funds to within 3% of fund owners, banks, and capitals. The role of the Federal Deposit Insurance Corporation (FDIC) was expanded and reinforced. The Deposit Administration was closed down by transferring its functions to the Federal Reserve, the Office of the Comptroller of Currency (OCC), and the FDIC. The regulatory function of the Securities and Exchange Commission (SEC) was intensified for securities companies, listed companies, and credit rating institutions with the establishment of the filing system of private equity funds and new organizations under the SEC, including the Investors Solicitors Office, Investors Consulting Committee, and Credit Rating Bureau. More regulatory power was granted to the Commodity Futures Trading Commission (CFTC) with respect to transactions involving derivative products and swaps. The Federal Insurance Agency was established under the Department of the Treasury to supervise the insurance industry at the federal level. Previously, the states, rather than the federal department, exercised independent supervision. All this contributed to facilitating the effective operation of the entire financial regulation regime, identifying and preventing systematic financial risks, promptly disposing of any potential emergency risks and incidents, and maintaining the stability of financial markets. (See the figures that compare the US financial regulation systems before the 2018 crisis and after 2010.)

Figures 2.1 and 2.2 demonstrate that prior to the 2008 international financial crisis in America: (a) regulatory relations were complex and lacking in coordination; (b) there was low efficiency due to the fact that one organization was under the supervision of several regulators; (c) the SEC was once a major regulator but lacked the capability and expertise for prudential supervision of investment banks, such as Bear Stearns Cos. and Lehman Brothers Holdings; (d) insurance supervision at the state level lacked the expertise for supervising complex products, such as the CDS sold by AIG; (e) unaccountability existed with quite many regulators.

As Fig. 2.3 demonstrates, subsequent to the 2008 International Financial Crisis, America passed and implemented the *Dodd-Frank Wall Street Reform and Consumer Protection Act* in July 2010. The biggest modification made in the Act was its restructuring of the financial regulation system and the reform of the entire American financial regulatory framework to prevent potential systematic financial risks.

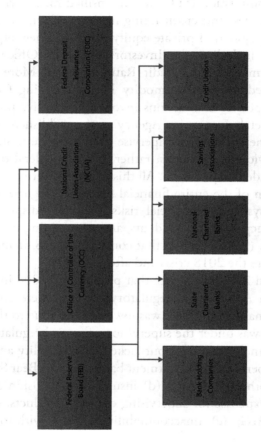

Fig. 2.1 American financial regulation regime—depository institutions (before the 2008 international financial crisis)

2 The "Twin-Peak" Model for Financial Regulation—A Review...

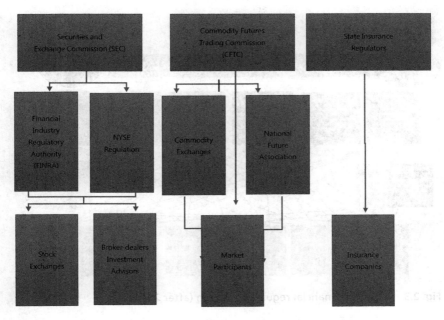

Fig. 2.2 American financial regulation regime—securities, futures, and insurance (before the 2008 international financial crisis)

First, the prolonged absence was remedied of a nationwide, universal regulation system and legal system framework in American financial industry.

Second, the Financial Stability Oversight Council (FSOC) was set up for the purpose of promoting the three cores of financial stability, that is, preventing systematic risks, protecting consumers, and improving the accountability system and transparency. Accordingly, the FSOC was endowed with three major functions: (a) identifying the risks that endangered American financial stability, (b) promoting self-restraints in financial markets, lowering expectations for government relief reducing and moral risks, and (c) effectively responding to new risks that endangered the stability of American financial system. Three corresponding powers were delegated to the FSOC: (a) promoting the collection and sharing of information and, on this basis, boosting regulatory coordination; (b) strengthening the identification and prevention of systematic financial

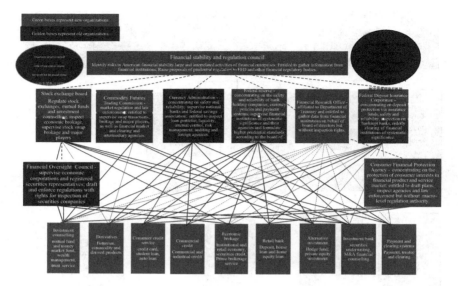

Fig. 2.3 American financial regulation system (after 2010)

risks in an all-encompassing manner based on the actual conditions of American financial market, to be more specific, at the institutional level identifying systematically important non-banking financial institutions and classifying them into the regulatory scope of the Federal Reserve, at the level of financial markets, empowering them to recognize the facilities of systematically important financial markets together with their payments, clearing, and settlement systems, with regard to financial regulatory standards empowering them to propose the implementation of stricter prudential supervision standards for institutions on a larger scale and for strong, relevant, or compulsory spin-offs for any institution that constitutes a serious threat against American financial stability; (c) possessing the right to recommend that American Congress amend laws and reduce any gaps in regulation.

Third, this act streamlined previous regulatory bodies through restructuring and strengthened inter-institution cooperation for closer supervision of separate operation. First, within the Department of the Treasury, the Federal Insurance Office (FIO) was set up to expand regulatory powers of the federal government over insurance institutions. Second, within the Federal Reserve, the Consumer Financial Protection Agency (CFPA) was set up to centralize financial protective authorities that were originally distributed to the Fed and SEC to supervise such financial institutions as banks, credit cooperatives, securities companies, and mortgage loan service agencies with the intent to protect the interests of financial consumers from damages caused by unfair or fraudulent financial transactions. Third, the Office of Thrift Supervision (OTS) was closed and most of its authorities were incorporated into the Office of the Comptroller of the Currency (OCC). Fourth, the Federal Reserve's range of authorities was broadened to intensify its core position in the umbrella-shaped system of financial regulation and turn it into a comprehensive regulator that could play a more significant role as a systematic risk administrator in steadily regulating financial institutions, products, and markets.

2.2 The UK Financial Regulation System

The financial regulation system in the UK developed from complete "self-regulation" to central bank intervention and mixed operation and then to separate operation and supervision.

In 1979, the UK issued its first bank act requiring institutions receiving public deposits to be examined and approved for their license. In 1987, articles concerning regulations on the Bank of England were added, together with the rights to examine bank shareholders and investigate bank executives. In 1998 and 2000, the *Bank of England Act* and the *Financial Service and Market Act* were passed. The former vested the Bank of England with the decision right of monetary policies to set interest rates according to the inflation targets of the government and monitor the flow of deposit funds. The latter set the rules for mixed operation and supervision and incorporated guarantee and insurance businesses into supervision so as to ensure the stability of the financial system, protect investor interest, and fight against financial crimes.

In 2012, the UK passed the *Financial Services Bill*, which consists of two parts. Part one contains provisions for (a) completing the separate management of the banking sector from the securities sector in 2019, (b) ensuring that depositors have priority for compensation in case of bankruptcy, (c) empowering the government to protect banks and dispose of losses, and (d) proposing a higher capital adequacy ratio standard for banks after the separation of businesses. Part two contains provisions for the regulation system composed of the Bank of England, the Financial Policy Commission (FPC), the Prudential Regulation Authority (PRA), and the Financial Conduct Authority (FCA). The Bank of England was granted the rights of the central bank by the Parliament to implement a system of board of directors, formulate and implement monetary policies, exercise micro- and macro-prudential supervision, and supervision of financial market infrastructure on behalf of the central bank. The FPC was established as part of the central bank composed of 13 members.

Among them six are from the central bank, five independent experts, one from the FCA, and one from Her Majesty's Treasury. Its initial primary objective was to review the likely risks of the financial system and provide a strategic direction for full-time regulators, and its secondary objective was to enforce the use of macro-prudential tools, for example, restrictions on bank leverage ratios and compulsory capital requirements for different types of assets, which were designed to offset financial risks and provide underpinnings for government economic policies. Its ultimate objective was to assume general responsibility for the identification, monitoring, and prevention of systematic financial risks.

The FPC can guide and is entitled to instruct the PRA and FCA to take risk mitigating measures, put forward suggestions on fluidity and other matters to the central bank, inspect the payment and settlement systems and clearing companies, and offer suggestions to Her Majesty's Treasury on adjusting the requirements for industrial capital and other related matters with focus on addressing the key issues of financial stability and removing potential barriers to the implementation of macro-prudential policies. The PRA is composed of the legal corporate institutions under the central bank. Its focus is laid on supervising and managing the implementation of prudential policies in the banking industry and in the insurance system, passing judgment about whether they are in healthy condition, evaluating their current and potential risks, and taking preventive measures for risks to the stability of the financial system in financial institutions, especially banks and insurance agencies. The FCA regulates independently, and its head is appointed by Her Majesty's

Treasury and is held accountable to Her Majesty's Treasury and the Parliament. It chiefly supervises the business behavior of financial institutions (including consulting companies) that rely chiefly on the capital market.

The FCA's focus is on (a) effectively supervising the activities of the capital market, (b) adjusting any conflicts of interests, (c) disposing of customers' assets in an orderly manner, (d) maintaining market credit, opposing market fraud, and preventing systematic risks and financial crimes, (e) giving top priority to customers' interests, (f) preventing dumping and protecting the interests of retail consumers, and (g) promoting effective competition. The major measures involved include: (a) examination and approval or cancellation of corporate licenses, (b) prevention of admittance to individuals, (c) suspension of corporate or personal underwriting qualifications, (d) imposition of fines on companies or individuals for violations, (e) punishment for companies that violate competition laws, (f) advance notification of rules before implementation, (g) application to the courts for bankruptcies, (h) punishment of insider dealing and other financial crimes, and (i) warning to those companies or individuals who violate network rules with a view to protecting the rights and interests of investors, maintaining financial stability, and promoting healthy and effective competition. (See figures comparing the UK financial regulation systems before and after the 2008 international financial crisis.)

The figure shows that before the 2008 international financial crisis in the UK (1) the tripartite coordination was weak as none of the institutions bore the responsibility for the overall supervision of the financial system; (2) between 1998 and 2000, the administration of financial regulations was not integrated, and the Financial Services Authority (FSA) only played a minor role in internal organization; (3) within the FSA, the numerous supervisory tasks required of it caused its resources and assets to become over-stretched, resulting in inadequate powers needed for prudential supervision; (4) its focus on financial stability was distracted by its goal of turning London into a global financial center; (5) the Labor Party announcement of the FSA in 1997 lacked legality due to its failure to pass an initial consulting procedure, and its release met with great public shock and controversy.

As can be seen from Figs. 2.4 and 2.5, there evolved in the UK a system of weak regulation to a system of twin-peak regulation. Its financial regulation was accompanied by transformations in the operation mode of the financial industry, which developed from self-regulation, to intervention by the central bank, and then to the twin-peak regulation of mixed operations (see Table 2.1).

In 2012, the UK introduced a new regulatory framework marked by *The Financial Services Act*. As the key to Britain's financial regulation reform, it set forth the statutory duties of regulatory organizations and created the "twin-peak" regulatory architecture, which placed the PRA directly under the central bank and the FCA directly under Her Majesty's Treasury and Parliament, which function like two wings. The PRA implements prudential regulation and is mainly responsible for the banking and insurance industries. The FCA reports to Parliament and Her Majesty's Treasury provides consumer protection and is mainly responsible for the regulation of the securities market. The FPC typically handles systematic risks as an internal organization of the central bank and provides guidance for the PRA and FCA.

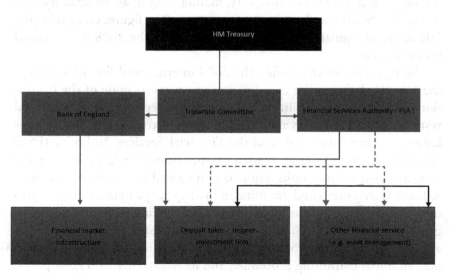

Fig. 2.4 UK financial regulation systems—pre-crisis-tripartite model

2 The "Twin-Peak" Model for Financial Regulation—A Review...

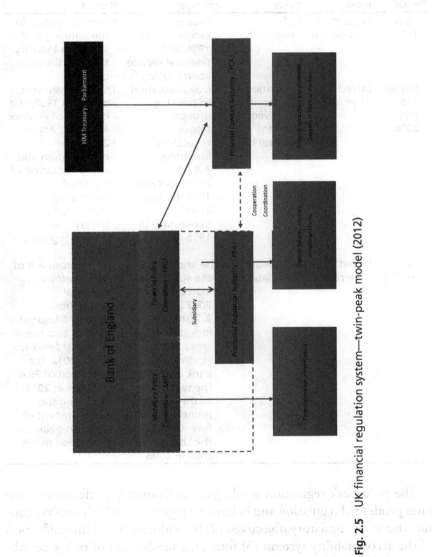

Fig. 2.5 UK financial regulation system—twin-peak model (2012)

Table 2.1 Historical stages of British financial regulation

Period	Operation mode	Regulation mode	Background for regulatory changes	Results
Before 1987	Separated operation	Self-regulation	"Financial explosion" in 1986 and financial service liberalization	Mixed operation in the banking and securities industry through financial groups
Between 1987 and 2000	Mixed operation	Regulation under intervention by the central bank	Weak regulation of banking groups, frequent regulatory loopholes, B.B.C.I. bankruptcy in 1991, Barings Bank bankruptcy in 1995	The establishment of FSA in 1998; the issuance of *Finance & Market Act* in 2000, the confirmation and implementation of a unified regulatory framework, and the creation of unified regulation by 2004
After 2012	Mixed operation	Twin-peak regulation	The impacts of the sub-prime loan crisis in 2007 upon the British financial industry, the crises of the Northern Rock Bank and RBS, the worsening of the British economy and finance after the Lehman crisis in 2008	The enforcement of *New Method of Financial Regulation: Reform Blueprint* in 2011 and *The Financial Services Act* in 2012, the operation of *PRA* and *FCA* in 2013, signifying the establishment of the twin-peak regulation mode

The twin-peak regulation mode goes as follows: (1) effectively separates prudential regulation and behavioral regulation, which resolves conflicts between regulatory objectives; (2) is conducive to the intensification of the accountability system; (3) forms the mechanism of policy coordination and information sharing; (4) coordinates monetary policies and prudential regulation; (5) facilitates interaction between macro- and micro-prudential regulation; (6) unifies the regulation of conduct in the securities market while protecting consumers' interests; (7) reveals serious defects in the existing British regulatory mode, represented by the absence of top-level coordination mechanisms for solving conflicts between prudential regulation and behavioral regulation in times of major economic and financial crises.

2.3 The Financial Regulation System in the EU

From 2012, the EU financial regulation system is divided into macro-prudential regulation and micro-prudential regulation, and its financial regulation shifted from mixed regulation toward separated regulation, as is shown in Fig. 2.6.

The European Systematic Risk Council (ESRC) takes responsibility for macro-prudential regulation and is composed of the EU Central Bank, the central banks of EU member countries, the European Supervisory Authorities (ESA), and the European Commission. Its chairman is the governor of the EU Central Bank, which performs the functions of macro-prudential regulation, administers monetary policies and

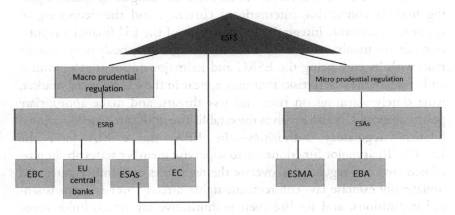

Fig. 2.6 EU financial regulation scheme: EA

other functions in association with a central bank. In 2015, it set up a dedicated regulatory organization composed of 127 joint regulation teams. Each saw the exclusive regulation of each of the 127 large commercial banks within the EU and reported to the EU Central Bank. The ESRC decides on matters related to the prevention and mitigation of systematic financial risks and is responsible for the coordination and cooperation with other internal and external regulatory organizations.

The ESA takes responsibility for micro-prudential regulation. The vice chairman of the ESRC acts as its chairman. The ESA consists of the European Securities & Markets Authority (ESMA), the European Banking Authority (EBA), and the European Insurance and Occupational Pensions Authority (EIOPA). The ESMA is responsible for regulating the securities market operation, the EBA small- and medium-sized commercial banks of EU member states through the regulators of EU countries, and the EIOPA insurance business and the pension fund investments.

According to my observations, it is high time for the EU to reform the EU financial regulation scheme, as the EU debt crisis has fully exposed its defects. The EU member states each acted in their own way with regard to financial regulation. They lacked unified means of macro-regulation, which made it difficult to conduct a comprehensive assessment and disposal of systematic risks. The EU accelerated the establishment of a unified financial regulation scheme in response to the spreading of the sovereign debt crisis of member states, the weakening of its speech righting matters concerning international currency, and the deepening of European economic integration. The reform of the EU financial regulation scheme involves the establishment of a regulatory body of systematic risks with its core being the ESRC and its major duties are to monitor and evaluate the macro risks that may appear in the EU financial market, issue timely warnings on risks and risk threats, and make appropriate policy proposals. It also involves the establishment of three super-national financial regulatory authorities—the EBA, the ESMA, and the EIOPA. Their major functions are to supervise member states abiding by related laws and regulations, oversee the regulators of member states and unilaterally exercise law enforcement rights directly over relevant financial institutions, and finalize their authoritative say which holds more weight than that of the member states regulators. In addition, "consumer protection" was established as the central objective of financial regulation intended to prevent and combat irrational and fraudulent behavior that was often found in financial operation. The core of the EU financial regulation scheme reform is to advocate the building of a framework of macro-prudential regulation based on strengthening micro-prudential regulation. Given the differences of macro- and micro-prudential regulation in the objects of regulation (i.e., the whole financial system vs. a single financial institution), the objectives of regulation (i.e., systematic risks vs. individual risks), and the mechanisms of regulation (including the macro indicators of asset prices, total credit and institutional leverage ratio, micro indicators of asset adequacy ratio, and the fluidity and non-performing loan ratio), such regulatory arrangements of the EU integrating macro- and micro-prudential regulation have become the mainstream legislation for the international financial regulation in the era of the post-2008 crisis. Finally, the EU countries are reluctant to discard their regulation rights, which make it difficult for a unified financial regulation scheme to effectively play its role.

2.4 Differences and Similarities in Financial Regulation Schemes

A comparison between the UK, USA, and EU in the evolution and current situation of their financial regulation schemes displays the following common features. First, transformation in financial regulatory legislation has been a dominating theme. After the 1929–1933 economic depression, America proclaimed *The Glass-Steagall Act*—a fundamental law that stipulated separate operation and management in the financial sector. Faced with fierce competition in the international financial industry during the 1980s and 1990s, America issued *The Gramm-Leach-Bliley Act* in 1999, which restored mixed operation and management in the financial sector. In response to the 2007–2008 financial "tsunamis," *The Dodd-Frank Wall Street Reform and Consumer Protection Act* was passed to impose strict regulatory restrictions. The UK financial market had always upheld the notion of "self regulation." In 1979, the UK passed its first act but exercised limited regulation on the institutions that absorbed public deposits. In 1987, a banking act was passed to call for the Bank of England to practice regulation. Between 1998 and 2000, *The Bank of England Act* was enforced, followed by *The Financial Service and Market Act* in 2012. After experiencing the world financial tsunami, the UK passed *the Financial Services Act*. In the EU, continuous improvement was made in financial regulation through legislation in 2012 and 2015. Apparently, legislation reform and improvement have been made continuously in America, Britain, and the EU to enhance their financial regulation schemes.

Second, a coordinating mechanism that gave equal focus to micro- and macro-prudential regulation was established. The former concentrates on individual financial institutions, with focus on micro-level indicators, such as capital adequacy ratio, fluidity, and non-performing loan ratio, and on the prevention of risks in individual institutions. The latter concentrates on the entire financial system and its relevance to the real economy, with focus on macro-level indicators, such as asset prices, total credit, and institutional leverage ratios. It lays emphasis on the entire financial market, systematically important financial institutions, and the shadow banking system, and regards it as its priority to prevent systematic risks. The 2008 financial crisis alerted the UK, USA, and the EU to the strengthening of macro-prudential regulation on the basis of intensified micro-prudential regulation and to the facilitation of the integration of micro- and macro-prudential regulation. In 2010, the Financial Stability Oversight Board was set up in USA and was empowered to collect information from financial institutions and make proposals to the Federal Reserve and other major financial regulators regarding standards for prudential regulation. In 2012, the UK set up the Financial Policy Committee, which was given the right to make suggestions and take measures in relation to prudential and behavioral regulation. Additionally, the UK established the "Prudential Regulation Authority" with the intent to implement macro- and micro-prudential regulation. The EU financial regulation scheme is directly practiced on both micro- and macro-levels, with equal focus on both levels.

Third, the protection of the rights and interests of financial consumers was intensified. The 2008 financial crisis caused financial regulators to suffer a spate of criticisms owing to inadequate protection for consumers. The experience and lessons gained from the financial crisis led to a series of measures being taken to strengthen consumer protection. The Consumer Financial Protection Bureau (CFPB) was founded in America and was dedicated to the protection of consumer rights and interests. It has the right to make rules, carry out inspection, and take punitive measures, such as fines, sanctions, and other penalties for rule violation. After the establishment of the CFPB, the American Congress introduced *The Financial Consumer Protection Agency Act*. In the UK, *The Financial Services Act* was enforced, which quickly triggered off a thorough reform of British financial regulation scheme by founding a new special organization—the FCA, responsible for the protection of financial consumer rights and interests. In the EU, a series of new regulators were put in place, such as the ESRC, ESMA, EBA, and EIOPA, and they regard the protection of financial consumers as the primary role of their work.

The above comparison also demonstrates the following major differences. First, while USA went from separate to mixed operation, the UK and the EU went from mixed to separated operation. In 1933, USA started separate operation and management of financial institutions but returned to the mode of mixed operation and management in the 1990s. There coexisted regulatory overlapping and vacuum in its regulation system for historical and realistic reasons. *The Dodd-Frank Act* of 2010 vested the newly established FSOC with the special power of coordinating and promoting the sharing of information between regulators. However, it failed to make substantive integration in addressing the "buck-passing" or overlapping of the institutions involved in system regulation. What it presented was a track of "crisis orientation" and "patch upgrading," which has given rise to theoretical controversies. It remains to be observed whether that act will ensure no systematic financial crisis, like the 1929–1933 economic depression and the 2007–2008 financial crises, in USA and for how long. *The Financial Services Act* issued in 2012 in the UK explicitly stipulates that the separation operation of the banking industry from the securities industry be completed in 2019, and under that framework were established the Prudential Regulation Authority (PRA) and the Financial Conduct Authority (FCA), both of which developed from the Financial Service Authority. The UK blazed its own way of preventing financial risks from its disposals of several crises. In 2012, separate regulation and administration were also practiced in the EU.

Second, the most remarkable characteristic of American financial innovation is the cross-industry creation of derivative products, that is, the so-called shadow bank. The financial technology of "Firewall" has been implemented for the regulation and supervision of such "shadow banks." There appeared prior to the outbreak of the 2008 crisis a few special investment banking companies and financial derivatives, such as Special Purpose Vehicles (SPV), Asset-Backed Securitization (ABS), Mortgage-Backed Securitization (MBS), American Depository Receipts (ADR), Residential Mortgage-backed Securities (RMBS), Commercial Mortgage-Backed Securities (CMBS), Credit Default Swap (CDS), and Collateral Debt Obligation (CDO). They embraced the enthusiastic participation of commercial banks, investment banks, and insurance companies. After the outbreak of the 2008 crisis, under the "Walker Rule," USA imposed strict restrictions on cross-industry investments, established a strict inspection system that integrated on-site and off-site regulation to control the leverage ratio of financial products, and provided timely disclosure of relevant information concerning the design, sales, and transactions of derivative products. By so doing the UK has realized the separation of prudential regulation from conduct supervision. The EU has stuck to the path of mixed operation and separate regulation. That demonstrates that the paths of operation and regulation vary from the UK, USA, and the EU.

However, practices have turned out that the separate management of banking and securities industries should be ensured in terms of legal provisions, accounts, clearing and settlement infrastructure and that technical "firewalls" for financial regulation should be established so that disputes and doubts can be removed regarding separate or mixed regulation. Technologically, "firewalls" should be installed between the banking industry and the securities industry so as to guarantee the fundamentally effective prevention of systematic financial risks. It is for the financial regulators to determine according actual circumstance whether banks, securities brokers, and insurers should coexist or should be unified and whether banks and insurance companies should be placed under the supervision of the central bank while securities brokers be regulated separately. There should be adequate certainty that whatever ways of regulation and supervision will not reduce the effect of "firewalls." The crucial issue resides in the effects of technical barriers, and institutional change is merely a matter of cost and efficiency. Technologically effective financial "firewalls" must be in place for lack of criteria for macro- and micro-prudential regulation with regard to the securities industry and its derivative products and more in-depth explorations about how to make improvements on financial markets. In addition, the existing financial groups of mixed businesses should be regulated with respect to their internal measures for the system and technology that are implemented for separate operation and management and the early defining of the nature of newly created financial businesses and their effective categorization within the technical framework of separate operation and management of accounts and clearing and settlement systems. It should be a general rule for worldwide financial development and regulation to boost competition under planning and secure stability through development.

Third, a clear framework of regulation has been identified in *The Financial Services Act* in the UK in 2012, which marked a gradual shift from self-regulation of financial markets to sound law-based regulation. The bankruptcy of the Bank of Credit and Commerce International (BCCI) and Barings Bank in the 1990s, together with the crisis of the Royal Bank of Scotland in the 2008 financial tsunami, led the UK to put the intensification of macro-prudential and separate regulation on the list of top priorities in financial risk prevention, confirmed by a "twin-peak" regulation system, which has laid a sound legal foundation for further consolidating and enhancing its position in the global financial market.

2.5 Selection of Modes of Financial Regulation in China

2.5.1 The "Twin-Peak" Mode of Financial Regulation

There are generally three types of financial regulation schemes, that is, single, multiple, twin-peak. The single regulatory scheme refers to a single financial regulator implementing highly centralized regulation for the financial industry, which was the case with the UK before 1998 and is currently the case with most small- and medium-sized countries. The multiple regulatory schemes refer to the regulation of different financial businesses by different institutions, which is currently practiced in America. The twin-peak regulatory schemes refer to the separation of prudential regulation, which is exercised over the banking and insurance industries, from conduct supervision, which is exercised over the securities industry, under which circumstances either separate operation and regulation or mixed operation and separate regulation can be pursued, which can be found in the UK, Canada, and Australia.

A comparison of financial regulation schemes shows that there is no absolutely "best" mode but more effective modes that are time-tested. The key to measuring the success of a regulatory mode resides in its efficiency, professional technology, coordination, legality, and accountability. Efficiency comes from coordination. Legal provisions enable regulators to effectively share and analyze information across departments so that staff members at all levels are able to work together for consensuses and create an atmosphere of trust. That is crucial in times of urgent disposals of financial risks and even crises. In addition, it is of great importance for financial regulators to maintain open dialogues with financial institutions. Efficiency also comes from competence and expertise. Such financial regulation mechanisms can more effectively attract, retain, and cultivate talents and give full play to the role of professionals, as well as facilitating the employment, promotion, and exchange of professionals between regulators. Additionally, efficiency comes from accountability. The members of financial regulatory bodies, especially those on decision-making committees, should avoid groupthink, continuously expand visions, and encourage diversified insights. Within an accountability system members should internally report to its committee or board and externally to the Parliament and the public. Coordination, legality, professional technology, and an accountability system are key to the efficiency of regulation.

After a comparison of financial regulation schemes and modes in the UK, America, and the EU, let us proceed to see what went wrong with their regulatory frameworks before the 2008 financial crisis. In Canada, the northern neighbor of America, its financial regulation scheme (see Fig. 2.7) fared well during the crisis. As a result of a crisis in the 1980s in

2 The "Twin-Peak" Model for Financial Regulation—A Review...

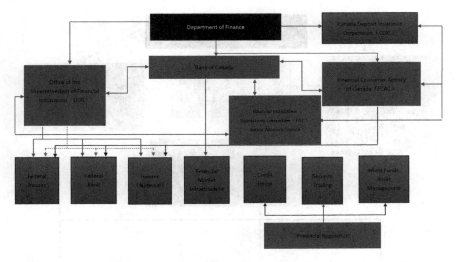

Fig. 2.7 Canada financial regulation system—twin-peak model. (Source: Rotman School of Management, University of Toronto, Canada)

the Canadian banking industry, the Canadian government set up a new prudential regulator in 1987, which was known as the Office of the Superintendent of Financial Institutions (OSFI). This new regulator was granted greater powers (including preemptive action rights) and more resources. It eventually set higher capital standards, laid focus on supervision, and pursued strong regulatory cooperation, which reveals Canada's way of creating their own "twin-peak" mode of financial regulation. Figure 2.8 shows Australia's "twin-peak" mode for its financial regulation scheme, and within the system every regulator has clear missions, task focuses, and tools for advancing effective regulation. As Fig. 2.5 has already indicated, the UK reformed its financial regulation scheme in 2012 and selected the "twin-peak" mode of regulation. It identified prudential regulation from conduct supervision and separated commercial banks, the insurance industry, and the capital market for separate regulation on the basis of industrial categories. That simple clear-cut scheme ensures proper division of work, coordination, and accountability, which is a good example for China to follow in achieving high efficiency.

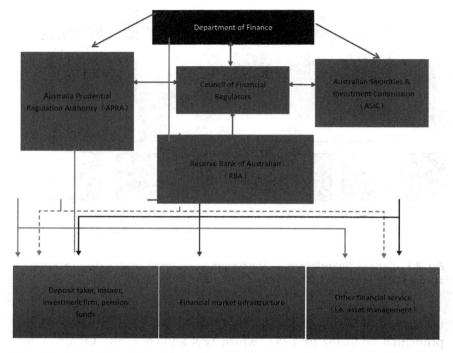

Fig. 2.8 Australian financial regulation system—twin-peak model. (Source: Rotman School of Management, University of Toronto, Canada)

2.5.2 Top-Level Decision-Making Body

The design of financial regulation modes or the creation of financial regulation schemes entails the national-level setup of coordinating, disposal, and decision-making mechanisms for financial regulation, which turns out to be of vital significance. In order to address potential systematic financial crises, America founded the Financial Stability Oversight Council (FSOC) in 2010, followed by the Financial Policy Committee (FPC) in the UK in 2012 and the European Systematic Risk Council (ESRB) in the EU in the same year. They represent the federal or national government in matters of coordination between financial regulators, policy measures, information sharing, and crisis disposals. In China the National Financial Stability Development Committee (NFSDC) was set up in 2017 to address a series of major issues in financial regulation with focus on functions and positioning and the composition of its members, for example, the FPC under the UK central bank composed of 13 people with six from the central bank, one from the FCA, one from Her Majesty's Treasury, and five independent experts. Its functions and structural proportion of members determine its orientation toward coordination, policy, and disposal of financial issues. It should be noted that in addition to formulating monetary policies, the UK central bank has been exercising substantive regulation over the banking and insurance industries.

2.5.3 Interaction of Financial Regulation Policies

Under the Chinese context the concept of "big finance" is to be strongly advocated. It requires the coordination, supplementation, matching, and interaction of fiscal, monetary, and exchange rate policies with regulatory policies for China to strengthen macro-prudential regulation and conduct supervision, develop regulatory tools, make regulatory rules, introduce regulatory measures, and prevent and dispose of financial risks. This is especially true in times of major financial events. For example, monetary policies and macro-prudential regulation have their respective policy objectives and policy tools, and they are generally not replaceable to each other. Therefore, it is highly necessary to strengthen their coordination. In fact, the core issue that the Central Bank of China is faced with is not a choice between the stability of commodity prices and financial stability but a decision-making concerning present and future economic stability. In other words, the implementation of policies must depend on a universal evaluation of the economic situation from the dual perspectives of the stability of commodity prices and financial unbalance. When signs indicate that the Chinese economy has overheated, then it will become problematic to use any macro-prudential tools to make a meaningful difference if monetary policies remain lax and unenforceable. To put it another way, the advantages of macro-prudential regulation in structural adjustment must be based on the appropriate adjustment of monetary aggregate. Therefore, to maintain the stability of the financial environment, it is necessary to take appropriate actions, such as joint top-level financial meetings to promptly digest major problems in financial operation or regulation, to address system issues and exchange ideas about the implementation and orientation of fiscal policies, and to discuss appropriate amendment of monetary, exchange rate and financial regulation policies. These meetings will strengthen the sharing of information, prevent financial institutions from transferring financial assets at will, and investigate rule-breaking operations to prevent individuals from dodging financial regulations. Regular releasing must be made of the facts on the operation of financial policies and financial regulation by using higher grade transparency and guidance of public expectations to make public the attitude and views of the state and financial regulators regarding current financial operation. Effective disposal of major financial events will prevent or alleviate the potential impacts of financial markets on the expectations for financial policy with a view to maintaining the stability of financial markets.

2.5.4 Regulation of Systematically Important Financial Institutions

In China, "one-to-one" regulatory measures should be taken for systematically important financial institutions, which appear to be similar in scope and range to those taken in the EU. A total of 127 work teams were formed in the EU for joint regulation after 127 important financial institutions were identified and confirmed. These teams implement a special system of "one-to-one" regulation and report directly to higher regulatory authorities under accountability. If continuous improvement is made on related measures, "one-to-one" regulation of large important financial institutions will facilitate the enforcement of laws and rules and the suppression of risks, in particular systematic risks, in the financial industry in their budding state.

2.5.5 International Cooperation in Financial Regulation

From a global perspective, financial development goes hand in hand with financial risks. Financial regulation necessitates both regulation schemes and international cooperation in China. Currently, three international organizations have been designed for the coordination of financial regulation. The Basel Committee on Banking Regulation (BCBR) was set up in 1974 to coordinate regulation in the banking industry, the International Organization of Securities Commissions (IOSCO) was set up in 1983 to coordinate regulation in the securities industry, and the International Association of Insurance Supervisors (IAIS) was set up in 1994 to coordinate regulation in the insurance industry. In addition, the Financial Stability Board (FSB), a global organization for coordination in regulating systematically important financial institutions, was set up in 2009 to substantively promote the formulation and implementation of regulatory policies and measures for the purpose of advancing financial stability and addressing problems of financial vulnerability. China's financial regulation scheme will be strengthened in regulation and ameliorated in international cooperation.

3

Local Economic Development and Financial Support—A Study of Chinese Financial Hierarchy

Financial development plays an indispensable role in China's economic growth. Financial repression is typically manifested by singularity of financial assets and institutions, incompatible environment, excessive regulation, backward financial infrastructure, and low financial efficiency, which impede innovation and economic development. The crux of financial liberalization is "relaxed control." Financial development involves interest and exchange rates, currency and capital markets, organizations, tools, derivative products, systems and rules, while financial authorities become fond of relaxing controls, constraints, censorships, and penalties, a typical laissez-faire style. Over a certain period of time, policies of financial liberalization and their matching measures can generate beneficial effects on savings, investments, employment, and economic growth. However, in the long run, they bring about inflation, economic recession, and financial crises.

3.1 Financial Liberalization and National Instability

By the end of the 1980s, economic problems persisted around the world, such as decline in economic growth rates, inadequate momentum to drive economic growth, sluggish demand, decline in population growth rates, twists and turns in economic globalization, turbulent financial markets, and sustained depression of international trade and investment. In 1990, the US Institute for International Economics (IIE) took the lead in formulating ten economic policy prescriptions, that is, the *Washington Consensus*, with support from the International Monetary Fund (IMF), the World Bank, and the US government. The prescriptions read as follows: fiscal policy discipline, with avoidance of large fiscal deficits relative to GDP; redirection of public spending from subsidies ("especially indiscriminate subsidies") toward broad-based provision of key pro-growth, pro-poor services like primary education, primary health care, and infrastructure investment; tax reform, broadening the tax base, and adopting moderate marginal tax rates; interest rates that are market determined and positive (but moderate) in real terms; competitive exchange rates; trade liberalization: liberalization of imports, with particular emphasis on elimination of quantitative restrictions (licensing, etc.); any trade protection to be provided by low and relatively uniform tariffs; liberalization of inward foreign direct investment; privatization of state enterprises; deregulation: abolition of regulations that impede market entry or restrict competition, except for those justified on safety, environmental and consumer protection grounds, and prudential oversight of financial institutions; legal security for property rights. The core of the *Washington Consensus* was to advocate the minimization of government role while accelerating privatization and promoting financial liberalization. In theory, that consensus called for a new model for completely free market economy and the minimization of government role to the greatest extent possible on the assumption that economic growth is possible if the market can freely allocate resources. In policy, it implies the rapid liberalization of markets and internal and external trade, the rapid privatization of state-owned enterprises, and the financial liberalization and market-determined interest rates for promoting economic development.

The Washington Consensus aimed to provide economic reform plans and countermeasures to those Latin American countries that were entrapped in debt crises and a political and economic theoretical basis for transformation in eastern European countries. There was strong justification for the ten policy prescriptions to stimulate economic development over a definite period of time. However, the *Washington Consensus* overlooked the government role which proved to be critical in improving world market system construction, especially in building up a modern financial system, which led to government failure in playing its regulatory role in economic and financial liberalization. The mechanisms of financial market competition failed to function owing to immaturity of financial market, lack of financial legislation and financial disorder. They failed to exert long-lasting influence and ended up in dilemmas.

In 2006, the World Bank came up with the concept of the "middle-income trap." In the transformation of middle-income countries into high-income countries, that is, after breaking through the "poverty trap" of the US$1000 per capita GDP level, developing countries may enter into the "takeoff" stage. However, when they get close to the per capita GDP level of US$ 3000, problems and contradictions that have accumulated in that process, such as increasing costs of resources, management, shortage of core technology, difficulty in innovation, frequent corruption, reduced faith in system, and social unrest, may erupt in succession, which are likely to slow down economic growth and even cause stagnation, thus the "middle-income trap." Such countries typically linger long in the middle-income stage and it takes quite some time for them to reach the high-income level, which is typical of those Latin American countries that pushed forward economic and financial reforms in the light of the principles of the *Washington Consensus*. As early as 1964, Argentina's per capita GDP exceeded US$ 1000 and rose to over US$ 8000 by the end of the 1990s. It fell to just over US$ 2000 in 2002 but bounced back to US$ 12,873 in 2014. It went down to US$ 14,590 in 2017 and 11,600 in 2018. Mexico's per capita GDP reached US$1000 in 1973 and 10,718 in 2014, but it went down to 9811 in 2018 and remained a little over the middle-income level after 45 years. The same is true of several other Latin American countries, which failed to surpass the threshold of US$ 20,000 for developed countries despite their efforts over the past few decades.

An analysis of economic slowdown or stagnation in Latin American countries like Argentina over that period shows the following causes. First, drastic fluctuations occurred in the growth rate of real economy. Between 1960 and 2018, Argentina experienced an average annual growth rate of only 0.55% and 23 years of negative growth in per capita GDP. In 1963 Argentina's per capita GDP was US$842, which was already somewhere above the level of middle- and high-income countries. By 2008, its per capita GDP grew to only US$11,600 but remained at somewhat the same level. Second, the driving force of scientific and technological engines was weak. In 2003, Argentina's proportion of R&D expenses to its GDP was only 0.41%, which ranked after the 40th place in the world. In 2006, there was a merely 1.1 R&D professional out of every 1000 Argentineans, and statistics from 2007 indicated that only 29.5% of Argentinean workforce received university degrees or higher education. There were no apparent advantages in Argentina's manpower. Third, there was severe polarization between the rich and the poor as well as prominent social conflicts. Argentina's Gini coefficient was around 0.45 in the mid-1980s, got close to 0.50 at the end of the 1990s, and reached 0.51 in 2007. The income ratio of the highest 10% income class and the lowest 10% income class was 40.9% in Argentina. Such unbalanced income distribution finds expression not only in property income but in wage grades as well. Additional causes, such as poor public security and backward urban infrastructure and public services, added considerably to social contradictions and income gaps. Finally, government administration turned out to be ineffective. Argentina was plagued by prolonged instability in macroeconomy, chaotic financial market, violent fluctuations in exchange rates, high inflation, chronic fiscal deficits, supply-side problems, and weak legal and economic means for macro-level administration. All this combined to bring about stopgap measures, economic ailments, social imbalance, and other derived problems.

It is assumable that *The Washington Consensus*, which called for minimized government role, rapid privatization, and financial liberalization, has proved to be a failed strategy, and its "shock therapy" a policy failure.

The modern market system or modern financial system features markets of adequate competition, orderly law-based regulation, and sound social credit. *The Washington Consensus* only focuses on the essential functions of markets or financial systems, that is, the competition and enhancement of market factors and organization systems. It overlooks the integrity of the underlying order of markets and financial systems of individual countries, that is, legal and regulatory policy systems for markets, as well as the development and improvement of the environmental foundation of market, such as social credit system and market infrastructure. Therefore, the market economy in the *Washington Consensus* is free market economy rather than modern market economy and modern financial system with sound systematic functions.

Globally, government should abide by rules of the market and the financial system, maintain proper order, and take part in administration thereof. The *Washington Consensus* only acknowledges the provision and support of public products by government but completely ignores proper government adjustment, supervision and administration in industrial resources and enterprise competition apart from allowing freedom and financial liberalization. Relaxed government control, rapid privatization, and financial liberalization prescribed in the *Washington Consensus* are examples of anarchism. Its inadequate view is exceptionally deficient in its theoretical expression compared with the realistic requirements for the structural development of modern market economy and modern financial system.

In the pursuit of economic and financial growth, the top priority, in addition to improving modern market and financial systems, is to strengthen government capabilities in constructing market and financial systems, in policy making and arrangements, and in converting economic and financial development modes to the greatest benefit. No mention was made of that in *The Washington Consensus*. Government capabilities include their abilities to comply with the rules of market economy and financial development, keep market economy and financial development well in hand, and play a part in their proper adjustment, supervision, and management. The creation of institutional environment requires improving legislation, law enforcement, judicature of the market and financial systems and legal education concerning markets and finance, and forming regulatory bodies, supervision range, and modes of regulation in accordance to the requirements of market economy and modern finance so as to exercise supervision over capital markets, financial institutions, business transactions, and enforcement of policies, laws, and regulations. The development modes of world economy and finance should undergo a substantive shift from Adam Smith's invisible hand and Keynes' government intervention to the construction, regulation, supervision, and administration of modern market economy and modern financial systems. Although such measures as relaxed government control, rapid privatization, and financial liberalization can indeed exert positive effects upon investment, employment, and development in the short term, they will eventually bring about economic fluctuation, inflation, financial risks, social instability, as well as difficulty in achieving sustained development in the long term. Such policies of "crisis orientation," "patch upgrading," and "shock therapy" are not to be advocated or adopted in China, as they may turn out to be detrimental to financial health and national stability.

3.2 Financial Repression and Regional Lack of Vitality

3.2.1 Financial Development—A Choice for Regional Economic Transition

Most of the countries in the world are undergoing economic transition and social transformation with the attempt to get over the "middle-income trap." It has become one of the chief strategies adopted in some regions in China and the world to promote industrial transition and upgrading by financial means. My own experience as chief executive and mayor of Foshan can be taken as an example here.

Foshan is economically one of the most significant municipalities in Guangdong Province, with an area of 3800 km^2 and 5.9968 million registered residents. In 2009, its GDP was close to RMB 500 billion and ranked 11th in China, but it more than doubled by 2018, with its total volume amounting to RMB 1055 billion, and ranked 16th, which signifies the entry of Foshan's industrial development into the late stage of industrialization and the early stage of post-industrialization. Under the context of industrial transformation, urbanization speedup, and internationalization, it has become an urgent issue how Foshan can expedite its transformation of economic development modes. Five major strategies have been proposed and adopted to promote industrial transition and upgrading through leveraging financial means in Foshan on the basis of actual conditions, in-depth investigations, and experiments.

The first strategy is the "dual transfer" and "cage vacation for new birds." In addition to the active implementation of "dual transfer," Foshan resorted to bank loans, local discounts, and financial guarantees to carry out the "three-batch approach" so as to lead its industrial transition and upgrading. The first approach was enterprise close-down and transformation. Foshan shut down and transformed over 1200 enterprises to reduce backward production capacity. Most of them were of heavy pollution and high energy consumption in ceramics, cement, bleaching and dying, small aluminum profile castings, and glass production enterprises. Meanwhile, guidance was provided for labor-intensive enterprises to transfer to less developed areas. Over recent years, about 460 projects were relocated in newly established industrial parks, which allowed for vacated spaces for high-tech firms and provided new driving forces for industrial upgrading and economic development.

The second approach was enterprise upgrading. By integrating information with industrialization and aligning services with the manufacturing industry, Foshan promoted massive, high-tech and high-end industries. Take the ceramic industry for example. In 2007, it had more than 400 ceramic. After three years of transformation and enhancement, 50 continued as a result of technological transformation. They adopted clean production methods and reshaped production processes. For some, their production bases were converted into headquarters, convention and exhibition centers, R&D offices, and logistics and information centers. In the past three years, despite a 40% reduction in its ceramic output, Foshan has witnessed an increase of 33% in output value and tax revenues, with a corresponding drop of 25% in energy consumption and 20% in the emission of sulfur dioxide.

The third approach was enterprise cultivation. By attracting new investments and focusing on photo-electricity, new materials, and modern services, new innovative industries have been cultivated and developed, such as those involving photo-electricity, medical technologies, environmental protection, electrical vehicles, solar energy technology, and photovoltaic applications, which have substantially reduced the proportion of traditional industries. Foshan is now the home for national demonstration of new industrialization and the national demonstration base for photoelectrical industry. In addition, by leveraging the transformation of old towns, factory buildings, and villages, Foshan has been able to develop new cities, industries, and communities for the purpose of increasing land utilization efficiency and further promoting industrial and urban transformation and environmental conservation.

The second strategy is soliciting new projects and boosting industrial transformation and upgrading. Foshan has given due focus to the attraction of investments, the direction of financial management, the maintenance of PE and VC, with prominence given to leading-edge projects in emerging strategic industries, advanced manufacturing industries, and modern service industries. Foshan has quickly fostered new industrial clusters and seized on the most vital points of industrial development through international leading project investments. For example, by introducing the high-tech Qimei flat panel display module (TFT-LCD), Foshan has attracted the upstream matching manufacturers of chips, panels, molds, and plastics that are needed for the manufacturing of these modules, as well as downstream TV set manufacturers. All these help to form a complete industrial chain of LCD flat displays and to upgrade local household electrical appliance industry. Other examples are the introduction of the Rainbow OLCD project, which has helped to promote the third-generation display industry, and the introduction of the FAW Volkswagen project, which has driven forward the entire manufacturing industry, industrial clusters, and chains of auto parts. So far, 47 of Fortune 500 enterprises have invested in 87 projects, and 99 of top 500 domestic enterprises in 167 new industrial projects in Foshan. They have formed a good number of backbone enterprises that are leading domestic industries in terms of technology, standards, and brands and have significantly elevated Foshan's industrial structure and level of development.

The third strategy is advancing science and technology and self-motivated innovation. Foshan boasts 347,000 enterprises under industrial and commercial registration, including more than 100,000 industrial enterprises. However, over 2200 of these enterprises have an output value of RMB 100 million or more. Small- and medium-sized enterprises, with less than RMB 100 million in output value, account for over 98% of the total. Considering its current industrial structure, Foshan has leveraged the combined innovation services of finance, technology, and industries to enact incentive policies aiming at creating strong foundations, establishing brands, registering patients, setting standards, and exporting its well-known brands. Foshan encourages and supports these enterprises in creating industry standards, national standards, and even international standards by utilizing its product standards, forming its core technologies, and using its brands, patents, and standards so that other enterprises can carry out the original equipment manufacturer (OEM) production of Foshan-based enterprises.

Over recent years, RMB 1 billion is allocated each year in Foshan to directly reward and guide those enterprises striving to strengthen technological progress and develop independent innovation. Take 2008 and 2009 for example, over 22 billion of enterprise investment was in place in 2008, an increase of 47% over the previous year, and over 30.8 billion in 2009, an increase of 39%, despite the strong impacts of the concurrent international financial crisis. Thus, financial means, along with technological progress and independent innovation in leading industrial transformation and advancements, have earned Foshan titles such as "Top 10 Innovative Cities of China," "Chinese City of Brand Economy," and "Capital of Chinese Brands." Foshan is the only demonstration city for well-known national trademarks and famous brands among prefecture-level cities of Guangdong province. The city has cumulatively filed 130,000 patent applications and has granted 86,000 patents, which ranks first among all the prefecture-level cities in China. Foshan is the home for 42 well-known Chinese brands and 65 brand-name products of China, which ranks it in the fourth place in China.

The fourth strategy is the employment of financial measures to build up its industrial highlands. Foshan draws upon capital power and financial means to integrate enterprises with capital markets so as to make them grow in size and strength. Internally, Foshan has implemented three schemes for financial development. The first is to increase the number of listed enterprises in Foshan from 13 in 2007 to 26 by implementing the 463 Plan for enterprise listing.[1] In this way, it has formed a registration listing of 102 enterprises. Meanwhile, support is provided for mergers and acquisitions in the hope of discovering good strategies, new transition platforms, and additional upgrades for enterprises. The second is to advance a valid link between industry and finance by fostering an equity investment fund, an SME guarantee fund, and a talent fund. Currently, 15 funds are in place, including an equity investment fund with a scale of about RMB 1.2 billion, with 126 million from local government as a guidance fund and a generation of RMB 1.1 billion of nongovernmental capital. All this has quickened the steps of enterprises going listed on the SME and GEM boards. So far, 45 enterprises have been prepared to apply, and over 30 enterprises have received coaching for restructuring or prospective restructuring. The third is to provide financial support for industrial transition and development through financial innovation, including developing rural banks and petty loan companies.

Externally, Foshan was designated by the United Nations Industrial Development Organization (UNIDO) as the only model city for effective operation of industrial clusters and capital markets in China. Taking advantage of this opportunity, Foshan has actively introduced overseas banks into the Foshan Financial High-Tech Service Zone. Agreements have been signed for 28 projects with a total investment of RMB 6.579 billion. Since the implementation of the CEPA Supplementary Agreement VI in October 2009,[2] four Hong Kong–based banks have opened their offices in Foshan, which is an excellent example of actively promoting closer connection between capital market and enterprise

---

[1] The 463 Plan means that, in the four years beginning in 2008, Foshan was the catalyst for at least 100 Foshan-based enterprises that carried out the transformation of a joint-stock system or started public listing procedures, including 60 companies that went public. If they proved successful either at home or abroad, they would raise about RMB 30 billion.

[2] CEPA Supplementary Agreement VI was introduced on May 9, 2009, and was officially enacted on October 1, 2009. It was designed to further enhance economic and trade exchanges as well as cooperation between mainland China and Hong Kong. Under the agreement, mainland China agreed to take 29 market-opening measures, one-third of which were to be tried first in Guangdong province. These measures cover aspects of law, convention and exhibition, public utilities, telecommunications, banks, securities, maritime transportation, and railway transportation.

transformation and upgrading, helping enterprises set up management mechanisms that dovetail with international practices, encouraging private enterprises to establish modern enterprise systems, enhance development transformation, and generate new economic vitality. Consequently, the contribution rate of private sector to Foshan's economic growth has reached 61.8%.

The fifth strategy is the "fourization integration and smart Foshan." In the wake of the global tide of IT revolution and smart city construction, Foshan has resorted to financial rewards, discounts, guarantees, investments, and services in promoting the integration of fourization, that is, incorporating informationalization into industrialization, urbanization, and internationalization, and the build-up of smart Foshan. Foshan was the leading city in China in terms of strategic breakthrough and economic development during the 12th five-year plan period and continues to be a role model in regional development.

Fourization first involves the integration of informationalization and industrialization, which actively fosters emerging industries related to informationalization, such as photo-electric display, radio frequency identification (RFID), Internet of things (IOT), industrial design, and service outsourcing for the purpose of transforming and upgrading traditional industries. For example, more than 1700 furniture manufacturers are located in Longjiang, Shunde, with only a few generating an output value of more than RMB 100 million. However, The Vizanne Group has turned itself from buyer market into seller market by means of 3D technology, customized manufacturing, and transformation of traditional furniture sales mode of "goods for purchase." In two to three years, its sales scale has topped RMB 300 million. Another case in point is the Midea Group, which uses IOT technology to transform traditional home appliances into intelligent home appliances. These "smart" appliances bring a new revolution to the home appliance industry.

Second, it involves the integration of informationalization and urbanization, which actively promotes the integration of telecommunication networks, television networks, and the Internet and conduces to the development of intelligent services and management systems, ranging from traffic, public security, urban management, education, medical care, culture, commerce, and government affairs. The synergy of such services and systems helps to build up the omnipresent U-Foshan and drive its transformation from partial application to integrated services in terms of administration, governance, and operation so that Foshan will become an intelligent homestead suitable for residence, commerce, tourism, and career development.

Third, fourization involves the integration of informationalization and internationalization. At micro level, enterprises are guided to set up internationalized R&D, production, and sales and service systems with resort to IT, IOT, Internet, and RFID so as to strengthen their capabilities of expanding into new international markets. IOT, for example, has transformed Foshan into an international procurement center for ceramics and home appliances. At macro level, the creation of a large trans-department, industry, and region clearance information platform or an electronic port provides enterprises with one-stop clearance services in electronic payments, logistic distribution, electronic customs declaration, and inspection, thus paving an expressway for enterprises to reach for the international market.

In the first half of 2010, Foshan achieved RMB 265.1 billion of GDP with its growth rate reaching 13.8% and a continuous rise in the proportion of advanced manufacturing industry, high-tech emerging industry, and modern service industry, displaying the excellent structure and development trend of the current industrial system. It is believed that the effective use of financial means in seeking financial development and promoting changes in the development mode of a local economy has considerably boosted and sustained the scientific, technological, and economic development of Foshan.

3.2.2 Eight Types of Competition in Local Economy

In seeking to overcome the "middle-income trap" and reinforce industrial and economic transformation, eight types of competition have been going on in Foshan's economic and financial development.

Project competition Project competition falls into three major categories: key national projects, social investment projects, and foreign investment projects. The first category covers major national projects, including projects in national programs for science and technology, construction projects for scientific and technological infrastructure, engineering and industrialization projects subsidized by national finance. The second category covers high-tech, newly emerging, equipment manufacturing and service industries, including raw materials, finance, and logistics. The third category covers intelligent manufacturing, cloud computing, and big data, IOT, and intelligent urban construction.

Local competition projects can introduce new sources of funds, unique talents, and industries, leverage the legality of project policies and the rationality of public services to adequately address problems concerning local fundraising, financing, and land requisition, and take advantage of those projects to guide land development in the locality, construct urban facilities, promote investments and industrial development, optimize resource allocation, enhance policy capacity, and facilitate sustainable development. Therefore, project competition has become the focal point and orientation for local economy. It has become essential for the market-based competition of Foshan economy to cultivate a strong sense of projects, development, efficiency, superiority, conditions, policies, and risks and increasingly strengthen their awareness.

Competition for chain matching All localities have their technical foundation and characteristics. However, most of them depend on the endowment of natural resources. The key for a city to retain resources and pool high-end funds from external sources is the optimization of industrial structure and the effective allocation of the industrial chain. The breakthrough point is tearing through high-end industrial development, forming industrial agglomeration and guiding industrial clusters. Local competition for industrial chain matching takes place in production factors and in industrial agglomeration and matching. In terms of production factors, low-end or primary production factors will not bring about a stable and lasting competitive force. Only through investment in high-end and sophisticated production factors, such as industrial technology, modern IT, network resources, traffic facilities, professionals, and R&D think tanks can a robust and competitive industry be developed and established. As far as industrial clusters and matching are concerned, territorial competitiveness reveals that effective industrial matching based on the existing industries within certain jurisdiction can reduce the transaction costs of enterprises and enhance their profitability. The industrial smile curve demonstrates that the highest value resides in both ends of industrial value chains, that is, R&D and market. An important path for the sustainable development of enterprises in Foshan is fostering advantageous industries, forming complete industrial chains and attracting investment in a targeted manner matching the industrial structure.

Competition for talents and technology The most fundamental ideology of localities is that labor force is the primary resource and that science and technology are the primary productive force. The key investment of localities should be in the cultivation and training of talents and technological innovation, while continuous improvement is to be made in talent cultivation and training, and the most essential measure is to create conditions for the attraction, introduction, cultivation, and employment of talents. The competitiveness of talents in science and technology is measured through a variety of indicators, including scientific and technological talent resources, the number of employers in scientific and technological activities for every 10,000 people, the number of scientists and engineers for every 10,000 people, the total number of scientific and technological personnel for every 10,000 people, the number of college students for every 10,000 people, the indicator of investment in scientific and technological talents for every 10,000 people, the total expenditure of scientific and technological activities, the proportion of scientific and technical expenses to GDP, the percentage taken up in local finance by per capita of scientific research funds and local financial appropriations for science and technology, the per capita expenditure of financial education funds, the total education expenditure in local finance, the number of full-time teaching staff in universities and colleges, and so on. It is Foshan's policy to continue to improve and enhance relevant indicators with a view to elevating the overall scientific and technological competitiveness of local talents.

Competition for public finance Widespread economic competition also takes place in financial income and expenditure. Financial revenues come chiefly from economic growth and tax collection. Apart from social consumption expenditure and transferred expenditure, competition for financial expenditure is mainly manifested through local economic investment, such as infrastructure, scientific and technological R&D,

policy funds invested in industries that need urgent development, and other financial investments in combination with social investments driven by the investments listed above. Financial investment expenditures drive the growth of social investments to boost economic growth. This is an important driving force for economic development, which must not be overlooked. The overall scale of financial income and expenditure is limited, which makes it necessary for local economies to erect investment and financing platforms to mobilize and attract domestic, regional, and even global financial resources, such as financial institutions, funds, talents, and information, to utilize them to the greatest possible extent and to improve local economic development, urban construction, and livelihood of citizens. The preferential policies and means for local economic and financial development have enabled Foshan to carry out active competition in financial expenditure and social investment absorption.

Competition for infrastructure Competition for infrastructure takes place in urban infrastructure hardware and software conditions for intelligent cities. The former provides transportation facilities (i.e., expressways, ports, and aviation centers), energy (i.e., electric power, natural gas), information platforms (i.e., cables, networking), scientific and technological parks, industrial parks, and creative industrial parks. Urban infrastructure software encompasses big data, cloud computing, IOT, and other intelligent platforms. They are critical, cutting-edge platforms for intelligent city construction. The urban infrastructure systems of localities, which drive forward local economic and social development, are divided into look-ahead, adaptive, and lagging-behind types. The moderately look-ahead supply of local urban infrastructure provides quality services in urban structuring, facilities scale, and spatial layout for market competition, which serves to reduce enterprise costs, improve productivity, and promote industrial development. It exerts direct impacts upon the diversity and future of local economy and national economy.

Competition for environmental system In addition to urban infrastructure, environmental system also involves ecological, humanistic, policy, and social credit aspects. It is crucial for local economic competition to harmonize economic investment development and ecological protection, match attractive investments to policy services, align wealth pursuit with social reinvestment, and facilitate interaction for legal supervision and social credit. Foshan's experience has proved that good environment is key to its success in attracting investors and projects and in boasting sustainable growth.

Competition for policy system Local economic policy system consists of external and internal levels. Between regions, as a public product characterized by exclusiveness and emulability, competitive policy systems must be (a) realistic to meet actual requirements for social and economic development; (b) sophisticated so as to be forward-looking and innovative in policy making; (c) operational to ensure that policies are clear, pertinent, and enforceable; (d) well-organized so as to secure performance by responsible agencies and people; (e) effective so as to realize their goals via mechanisms of inspection, supervision, examination, and evaluation, as well as the role of third parties. Sound policy systems have played definitive roles in Foshan's enhancement of economic competitiveness.

Competition for administrative efficiency Administrative efficiency is a concentrated reflection of administrative activities together with their speed, quality, and efficiency. It considers four aspects: macro efficiency, micro efficiency, organizational efficiency, and individual efficiency. In terms of administrative norms, local economies should try to meet standards of law enforcement, interests, and quality. In terms of efficiency, they meet standards for quantity, time, speed, and budgets. Competition for administrative efficiency is by nature competition for organizational systems, subjective responsibilities, service awareness, work skills, and technological platforms. Foshan has set a precedent in the race for administrative efficiency through adopting "parallel" and "integrated" service modes.

3.2.3 Local Economic Development Requires Financial Underpinning

Whether it is industrial transformation and upgrading or regional economic competition, local economic development needs financial support to make it dynamic. Financial growth will eventually boost and promote local economic development in return.

Local financial development is always playing an increasingly significant role in facilitating local economy. In Foshan, for example, financial institutions take up more than 90% of its loans that go into agriculture, rural areas, and farmers as well as small- and medium-sized enterprises. Viewed from macro level, local finance accounts for an increasingly larger proportion in the entire financial sector of a country, and in China, for instance, local financial institutions, including regional joint-stock commercial banks, urban commercial banks, agricultural and commercial banks, and other financial institutions, account for as high as 60.86% of the financial assets of the banking industry. Local finance has been enjoying quality growth, rapid development, and high degree of marketization. Since 2013, the growth rate of local financial institutions in China has remained higher than that of large national institutions, as they are closer to market, more flexible in operational mechanism, and stronger awareness of competition. It is also notable that local financial development has provided diversified and differentiated services for entrepreneurship and people's livelihood, such as petty credit loans, syndicated loans, and financial leasing Nanyue Bank in Guangdong has introduced for the development of small enterprises. All this has effectively encouraged individual entrepreneurship and financing for small and micro enterprises.

There is another significant aspect to this issue. Institutions holding large amounts of nongovernmental capital have been seeking for financial investments. Nongovernmental capital has high expectations for financial investment. Private banks, petty loan companies, financing guarantee companies, pawnbrokers, mutual fund associations, and monetary brokers have been squeezing into this general financial flux. Industrial enterprises have been seeking for allocation of financial resources and stronger ties with financial institutions by establishing financial companies, financial leasing companies, and auto financing companies for the purpose of promoting efficient allocation of funds and enhancing industrial operation. Local economies need financial support and are at the same time improving the efficiency of resource allocation through financial institutions and financial markets to boost their sustainability. Institutions, such as local urban banks, rural banks, township banks, agricultural credit cooperatives, micro and small insurance companies, trust investment companies, credit rating agencies, industrial investment funds, and equity investment funds, have been playing an ever more critical role in promoting local economy. New developments in economy require new financial business modes. Modern economies, such as the Internet, have broken away from traditional models and have exerted strong impacts upon innovation and economy. New financial business modes have been generated in conjunction with finance, such as P2P loan platforms, licensed operation centers, third-party payment institutions, online payment, and wealth management. Those dimensions have helped to boost local economies.

As is obvious, the driving force for local financial development originates from local economies but requires local economies to weed out "financial repression" for the furtherance of local finance.

3.2.4 Stronger Measures Are Needed to Release Financial Repression

The interaction between local economy and finance stems from localities and social communities composed of individuals. The lack of corresponding financial functions and measures for local economic development will lead to insufficient supply of financial services and failures to fully meet the needs of multi-level development of real economy. With regard to micro-small finance, rural finance, and livelihood finance, it is hard for state financial regulatory bodies to make regulations that fit in with local situations and retain market involvement so as to meet diversified economic realities and multi-level financial needs. It is beneficial for local economies to engage in productive interaction with local finance so as to achieve more effective development.

However, the competitiveness and vitality of China's financial system, along with financial functions and development means of local economy, depend to a large extent on national financial regulations. Ways of allocating financial resources vary with financial regulation systems. A sound financial regulation system demands properly handling relations between government and market to enable market to play a decisive role in the allocation of resources and relations between central and local governments by clearly defining their respective responsibilities for more effective financial regulation and risk disposal. Excessive financial control and repression will result in the simplicity of financial institutions and financial assets, unhealthy financial environment, backward financial infrastructure and poor financial efficiency, thus impeding innovation and development of local economies. Stronger measures must be taken to define the financial responsibilities between central and local governments, set up hierarchical regulation, and induce more compatible financial regulation systems.

First, innovation should be encouraged, orderly competition ensured, an inclusive financial regulation system established, and more initiatives be mobilized for market entities to give full play to their innovative vitality in local economic activities. At present, financial powers, such as the US and the UK, tend to implement inclusive and innovative regulation by following the principle of "access unless prohibited" and "negative list." In some countries, financial regulation is both innovative and restrictive due to the fact that they are in the initial stage where market players and local economies have yet to develop their capabilities to manage risks. In some countries, market economies and governance capabilities are becoming more developed, but strict and excessive regulation will suppress financial innovation and run counter to economic transformation and financial competitiveness enhancement. On one hand, it has caused suppression upon normal financial innovation, which is detrimental to the efficiency of serving real economy and causes finance to fall far behind the needs of real economy. On the other hand, financial innovation has surfaced through "detours," frequent chaos in financial wealth management, disorder in inter-bank market, and serious interest arbitrage, which has severely disrupted the health of financial market. And in others, financial innovation mainly originates from local institutions, such as consumer finance companies, science and technology banks, community banks, and online finance. There is a stronger motivation for local economies to intensify the initiative, acuity, and sense of urgency in financial innovation. Therefore, it is time for China to drive its financial regulation from the innovation-based regulatory type to the innovation-based inclusive type, which requires the return of rights to market and stimulates the innovativeness of market players and requires the delegation of powers to lower levels of administration and mobilize local initiatives for economic and financial development. The differential regulation of local financial development is conducive for boosting business innovation and for preventing systematic financial risks on the national level.

Second, it is of equal importance for local governments to fulfill vital responsibilities of guarding against financial risks and maintaining stability and to vest them with authorities of financial regulation and disposal of financial risks that match their economy. It is obligatory for them to exercise authorities to standardize, regulate, and take effective measures to prevent and handle potential risks. These risks may give rise to new problems, especially in newly emerging financial areas, such as micro and small financial institutions, quasi-financial institutions and online finance, which have "blind zones" in the financial sector. Financial repression and excessive control will result in ambiguous boundaries of financial regulatory power between central government and local government, absence of supervision, insufficient innovation, low efficiency, and even the "Matthew effect" on financial resource allocation, suggesting a growing shortage of support in financial resources to less developed areas, rural areas, micro and small economies. Viewed from the global perspective, financial crises provide anti-driving impetuses for improvement on financial regulation systems highlighted by constant expansion of regulation scope, increasing convergence toward similar modes of regulation and hierarchical regulation. China has been following the general trend of world financial regulation by continuing to coordinate and mobilize initiatives on the part of both central and local governments, maintain balance between financial innovation and financial stability, wisely demarcate and delegate financial governance authorities to local administration, and set up financial regulatory systems that feature hierarchical regulation and harmonized incentives to adapt to the development demands of real economy and modern financial systems. All this has helped to better remove contradictions in current financial development, facilitate local financial development and stability, and establish modern financial systems with orderly development and responsible regulation.

3.3 Definition of Central and Local Responsibilities and Authorities

3.3.1 Overall Thinking and Basic Principles

By focusing on the decisive role of market in the allocation of financial resources, China should build up a hierarchical financial regulation system with "effective coordination, clear-cut responsibilities and authorities and efficient operation" so as to meet development needs of multi-level real economy and financial systems through sound division and demarcation of obligations and powers between central and local governments, enhance the modernization of financial systems and financial governance capabilities, ameliorate the efficiency of financial resource distribution, and strengthen the vitality and competitiveness of modern financial systems.

There are some fundamental principles China should follow in achieving its goal: (a) stick to the market-oriented approach and give full play to the decisive role of market in allocating resources; (b) continue with more effective coordination that ensures central government in the unified, vertical, and prudential regulation of nationwide, systematic, and trans-regional financial affairs to guard against high risks and vest local regulatory authorities rights to exercise hierarchical regulation of local, partial, and segmented financial issues within their respective jurisdiction; (c) strive for balance between financial innovation and assurance of financial stability, balance between risk control by central government and local financial development, and balance between macro unified regulation by central government and differential regulation by local government; (d) match authorities with responsibilities through scientific division of boundaries between central and local authorities to ensure correspondence between local authorities for financial regulation and local financial development along with their participation in risk disposal so as to achieve incentive compatibility; (e) abide by law-based regulation to clarify regulatory functions and powers of central and local government to make sure that financial regulators at all levels discharge their duties in strict compliance with laws; (f) stick to classified guidance and gradual progression. Central government may take steps to define authorities for financial regulation and risk control by level, by category, on the basis of financial management capabilities, localities, and areas.

3.3.2 Definition of Authorities and Responsibilities of Central and Local Governments for Financial Regulation

3.3.2.1 Authorities and Responsibilities of Central Government for Financial Regulation

First of all, the central government should formulate rules, guidelines, policies, and initiatives for financial operation, promote the legal system of finance, draw up negative lists for the financial sector, draft rules for business access, create regulations for financial institutions, and provide legal definitions for tailored local financial regulation.

Second, the central government should examine, approve, document, and regulate financial institutions of national, systematic, and trans-regional significance, in addition to those institutions that involve extensive public interests and may trigger off major financial risks with regard to their establishment, change, termination, and business scope.

The central government should examine, approve, put on file, and regulate the businesses of financial institutions, in particular financial businesses that are nationwide, trans-regional, widely ranging, and complex in function and may cause risks that are susceptible to spill over, as well as nationwide financial transaction markets, such as exchanges and inter-bank bond markets. Measures should be taken to strengthen those mechanisms of financial infrastructure and markets that have national importance.

To ensure coordination, supervision, and guidance of local financial development, central government should strengthen macro guidance and supervision of local financial work, inspect and guarantee the implementation of its financial policies by individual localities, and provide specific guidance and professional training of local financial supervision to elevate the level of financial regulation. The central government should produce qualification auditing, examination and inspection of financial institutions and businesses to which central government has delegated authorities, provide early warning against financial risks that may appear within the scope of local regulation to ensure proper handling of risks, and establish a system of consultation between central and local governments regarding the regulation of financial development.

From a longitudinal perspective, central government should define its obligations, responsibilities, and relations of risk control and regulation to local governments with regard to "institutional access" and "business examination and approval" through classification of financial institutions based on their statutory reserve on deposit or the ratio of it and formulate appropriate rules so as to form orderly and rule-based financial systems of regulation, better suit local differences and different levels of financial needs, and boost coordinated development. From a transverse perspective, full play should be given to the role of central government agencies in holding regular consultations with local government for the purpose of clarifying and specifying the responsibilities of central and local governments centering on financial regulation and crisis relief, such as the supervision of operation of institutions together with their shareholders and board directors, the monitoring, relieving, and disposing of partial and systematic risks, as well as the building of agencies and team.

Central government should safeguard national stability and security of finance by strengthening macro-level administration, prevent and dispose of national and systematic financial risks, and manage the risks that may appear in the financial institutions and their transactions central government has examined, approved, and documented. Measures must be taken to monitor and prevent international financial risks to help ensure financial security.

3.3.2.2 Authorities and Responsibilities for Local Financial Regulation

What should be first done is to formulate financial development plans and policies in the light of the actual conditions of economic development in question, introduce detailed rules and operational measures for the implementation of financial policies of central government, and formulate specific rules and norms for local financial regulation according to national laws and regulations.

Second, local government should take three measures to administer institutional entry and regulation. The first is to continue to examine, approve, and regulate financial institutions and quasi-financial institutions that have initially been placed under the jurisdiction of local government in respect to their establishment, change, termination, and business scope, including petty loan companies, guarantee companies, pawn shops, cooperation funds, and nongovernmental credit intermediaries. For those previously unspecified examination and approval, typically new financial modes that have appeared in local financial development, it is recommended that local government should take the responsibility for their examination, approval, and documentation, such as local Internet P2P lending platforms and licensed operation centers.

Central government may make access rules and authorize local government to examine, approve, and regulate local micro-, small- and medium-sized financial institutions that were previously placed under the examination and approval of central government but are closely related to local financial development without involvement of public interests, but they should be reported to financial regulatory bodies of central government (and its agencies) for qualification verification and documentation. That covers local small and medium private banks, rural banks, community banks, financial companies, financial leasing companies, consumption financial companies, auto financial companies, micro and small insurance companies, money brokerage companies, trust investment companies, factoring companies, credit rating companies, third-party payment institutions, and significant industrial investment funds. For some of them, the recording system may be considered in lieu of examination and approval.

Third, local government should examine, approve and regulate financial dealings within its jurisdiction, including deposit, loan, inter-bank, investment, trust, and intermediary business, equity management, as well as other financial businesses that are of local interest and whose risks that are hard to spill over, such as municipal bonds and collective bonds of micro, small and medium-sized enterprises. Local government should also examine, approve, and regulate local financial market platforms, including the over the counter (OTC) equity trading market; property rights trading markets; micro, small, and medium enterprise loan transfer platforms; and local government financing platforms.

Fourth, local government should shoulder the responsibility for the prevention and disposal of the risks that may stem from financial institutions, businesses, and market platforms it examines, approves, and regulates. It should strengthen cooperation with regulatory bodies of central government, its agencies, and related departments to crack down on illegal financial activities, create mechanisms for local financial stability, and enhance its ability to defuse and dispose of any group incident within its jurisdiction.

Finally, local government should strengthen its construction of financial infrastructure, including local financial credit systems, non-financial administrative penalties on acts of dishonesty, local financial legal system, optimization of operational environment of local finance, and creation of platforms for the release and exchange of financial information.

3.3.3 Central and Local Financial Regulatory Structure

The organizational structure of financial regulation on the central level consists of The People's Bank of China, which plays the role of China's central bank; enforces national monetary policies, prudential policies, and exchange rate policies; and performs regulatory functions of payment clearing, FOREX management, liquidity, money market, and lender of last resort that are oriented toward financial institutions and enterprises. Effective regulation should be exercised over banking, securities, and insurance businesses. Agencies of central financial regulation should exercise their authorities and responsibilities of central financial regulation within its jurisdiction; perform central inspection, guidance and regulation of local financial development; and promote stable development of local finance. Additionally, they should supervise local affiliates and businesses of nationwide financial institutions, as well as verify and record the qualifications of local affiliates and businesses that central government authorizes local government to examine, approve, and regulate.

The organizational structure of financial regulation on the local level consists of bureaus of financial regulation that perform three regulatory functions. The first is to undertake matters related to local financial stability, development, and supervision; assist central government in strengthening the supervision and service of local finance; maintain local financial stability; and dispose of financial risks. The second is to examine, approve, and regulate financial institutions, their businesses, and market platforms for which central government delegates authorities according to regulations and to report to central regulatory bodies or their agencies for qualification, auditing, and recording. The third is to regulate local financial assets, such as the founding of financial holding companies that manage local financial assets and carry out market-oriented investments and operations for value preservation and accrual.

It follows that relations between central and local governments should be clearly defined for financial regulation, authorities and responsibilities should be clarified according to laws and rules, and sound consulting mechanisms should be established for the purpose of coordination and cooperation in promoting financial development and stability.

3.4 Measures for Effectively Promoting Local Financial Development

The following measures should be taken in the light of actual situations to ensure the security and development of China's finance.

First, carry out orderly reforms and seek progress in stability. An overall plan for the hierarchical regulation of finance should be formed and outlined to identify the mechanisms, responsibilities, and powers of central and local governments for financial regulation. To this end, pilot units should be selected for step-by-step promotion. Once national schemes and layouts are introduced, local governments should promptly advance reforms for improvement on local financial regulation systems. Organizational plans should ensue to match central and local financial regulation to conclusively determine mechanisms for financial regulation, functions, internal organs, personnel, and relevant work.

Second, continuous improvement should be made on laws and regulations. Central government should introduce *Instructions on Local Financial Regulation* and *Regulations on Supervision and Management of Local Finance* to clarify the functions, obligations, objects of regulation, contents of authorization, work procedures, and guarantee mechanisms for local financial regulators. Accordingly, local bureaus of financial regulation should be established to conduct such reforms. Central and local organizations of financial regulation should be clearly defined, and amendments should be made in relevant existing laws, such as *Act on Commercial Banks*, *Securities Law*, and *Insurance Law*. Improvement should be made in standards for local financial regulation, and regulations should be established for supervision and operation. For example, for local financial institutions that absorb deposits, strict access and withdrawal mechanisms should be set up to examine not only hardware indicators, such as registered capital and operation sites, but also software indicators, such as shareholder qualifications, legal representatives, institutional capabilities to control risks, and overall employee caliber. Local legislation may take place within the existing legal framework or under the precondition of state legislation.

Third, prevent and control local financial risks. Priority should be given to building three secure networks of financial regulation. First, consideration may be given to setting up local deposit insurance companies to provide support for financial institutions with local and community deposits and operating from local reality under the restraint of a unified central deposit insurance system. Second, consideration may be given to setting up local financial assets management systems to dispose of possible non-performing financial assets and avoid fluidity and credit crises. Third, consideration may be given to setting up financial holding and re-guarantee systems to implement M&A through local financial holding companies for unstable financial institutions.

What should be done next is to establish three mechanisms for the management of local financial risks. First, the mechanism of financial risk monitoring should be set up to carry out the monitoring, evaluation, and early warning of local financial risks via specially created financial risk management committees so as to improve the security, stability, and vigor of the local financial sector through innovative and agile regulation. Second, a mechanism for the emergent disposal of financial risks should be set up to improve emergency response plans, intensify mechanisms of departmental coordination and joint action, and perfect the local system of financial risk reserves. In case of emergency, the local bureau of financial regulation should be allowed to get into two-way communication with local financial institutions and monitor the operation of financial institutions at any time. Third, a mechanism should be set up for the protection of financial investors and consumers. Investor protection funds should be established by following the practices of the securities industry as the risk reserve of local property rights trading markets to be used in the relief and compensation of major risk accidents so as to strengthen the protection of the rights and interests of financial consumers. Financial management mechanisms should be created to restrain local government from excessive intervention and credit overdraft.

Fourth, optimize local financial environment. Organizations should be established to exercise industrial self-discipline over local finance, give full play to its role in providing services, submitting appeals, standardizing behavior and implementing cooperation, exchanges, self-discipline, and self-supervision so as to regulate market, prevent risks, and ensure healthy development of the financial industry. It is feasible to develop third-party rating organizations for micro and small finance for the purpose of promoting ratings of micro and small financial institutions, improving operation management, accumulating credit, conducting orderly competition, and helping investors effectively assess financial risks and lower transaction costs. Additionally, measures must be taken to improve statistics system of local financial information and networking system. Local micro and small financial information centers may be set up to communicate with micro and small financial institutions within the region and facilitate access to the Internet for their core business information. Finally, improvements should be made in mechanisms of communication, coordination, consultation, and interaction between central and local financial regulatory bodies, such as the establishment of systems for communication, exchange, and sharing of crucial financial information across countries and regions, the establishment of interactive mechanisms for joint regulation, inspection, and meetings between central financial agencies and local bureaus of financial regulation, and risk disposal mechanisms for central financial development, coordination, and management.

4

The Establishment of an Onshore Transaction Clearing Center for RMB Offshore Business—Explorations in the Interactive Model for Internal and External Finance

An offshore financial center (OFC) refers to the premises where financial services are conducted and provided by institutions of a home country for overseas clients independently of the host country's financial legislation and regulation. OFCs are characterized by overseas currency, overseas banks, overseas markets, less monitoring by laws and regulation, low tax and even tax exemption, high efficiency, and ease and convenience.

4.1 Integration and Internationalization

Currently, the globalized integration of economy and the internationalization of financial markets are the striking features of economic development.

4.1.1 Globalized Integration of Real Economy

The globalized integration of real economy finds expression in the globalization of production and service trade, large-scale increases in foreign direct investment, the rapid development of science and technology, the ongoing formation of transnational corporations, and so on.

Take for example global transnational corporations, which are variously known as multinational enterprises, international firms, supernational enterprises, and cosmo-corporations. Based on their home countries, these enterprises set up affiliates or subsidiaries in different parts of the world. These subsidiaries are then established through direct foreign investments that engage in internationalized production and operation activities. Their strategic goal is to maximize global profits by orienting themselves to the international market. Their organizational mode is to control foreign affiliates or subsidiaries through holding shares. Their business covers all possible areas for the global pursuit of transactions, which involve capital, commodities, talents, technologies, management, and information. Additionally, such packaged and integrated activities are always under the control of the parent company and revolve around the overall strategic objectives of that company, adopting multiple, transverse (horizontal) operations. Each parent company and its subsidiaries typically engage in the production and distribution of a single product, rarely with specialized division of labor. They may also adopt multiple longitudinal (vertical) operations. Each parent company and its subsidiaries produce and distribute products from the same industry at different stages, thus making it possible to have comprehensive (mixed) multiple operations. This is where the parent company and its subsidiaries produce different products and operate various businesses, which are not mutually related, to form mixed transnational corporations.

With their increasingly expanding influence, transnational corporations have acted as the dominant power and vanguard in global economic integration. Starting in the early 1990s, many multinational corporations adjusted their past strategies for development in numerous countries. These strategies have been fine-tuned for better global development and operations. Tailoring one's business for global operations has become the norm. For many transnational corporations, their overseas assets, income, and employees have exceeded 50% of their total company-wide. Utilizing a strategy of global integration, an adjustment of management architecture and cultural ideas, they have successfully integrated global resources and significantly enhanced their global competitiveness and profitability.

On the global integration stage, transnational corporations have played a leading role as the organizer of world production, accompanied by the accelerating global integration. Currently, about 95,000 parent companies of transnational corporations are operating around the world, with about 950,000 overseas affiliates. Among them the output value of Fortune 500 enterprises accounts for 50% of the total global value output, with their internal and mutual trade taking up more than 60% of total global trade and their investments 90% of the accumulated global direct investments. Through globalized economic integration, they implement transnational M&A, adjust industrial structure, and optimize the allocation of resources. These factors allow them to contribute to the globalization of the industrial chain.

Transnational corporations promote international trade and economic growth. They have been a great promoter of the foreign trade of developed countries since World War II. They have enabled the products of developed countries to be produced and sold directly to host nations through direct investments. They obtain detailed business information that allows them to circumvent trade barriers and enhance the competitiveness of their products. They have accelerated the changes in the structure of the foreign trade commodities of developing countries. They are in control of the trade of many critical raw materials, manufactured products, and international technology. The inflow of transnational corporations has advanced a shift of industrialization from primary product exporting to importing substitution and then to exporting substitution of industrially manufactured products. These beneficial conditions have driven the establishment of the industrial system and sustainable trade growth of developing countries.

The globally integrated operations of transnational corporations have boosted the flow of funds, technologies, and advanced management modes around the globe. Oriented toward the pursuit of profit maximization, these companies have their needs met by the cheap resources, labor force, and broad markets in developing countries. They form a synergy between each other despite perceived contradictions and quarrels. In this way, developing countries have expedited the industrial restructuring of even less developed countries and regions. Indeed, they have been a catalyst for the sustained development of the economic integration of the world.

4.1.2 Internationalization of Financial Markets

The production, services, trade, investment, and advancements in science and technology as well as transnational corporations in global integration are without exception advancing the internationalized development of financial markets. The globally integrated development of real economy requires financial matching, services, and support. Conversely, finance has its own unique set of laws, and it is becoming continuously internationalized.

Primarily, the structure of the modern financial system is manifested as the increasing improvement on the internationalized structure of financial markets and the steady growth of currency, capital, and foreign exchange markets. For example, in response to different foreign exchange controls and the free convertibility of money in different countries, the Non-Deliverable Forwards (NDF) market was created in the 1990s. Under NDF, banks act as the intermediary for supply and demand parties. These parties sign NDF contracts by their exchange rate views (or purposes). These contracts explicitly set forth exchange rates which will be settled and cleared against the difference from the actual exchange rate upon the expiration of the contract. In these contract settlements, a currency that can be converted freely is used. The term of NDF contracts generally ranges from months to years. The principal varieties of rapid transactions under NDF are mostly of the varieties that have a run of one year or less. NDF provides hedge functions for the monetary support and services of emerging market countries worldwide. These hedge features support developing countries in their activities geared toward expanding real international economies. Thus, hedging is implemented to avoid exchange rate risks for trade contacts of enterprises in emerging market countries or those enterprises having overseas affiliates.

Second, it is manifested as the diversified internationalization of financial institutions. With global integration and transnational corporations, the steps taken by real economy toward comprehensive operations, high technology, and internationalization have accelerated the development of financial institutions, universal banks, transnational financial groups, online banks, and financial oligarchies. Such cases can be seen everywhere in the UK, the United States, and European countries. They are large in quantity and pursue profits as market players. Their internationalized entry can both strongly boost the globalized development of real economy and exert great impacts on real economy and financial markets.

Third, it is manifested as a diversity of international tools for financial services. They have emerged from an endless stream of innovative financial services. These include new commercial products, financial investment transactions, financing, and settlement, and management of exchange rate risks. For example, Cash Pooling, a fund management mode developed jointly by transnational corporations and international banks, provides businesses with numerous valuable services. These services include the transfer of account balances for transnational corporation members, overdraft coverage between member enterprises, current allocations and collections, entrusted loans between member enterprises, separate calculations of interest for deposited funds, and borrowing services for member enterprises from the headquarters of a group. Cash Pooling enables a transnational corporation to allocate global funds within a group and reduce the net position held by that group to the greatest extent possible. It also allows multinational corporations to form close strategic alliance relationships with international banks to form unique management effects, rendering the process more efficient.

Fourth, it is manifested as the increasingly improved internationalized rules for financial laws of governance. These include legislation, law enforcement, judicature, and education in legal systems. However, the prerequisite is that other laws and regulations may be established. An example can be found in the international coordination of the transnational tax payment standard and the preferential taxation policy for entity enterprises and financial institutions. According to the International Monetary Fund (IMF), a better taxation system should meet the following three conditions: (a) Taxes should be small in quantity and good in quality. Generally, these would include the following taxes: import tax, excise tax, general sales tax, personal income tax, and property taxes. (b) Preferably, there should be a minimal number of tax rate grades and they may not be excessive. (c) There should be a minimal number of tax preferences, exemptions, and reductions. The taxes paid by taxpayers to their income source countries are deemed to fulfill their tax obligations. When tax declarations are made to the residence country government, then they become revenues that are considered to have met tax payments and can be deducted from taxable income.

According to IMF standards, the international coordination of preferential tax policies covers tax categories, tax rates, and tax reductions and exemptions. The degree of coordination varies with its extents and can be classified into the modes of consultation, convergence, and integration. The routes of coordination for these modes include international tax treaties, regional taxation alliances, and the World Trade Organization (WTO). The international coordination and enhancement of transnational taxation and preferential tax policies have become an essential link for improving legislation and maintenance of the economic and financial order in the globalization of real economy and financial markets.

Fifth, it is manifested as the increasing attention to the internationalized financial regulation, which includes the internationalization of institutional regulation, business regulation, and market regulation. While gradually advancing the convertibility of capital accounts, countries around the world have intensified the convenience of specialized financial service, reinforced the vigor of their finance departments, enhanced the efficiency of global intermediary activities, promoted the diversification of global assets, and stimulated domestic and overseas investors. Conversely, they have also brought about financial risks, such as currency substitutions, capital flight, financial instability, and fluctuations in national monetary and exchange rate policies. For example, money-laundering activities that disrupt the order of financial management often take advantage of economic openings and the convertibility of capital accounts. These illegal activities may involve banking, securities, insurance, and real estate. They are often associated with smuggling, drug trafficking, embezzlement, corruption, tax evasion, and terrorism, disrupting the market order, damaging the reputation and normal operation of financial institutions, and threatening the security and stability of the financial system. In response to these conditions, monetary authorities in various countries have strengthened anti-money laundering under international finance regulation from organizational structure to system improvement. They have resorted to legislative and judicial resources and have mobilized relevant regulatory organizations, commercial institutions, and financial institutions, which identify any possible money laundering and punish organizations and individuals involved so as to effectively impede and crack down on criminal activities.

Finally, it is manifested as the continuous improvement on the internationalized financial infrastructure. This is not just a tangible benefit of international convenience in payment clearing and settlement systems between transnational enterprises of real economy, banks, and financial institutions, but it also includes the global application of the financial service system for accounting, laws, auditing, and evaluation, as well as the establishment and international recognition of the security, rules, and norms for the information technological security system between transnational enterprises, banks, and financial institutions. The internationalization of financial infrastructure has provided great ease and convenience in the application of both hardware and software financial infrastructure.

The global integration of real economic development and financial market internationalization has been pushing countries around the world to become active participants, reformers, coordinators, and organizers of the global economic and financial system. Now the creation and perfection of a sound global financial system with innovative governance have become an important subject and direction in international finance.

4.2 Offshore and Onshore Markets

For all countries, the global financial system governance resides primarily in the orderly linkup, interaction, and convenience between offshore and onshore markets.

4.2.1 Production and Capital Internalization Facilitate the Offshore Financial Market Formation and Development

Stage 1 Birth of international financial markets. Around World War I, London became the first international financial market, and after World

War II, New York became another important global financial market, followed by the establishment of other financial centers in Zurich, Switzerland, Frankfurt, Germany, and Luxembourg.

Stage 2 Continuous developments of offshore financial markets. In the 1950s, the implementation of the US Marshall Plan caused a huge flow of US dollars into Western Europe. Meanwhile, there continually occurred in the United States an international balance of payment deficits, thus another large outflow of US dollars. That brought into shape the European market of US dollars and signified the inception of the offshore financial market. Subsequent to the 1960s, the German mark, French franc, Dutch guilder, and currencies outside Europe started to appear on this market, which caused the European market of US dollars to develop into a European financial market. In 1968, Singapore set up the Asian financial market. Ten years later, Hong Kong relaxed its restrictions, and another international financial center came into existence in Asia. In 1986, the offshore financial market developed rapidly in Tokyo. By 2019, the number of offshore financial markets grew to 91 (see Table 4.1).

According to statistics, by the end of 2019, 70 countries and regions had set up offshore financial markets (see Table 4.1), and the scale of assets from those markets skyrocketed from less than US$ 1 trillion at the end of the 1970s to 18.454 trillion. The offshore financial market displayed the following characteristics: (a) Business activities were rarely overseen by laws and regulations, featuring simple formalities, low or no taxes, and higher efficiency. (b) An offshore financial market was comprised of "overseas banks," that is, the global network of banks engaged in overseas currency business. (c) The loan currencies of an offshore financial market belong to overseas countries. They enable borrowers to freely choose from a variety of currencies. The loan relationship of the market is the relationship between foreign lenders and foreign borrowers, which involves all parties concerned. (d) The interest rate of an offshore financial market adheres to the London inter-bank offered rate (LIBOR) as its standard. Its deposit interest rate is slightly higher than that of the domestic financial market, while its loan interest rate is somewhat lower. Both rates carry a minimal margin of difference from domestic rates, and they are highly competitive and appealing.

4 The Establishment of an Onshore Transaction Clearing Center…

Table 4.1 Distribution of global offshore financial markets by 2019

Africa	Asia-Pacific	Europe	Middle East	America
Djibouti (5)	Australia (18)	Austria (22)	Bahrain (5)	Aruba (21)
Seychelles	The Cook Islands	Andorra	Dubai	Bahamas
Tangier	Nauru	Luxembourg	Israel	Barbados
Liberia	Niue	Malta	Kuwait	Burritz City
Mauritius	Philippines	Monaco	Lebanon	Cayman Islands
	Singapore	The Netherlands		Bermuda
	Guam	Russia		Puerto Rico
	Macao	Switzerland		Uruguay
	Vanuatu	Cyprus		Grenada
	Western Samoa	Gibraltar		Panama
	Japan JOM	Jersey		Antigua
	Hong Kong	Hungary		Anguilla
	Malaysia (Namin Island)	Liechtenstein		Costa Rica
	Mariana	Madeira Islands		Dominican
	Marshall Islands	Guernsey		Caicos Islands
	Micronesia	London, UK		The British Virgin Islands
	New Delhi, Thailand	Dublin, Ireland		Montserrat Islands
		Channel Islands		Netherlands Antilles
		Paris, France		US IBFs
		Frankfurt, Germany		American Samoa

Source: Bank for International Settlement (BIS)

Furthermore, the development of offshore financial markets has broken through its original concepts and modes. The United States set up International Banking Facilities (IBFs) in 1981, and Japan set up Japan Offshore Market (JOM) in 1986, which caused a drastic change in the regionalist perception of offshore financial markets, which means that offshore financial markets may also be set up in home countries. That explains why major developed countries set up their offshore financial markets, which assumed diversified business modes.

International Banking Facilities (IBFs) is an offshore special financial account that was set up inside the US on December 3, 1981, with the approval of the Federal Reserve. The offshore business of that account is identified from domestic business, which falls into a different account used for and made available mainly to the domestic and foreign banks within the US according to the financial law. Through the offshore financial account, services such as deposits and loans are provided for non-resident customers in the US. That account (or facility) has the following functions to perform: (a) American banks and foreign affiliate banks within the US can provide convenient services for foreign deposits and loans. They are free from the restrictions imposed by the central bank on reserves against deposits, and the regulations of the Federal Deposit Insurance Corporation dictate that these banks do not need to pay the reserves against deposits. Customers may opt out of insurance; (b) each American state enjoys tax preferences by allowing the banks that have opened "IBFs" to be exempted from state and local taxes; (c) the scope of business is subject to the restrictions imposed by Bank of America and the Federal Reserve Bank.

JOM, that is, the Japan Offshore Market, refers to the offshore financial market established by Japan on December 1, 1986. The JOM has been an important symbol of its financial market internationalization. As a unique account of the Japanese offshore financial market, JOM was set up as an imitation of the IBFs of the US. First, the JOM market is subject to neither legal reserve requirements nor deposit insurance requirements. It has no interest withholding tax, nor is there control over interest rates. Additionally, the market allows neither bond business nor futures transactions. Second, the entities of JOM are the banks that have been licensed to operate FOREX businesses in Japan. They are required to separate their offshore accounts from their existing domestic accounts for "external-external" types of financial transactions. Third, their fund utilization method is limited only to loans for non-residents, the amount remitted to offshore accounts and the deposits of overseas financial institutions and their headquarters. Fourth, their fund-raising method is limited only to non-settlement deposits saved or borrowed from non-residents, other offshore accounts, and headquarters with a relatively free choice of currencies, such as yen or other currencies. Finally, JOM's financial tax measures, within the finance system, include policies for deposits into offshore accounts, interest cancelation as well as restrictions on the reserve

Table 4.2 Comparison of the scale of deposits and loans in major world offshore financial centers (US$ 1 billion)

	2000	2001	2002	2003	2004	2005	2006
Deposits							
Offshore centers	1642	2003	2163	2655	3143	3254	3799
All countries	9457	10,023	11,444	13,486	15,854	17,213	20,084
Offshore centers/all countries	17.36%	19.98%	18.90%	19.69%	19.82%	18.90%	18.92%
Loans							
Offshore centers	1085	1237	1276	1525	1857	2042	2411
All countries	8318	8872	10,059	11,869	13,820	15,202	17,876
Offshore centers/all countries	13.05%	13.94%	12.69%	12.85%	13.44%	13.43%	13.49%

Source: Bank for International Settlement (BIS)

system and the deposit insurance system, and within the tax system, they include policies for moderate tax reduction or exemption for deposits in offshore accounts and for local taxes and value-added tax (stamp tax), though a certain amount of such taxes is still required. Since the beginning of the twenty-first century, the offshore financial market of the world has shown a trend toward stable development (see Table 4.2).

4.2.2 The Orderly Connection Between Offshore and Onshore Markets

The internationalization of a country's currency is an essential indicator of its position among the world's economic powers, its influence upon global economic affairs, and its say on international financial matters. With the rise of a country's economy, the internationalization of its currency becomes its inevitable choice of merging into global economy and international financial market, developing itself into a global economic power, heightening its international economic position, and strengthening its competitiveness. It is also its inevitable choice to help improve the international currency system and fortify the governance of the global financial system in the period subsequent to the international financial crisis.

Developed offshore markets can further advance the internationalization of currencies of their home countries that can secure an advantageous position in the competition of major international currencies to the effect that primary global currencies be traded around the clock, international currencies have multiple third-party transactions, nonresidents request holding the assets of such currencies outside the countries that issue them, their "extracorporeal circulation" reduce the impacts on the monetary policies of the issuing countries, and the institutional advantage of an offshore market help enhance the extent of the internationalization of that country's currency. Experience in international finance has shown that an offshore financial market can play a critical driving role in the internationalization of a country's currency. Just as discussed above, the internationalization of US dollar has proceeded continuously through the development of IBF markets throughout its territories and the establishment of London-based US dollar market in Europe. Currently, the international use of major global reserve currencies is primarily through offshore markets. Offshore financial centers are where wealth is typically concentrated and financial activities are carried out. These financial centers circulate 50% to 70% of the world's money stocks. Offshore financial market investments account for one-third of the total assets of the World Bank and 30% to 40% of the private wealth.

The orderly connection between offshore and onshore markets is driven by both the internal needs for the internationalization of a country's currency and the external pressure for the global integration of real economies and financial markets. The internal need for the internationalization of a country's currency finds expression in the following: (a) The economy's global integration and the financial market internationalization have reinforced the accelerated needs for the offshore-onshore connection of a country's currency, the improvement on its internationalized development, and the enhancement of its rights of speech in international economic affairs; (b) the effectiveness of onshore regulation is under challenge; (c) the cost of onshore regulation is increasingly harder to bear. The external pressure for an active offshore-onshore connection stems mainly from the promotion of WTO and other international organizations involved, which require a country to undergo a shift from its current account convertibility to its capital account convertibility and to full convertibility. Consequently, in order to implement the internationalization strategy for a country's currency, it is necessary to make efforts to create for its home currency a globalized financial market with an interactive offshore-onshore connection.

To this end, China should plan and organize an onshore transaction and settlement center for RMB offshore business, which will bring about more effective RMB internationalization. So far, three RMB offshore business centers have been created in Hong Kong, Singapore, and London. RMB offshore business can be conducted in Shanghai, Shenzhen, and Zhuhai. For a currency issuing country, the key is to guide the orderly development of the offshore market to prevent possible impacts of offshore home currency upon domestic monetary policies and financial stability, improve the flow channel and mechanism of offshore-onshore connections, and boost the interaction between the development of offshore markets and the opening of onshore markets. The set-up of the onshore transaction and settlement center for RMB offshore transactions is exactly an effective way of achieving the goal of helping China accelerate its offshore financial market development.

First, its setup can drive the RMB offshore market development in Hong Kong and expedite domestic onshore financial market construction. In recent years, with the continuous reinforcement of China's national strength, the demand by non-residents for China's financial assets has been on the increase. As an essential RMB offshore center, Hong Kong owns more than 1 trillion yuan of RMB, which is expected to exceed far beyond that if RMB assets that exist in the form of bonds and notes are added. However, Hong Kong is now faced with a bottleneck in its RMB offshore business, as it is experiencing a slowdown in RMB stock with signs of weak fluidity. The main reason is that Hong Kong implements a linked exchange rate system that is tied to the US dollar, resulting in a weak and murky environment for the establishment of an RMB center. On this downside are pitfalls, such as blocked channels for RMB investment and financing, small quantities of RMB financial products, small cash pools, and an imperfect back-flow pipeline and mechanism.

It has become an urgent issue in Hong Kong's RMB offshore market how to design and construct a system that actively and effectively utilizes a huge amount of RMB funds. If it is well utilized, Hong Kong will become a global RMB offshore trading center that will provide strong support for the construction of the mainland capital market, and if not, offshore RMB may become stagnate and inactive or become a tool for underground financial transactions and arbitrage that will harm the stability of onshore domestic finance. Its establishment in the mainland will accumulate a good number of domestic and foreign financial institutions, transnational corporations, and intermediary service organizations, which will bring about changes in the situation of one mainland bank versus many foreign banks in the Hong Kong market, equality in competition between domestic and foreign financial institutions on the same platform, and more effective provision of diversified RMB financial services. A sound connection between RMB onshore and offshore markets will accommodate offshore RMB funds, providing good foundations for real economy, practical demands for enterprises, enough depth and breadth for the financial market, adequate fluidity for Hong Kong and other RMB offshore markets, and the enhanced desire for the international holding of RMB.

For Hong Kong, it is feasible to broaden the offshore RMB investment and financing channel, unblock the back-flow pipeline and regulatory mechanism, and stimulate offshore RMB transactions to form an offshore RMB center, which is more productive and generates positive economic circulation. For mainland China, it is feasible to fully utilize and effectively manage offshore RMB funds, control the dominant power for the favorable pricing of offshore RMB, and promote the construction of the domestic onshore financial market. Therefore, given the need for an offshore market and the ever-increasing demand on the onshore market, the establishment of an offshore center is a win-win initiative for RMB internationalization.

Second, its setup can strengthen the pricing power for the RMB exchange rate and enhance the independence and effectiveness of the national macroeconomic policy. At present, Chinese onshore RMB pricing takes place mainly at the interbank FOREX trading market located in Shanghai under the negative influence of policy intentions and short and sporadic exchange hours. The pricing of overseas offshore RMB (e.g., the NDF market) is also defective in that there is no offshore trading market concentrated in one area, that the laws and regulations of different countries have different requirements for the FOREX market, that there is no direct pricing mechanism between RMB and the currency of a trade or investment counter-party country, and that aggressive long or short trades by market traders are commonly encountered. One possible solution is to set up the center within the mainland for RMB pricing through a market-based mechanism, which can help hold the dominant power of pricing for offshore RMB and ensure the credibility and stability of pricing. Meanwhile, with the ongoing RMB internationalization, capital flow is bound to become more frequent and more extensive in scale. As a sizeable economy, China needs an independent and flexible monetary policy to ensure effective macro control. With that in mind, according to the exchange rate theory and the experience of a mature market economy, the exchange rate is no longer an appropriate primary policy objective of the central bank. A FOREX market needs to be created on the basis of market demand so as to realize a market-oriented formation of the exchange rate. Considering that the financial reform of China has arrived at a "deep water zone" and it has become necessary to effectively identify and manage exchange rate risks and external impacts, the setup of the center will provide a shield against external impacts under the monitoring and administration of the country's monetary authorities and a stabilized market-oriented RMB pricing mechanism, while ensuring the independence and effectiveness of its national macroeconomic policy.

Third, its setup can effectively serve the real economy and accelerate the internationalization of onshore financial institutions. In 2013, China absorbed US$ 117.586 billion of FDI, more than 87% of which came from ten countries or regions in Southeast Asia. However, the transactions between the RMB and other Southeast Asian currencies, including the HK and Singapore dollar, have not taken up most of the FOREX transactions of China. This shows that dual currency transactions are bound to appear in investments, which involve the transactions between the home currencies of different economies and the US dollars and between the US dollar and RMB. It has invisibly increased transaction costs and the exchange rate risks to both parties. The danger has been even more significant due to the recent period of drastic USD exchange rate fluctuations. As a useful addition to the interbank FOREX trading market, its setup is focused on multiple currency transactions catering to the needs of real economy. That will help find out the exact transaction price between RMB and other currencies, lower transaction costs for traders and investors, reduce exchange rate risks, and better serve real economy. In the meantime, both outgoing Chinese enterprises and incoming foreign enterprises give birth to significant needs for international financial services. The establishment of the center and development of the international banking business can fully satisfy the needs of enterprises and open up international business space for onshore financial institutions. Given the current continuous acceleration of overseas investment for M&A and the outward transfer of labor-intensive industries, there is an even greater need for the support of domestic financial platforms and financial institutions, which can spur onshore financial institutions to quicken their strides toward internationalization and further strengthen their ability to serve the transition and upgrading of the real economy.

Fourth, its setup can reinforce service trade competitiveness and assist the country in actively responding to the challenges of restructured international economic and trade order. Currently, China finds itself at a crossroads where it must undergo a shift from advancing goods exporting with a weak currency to boosting the competitiveness of the service trade with a strong currency. Generally speaking, the homogeneity of goods is the primary determining factor in price competition, while services enable a country to break away from its reliance on low-price competition owing to their inherent exclusivity differences. Economic restructuring and transformation in development modes will certainly require China to build up competitiveness in its service trade. Overall, the competitive edges of service trade should be based on the objective foundation of the RMB becoming a strong currency underpinned by powerful trade strength and the steady internationalization of RMB.

Starting in 1993, the US fortified its competitiveness in service trade by adopting a national policy of strong dollar. As a result, the service trade enhancement consolidated the strong position of the US dollar. In 2018, China vaulted itself into the enviable position as the largest goods trading country in the world. The total goods trade was worth

4.623 trillion US dollars. However, its service trade lagged far behind. Its total service trade import and export was only 791.9 billion US dollars, with a deficit of 291.3 billion US dollars, which means that China had the largest service trade deficit in the world. To strengthen the competitiveness of its service trade, China should immediately advance cross-border service trade through free trade zones (FTZ) and accelerate the RMB internationalization, which are the two sides of the same coin. On one hand, FTZ usually go along with the construction of currency financial markets. The higher the extent of financial market development and currency internationalization, the more likely it is for FTZ to become the industrial and trade centers in the world. Such a center within the territory, preferably within FTZ, can become a bridgehead deeply embedded into the global financial and trade value chain, lead China's outbound service trade and capital exports, and induce China to move toward a strong power of service and capital trade.

Alternately, with the global economic and trade order reshuffling in this era of the post-financial crisis, developed countries in the Western world, as well as Japan, have been accelerating their marginalization of WTO. Great efforts have gone into promoting the Trans-Pacific Partnership (TPP), Trans-Atlantic Trade & Investment Partnership (TTIP), and Plurilateral Services Agreement (PSA) in an apparent attempt to seize back world economic dominance, establish new rules for international trade and service industries and leverage their advantages so as to force WTO re-entry upon emerging economies and restrict the development of huge manufacturing industries in other countries. In response to that, by developing FTZ and setting up such a center, China can better capitalize on its markets, expand its international trade, and further promote its openness and competitiveness in service trade and investment.

Fifth, its setup has fully drawn upon the practices and experiences of the developed economies, signifying innovation of China's financial reform. The outflow of US dollars and the American financial service industry in the 1960s–1970s awakened the US to the fact that reforms must be in place to increase the appeal of US dollars to the Europeans and ensure the competitiveness of its financial service industry. In 1981, the Federal Reserve revised its regulations and approved the Bank of

America, deposit organizations, and the affiliates of foreign banks within the territory to establish IBFs (International Banking Facilities), undertake such offshore US dollar transactions within the US as international deposits and loans, and attract the back-flow of offshore US dollars under strengthened administration. These offshore account systems, which provide non-residents with financial services, are strictly separated from onshore accounts, which was a huge leap forward in financial innovation. That sets the precedent of one country setting up offshore financial markets with its home currency through an onshore center, an outstanding contribution to the development of the American financial system and beneficial experience to other countries that were undertaking similar reforms. IBFs led to the rapid development of offshore finance in the US. Within two years, more than 500 IBFs were set up. Over half of them were in New York, and they have attracted large amounts of overseas US dollars and international banking business. In the late 1980s, the assets of IBFs accounted for half of the total outbound assets of the Bank of America. This catapulted New York's position as the world's international financial center.

In 1986, Japan modeled after the US in setting up the JOM (Japan Offshore Market) in Tokyo, and it played an essential role in the internationalization of the Japanese yen. In 1990, the proportion of yen in the international FOREX reserves rose to 8.0%. In 2012, the scale of overseas lending made by Japan through its JOM accounted for 21.4% of its total external loans. Currently, in the development of its RMB offshore market, China should fully draw upon their practices and experience. Through a fully functioning RMB offshore market, China will be able to expand its offshore business of home currency internationally, implement reforms and innovations that are proportional to its conditions, create an onshore transaction and settlement system for offshore RMB, and promote the outflow and back-flow of RMB.

To sum up, the establishment of such a center is a mandatory requirement for China to develop the RMB offshore financial market and to boost its RMB internationalization, as well as a rational, all-win choice for parties involved.

4.3 The Design of Offshore-Onshore Connections in China

4.3.1 Rationale

It is imperative for China to persist in financial service to real economy, in reform and innovation through experimentation, and in risk control and steady progress. China must take action to set up a multi-level and internationalized center to guide the outflow and orderly back-flow of RMB, trade multiple currencies, drive the development of diversified financial products with the primary use of RMB, spur the RMB exchange rate to achieve marketization and convertibility of capital accounts, and form an RMB offshore financial market that features offshore-onshore connections that can cover Asia, radiating to other parts of the world with a high degree of prosperity, expedite RMB regionalization and internationalization, enhance trade competitiveness and economic influence of China.

4.3.2 Mode Selection

According to the differences in market operations and regulatory modes, the offshore financial market is divided into four modes:

1. Internal and external body type, which is represented by London and Hong Kong. Markets spontaneously form this type with highly integrated and mutually infiltrated offshore and onshore financial businesses. It makes direct use of existing domestic onshore financial systems to carry out offshore financial activities. Note that domestic onshore financial laws and supervisory regulations do not restrain offshore financial activities.
2. Internal and external separation type, which is represented by American IBFs and the Japanese JOM. These are the world's first offshore financial markets of this type. Formed under the impetus of policies, it strictly separates offshore from onshore business, isolates

accounts, and has created offshore business for non-resident transactions.
3. Osmotic type, which is represented by Singapore. It is a hybrid of the above two types. It is based on the separation type with offshore and onshore businesses in relative separation and accounts in isolation. It allows moderate penetration and conditional interconnection.
4. Tax havens type, which is represented by the Cayman Islands and Bermuda. As an accounting center, it provides a trading site without financial services, and it uses extremely low taxation to attract transactions (see Table 4.3)

The selection of modes is determined by factors such as the opening degree of the financial market of a country, its risk monitoring level, and state of economic development. At this juncture, China's center should be designed according to the mode of internal and external separation type. Using the experience of the US in IBFs as a guide, although its financial industry was already highly developed in the 1980s, it still placed offshore businesses within the banking sector and strictly implemented internal and external separations. It did this as an essential transitional means of loosening financial regulations and developing financial markets. Therefore, it provided a buffer for the reform of domestic financial regulations and a change in monetary policies.

After the 1990s, the US financial system shifted from dominating the banking sector to taking over the capital market. With the development of direct financing, for example, money market funds and asset-backed securitization, the boundary of onshore and offshore USD business became blurred. The degree of market integration increased significantly. It was about this time that the functions of IBFs began to gradually fade out. Currently, the construction of the RMB offshore market in China has just started. The opening degree of the Chinese financial market is rather low, the system of regulations is imperfect, and free convertibility has not been realized for capital accounts. Given the factors above, the center needs to adopt the model of the internal and external separation type as an essential carrier of the national offshore market. This model is characterized by "government creation" and "internal-external separation." It can better prevent financial risks, protect independent onshore

Table 4.3 Modes of international offshore financial markets

Mode	Typical market	Transaction subjects	Scope of business	Method of formation	Characteristics
Internal & external body type	London, Hong Kong	Non-residents, residents, offshore financial institutions	Medium- and long-term fund lending & borrowing	Formed naturally	The offshore organization follows no strict application procedure, does not set up independent offshore accounts, operates with an onshore account, and imposes no restrictions on fund entry and exit
Internal & external separation type	IBFs of USA, JOM of Japan	Non-residents, residents, offshore financial institutions	Medium- and long-term fund lending & borrowing	Created artificially	The authority must examine the establishment of an offshore organization; offshore business may occur only in a special account (IBF); offshore transactions are separated from onshore transactions; offshore and onshore fund permeation is prohibited
Osmotic type	Jakarta, Bangkok, Singapore ACU	Non-residents, residents, offshore financial institutions	Medium- and long-term fund lending & borrowing	Created artificially	Three cases: OUT→IN type; IN→OUT type; IN←→OUT type
Tax havens type	Cayman, Bahamas, Bermuda	Non-residents, offshore financial institutions	Processes accounting only, without actual transactions	Created artificially	Bookkeeping type (Paper Company, Shell Branch), Anglo-American Legal System, low tax, primarily no financial regulations

financial market development, and stay clear of impacts of overseas financial fluctuations. Also, it can break the restraint of onshore financial policies, laws, and regulations, attract overseas financial institutions and funds, develop international financial business, and promote China's financial internationalization.

In the long run, given China's continued financial maturity, expanding markets, and refining of its regulatory system, this seems to be the best model for gradually changing from an internal and external separation type to an osmotic type. It should enable offshore funds to be used directly for onshore purposes. This will provide greater support for the overseas development of domestic enterprises and continuously enhance the competitiveness of the offshore market.

4.3.3 Basic Framework and System

(1) Regional layout: Consideration may be given to selecting either Guangdong or Shanghai as one of the pilot regions for the center. Guangdong can be a better choice for the following reasons.

(a) Guangdong possesses the economic and financial foundation for carrying out an offshore RMB business. Guangdong has already become a huge province in terms of economic and financial volume. This region is highly export-oriented with its total import-export volume that accounts for 26% of the national total. It attracts 21% of the total FDI of China. It has a well-developed manufacturing industry and a complete financial and industrial chain with policy advantages that have made it a comprehensive experimental zone for financial reforms and innovations in the Pearl River Delta.

(b) Guangdong is an important bridgehead for RMB internationalization, and it started RMB settlement experiments for cross-border trade in 2009. Currently, the settlement amount accounts for 30% of the national total, and this has allowed the RMB to become the second largest currency for cross-border income and payment, second only to the USD. A pressing direction of RMB internationalization is to move ahead with the Maritime Silk Road so that Southeast Asia becomes the top pick for building the RMB currency area. Guangdong has been an important starting point of the Maritime Silk Road since ancient times. It is in close economic and trade contact with ASEAN countries, and it plays an irreplaceable role.

(c) The joint construction of a global RMB offshore market by Guangdong and Hong Kong has natural advantages. Closely related to each other, the two places promote and complement each other. They have both been committed to advancing economic integration and liberalizing the service trade. It will present a limitless prospect to combine, superpose, and magnify the advantages of Hong Kong as an international financial center and an RMB offshore center. Such a synergy will bring about enormous prospects for the financial development of both places.

(d) If it is established in Guangdong, the center can divide the workload and cooperate with the China FOREX Trading Center in Shanghai. This will allow for staggered development and mutual enhancement. The two price systems, that is, the onshore RMB exchange rate (CNY) in Shanghai and the offshore RMB exchange rate (CNH) in Guangdong, can corroborate and support each other to jointly boost the exchange rate marketization.

(2) The content of services: As a multiple currency settlement center that intends to use offshore RMB for trade and investment between non-residents and between residents and non-residents, the center can provide flexible exchanges between RMB and other currencies, which are not restricted by quotas. However, in its early stage, it must rely on the foundation of real trade and investment before gradually unitizing the offshore convertibility of capital accounts. There are four aspects to that. The first is to influence enterprises to use RMB for pricing and settlements in foreign trade and investments so as to create a platform for comprehensive services for RMB to flow out and back. The second is to conduct cross-border RMB businesses and product innovation so as to create a service system of cross-border RMB investments and financing that promotes real economy and connects it with Hong Kong, Macao, and the rest of the world. The third is to introduce domestic and overseas market players to promote cross-border transactions between offshore and onshore RMB markets so as to become a major hub that connects those markets. The fourth is to form offshore RMB market prices and become a market weathervane for the formation of the RMB exchange

rate. Eventually, it is guaranteed that all mobile elements can achieve a barrier-free configuration through advantageous financial arrangements.

(3) Core system: It is suggested that the People's Bank of China, as the central bank, should approve the establishment of CIBFs (China International Banking Facilities). These may also be expressed in other forms of accounts. However, an account of this nature must be set up in advance. After the establishment of CIBFs, the People's Bank of China should allow domestic financial institutions (designated FOREX banks initially) to set up their CIBF accounts and take the lead in carrying out offshore RMB business in the center. These may be spread to other regions as conditions progress. This step is designed to attract the backflow of offshore RMB. CIBFs will be set up as an imitation of American IBFs. This means that they will function as an onshore asset-liability account of financial institutions dedicated to processing offshore RMB business rather than an independent bank system or an individual business organization. Its essential components are as follows. First, domestic banks and other financial institutions can use their domestic organizations and equipment to absorb deposits of foreign currencies and offshore RMB through CIBFs without being restrained by domestic statutory reserves and an upper limit of interest rates. This may also be done without the need to affect insurance with a deposit insurance fund. Second, loans may be issued to domestic onshore borrowers but must be used for overseas offshore purposes. Third, RMB deposits and loans in a CIBF account are deemed as offshore RMB and they are strictly separated from domestic RMB account management. Fourth, the tax due date and amount owed for the CIBFs net business income depend on the development and competitive state of the RMB offshore business. Fifth, residents can also open CIBF accounts, while IBFs cannot. Of course, the CIBF account must be used for the relevant business of offshore RMB and foreign currencies (e.g., the income from the overseas assets or investment of residents). Sixth, only by opening CIBF accounts can non-residents and residents use RMB for trade, investment, and settlement between RMB and other currencies at the center. In short, this is an individual asset-liability account and an institutional arrangement related to it for offshore RMB financial business conducted onshore within China.

(4) Pricing system: CIBFs are relied upon for transactions and settlements between offshore RMB and multiple currencies to form the prices of offshore RMB, which may go through several stages. Stage 1 involves the construction of a market for the circulation of various currencies. This construct would be oriented toward the transaction subjects of the real economy. It would be used to affect the free settlement between offshore RMB and multiple currencies by right of real trade and investment. As a result, transaction subjects would decide RMB prices according to the listed prices of banks. Stage 2 involves the construction of inter-bank money exchanges, that is, the construction of the spot goods market for transactions between offshore RMB and the currencies of the economies of Hong Kong, Macao, and Southeast Asian countries. This stage would be carried out under the support of the People's Bank of China as the central bank and Chinese or foreign commercial banks as members or market makers. They will affect inter-bank transactions within the exchange. At the same time, they will open the curb transactions of banks for customers. In the exchange, comprehensive indicators are formed and released reflecting the exchange rate between RMB and the currencies of neighboring countries. On this basis, transactions of derivatives and indicators will be developed for RMB and its neighboring currencies. The purpose is to establish a benchmark pricing system of offshore RMB. A benchmark pricing system will work in concert with the onshore RMB exchange rate in Shanghai. From a longer term perspective, a unified money exchange may also be set up in due course, which will be a physical transaction market with the participation of commercial banks, non-banking financial institutions, and qualified sectors of the real economy. Transactions of spot goods and derivatives between RMB and foreign currencies may occur without the need for a background of real trade investment. The formation program of the RMB exchange rate will become more market-oriented.

(5) Matching measures: Measures must be taken to strengthen the construction of infrastructure in the region where the center is located and optimize the investment development environment and attract more financial institutions and enterprises, to improve the physical trading facilities of the center as well as the network facilities that match the CIBF's account system and build an efficient, secure, and stable data system and clearing and settlement system, to guide financial institutions

within the region in setting up background organizations, that is, creating a data backup center and support the services for offshore financial data, and to attract international talents in the fields of finance, law, and accounting to fortify intelligent support.

4.3.4 General Principles

Promote the connection and interaction between the center and the offshore markets in Hong Kong, Singapore, and London for an all-win development.

The general principles include: (a) remain country-oriented with focus on holding the pricing power of offshore RMB, (b) deepen exchanges and draw fully on sophisticated overseas systems and practices, (c) strengthen cooperation by driving two-way investments and financing exchanges with Hong Kong and improving bilateral cross-border loans and other initiatives, while gradually extending these services to Singapore and London, (d) take joint action in regulations and accelerate the establishment of regulation coordination programs with these offshore markets, (e) seek simultaneous development and promote the orderly export, healthy back-flow, and extracorporeal circulation of RMB.

Specifically speaking, what should be first done is to strengthen connections with the Hong Kong offshore center and build through joint efforts between Guangdong and Hong Kong a global RMB offshore financial market for the Guangdong-Hong Kong-Macao Greater Bay Area with a view to invigorate the stock funds of RMB in Hong Kong and provide freer flow through the investment and financing channel and back-flow passage. This will demonstrate strong support for the construction of a purpose-built Hong Kong international financial center rather than a substitute with a waning-waxing situation. The center will unfold offshore RMB transactions and settlements against the background of real trade to form the spot goods market of RMB. It will also be able to fix the spot price of RMB versus neighboring currencies. This won't clash with the NDF market in Hong Kong.

Furthermore, RMB will be unable to play its due role if its fluidity is poor in Hong Kong. However, it may weaken the position of the HKD as an international currency if its circulation is excessive. CIBFs have formed a buffer zone between Hong Kong and mainland China and between the RMB and the HKD. The setup of the center in Guangdong is intended to promote the superposing advantages of Guangdong and Hong Kong and to jointly build a global RMB offshore financial market. The Hong Kong government may take a significant role in the development of the center, while Hong Kong-based financial institutions may set up CIBFs to become market makers. Such a joint offshore market should be designed to become a fluidity rallying point of the global offshore RMB, financing center, pricing center, trading center, and wealth management center. These functions will take over the "wholesale" functions of the RMB offshore business and provide diversified RMB financial products. They will carry out the transactions that use offshore RMB to directly purchase the assets and property rights whose value is indicated in foreign currencies. Other offshore markets located in Singapore and London mainly undertake the "retail" functions of offshore RMB and then grow into regional RMB offshore centers.

Second, it is imperative to strengthen connections with the offshore center in Singapore and the financial markets in Southeast Asia and advance Southeast Asia toward becoming an RMB currency area. With the on-time completion of the China/ASEAN FTZ, the scale of trade between China and ASEAN countries will continuously expand. The RMB will be fully capable of becoming a significant payment and reserve currency in the region. As Southeast Asia's RMB center, Singapore will be positioned as the platform that provides RMB financial trade and investment business throughout China and Southeast Asia. It will be an important regional market due to the investments in RMB financial products. Singapore will be able to strengthen RMB fluidity by setting up CIBFs at the center, which will then be able to reach out to the Southeast Asian region through its cooperation with Singapore, provide specialized services in China, especially those involved in transferring labor-intensive industries to Southeast Asia and promoting the use of RMB for investments and settlements, and communicate directly with the currency authorities of major Southeast Asian economies to attract a greater variety of currencies into the transactions of CIBFs. Consequently, local financial institutions and enterprises may be introduced to take part in RMB exchange rate pricing.

Finally, the connection must be strengthened with the offshore center in London to spur RMB on its way into the European market. London, a long-established international financial center, has a developed offshore financial industry and should be positioned to become a bridgehead for the RMB to work its way into Europe. In the short term, London's demand for RMB is mainly seen in the investment demands for RMB products, for London has gathered many institutional investors from around the world that invest in Asia. Additionally, historically, the close contact between London and Hong Kong will facilitate the marketing of Hong Kong's RMB products in Europe. In the medium to long term, Europe is China's biggest trade partner. However, there is only a meager quantity of RMB settlements for bilateral trade. In the future, London will provide RMB financial services for European trade and direct investment in China to become a major offshore market of the RMB in Europe. China should try to motivate London-based financial institutions to set up CIBFs at the center and advance the development of the RMB offshore market in London.

4.3.5 Effective Measures

Use the center as a platform capable of taking multiple measures to promote the effective combination and coordinated progress in internationalizing the RMB, local enterprises, and domestic banks.

The experiences of developed countries show that the internationalization of their currency is roughly in synchronization with that of its enterprises and financial institutions. First, the internationalization of our home currency will help native enterprises strengthen their overseas competitiveness, and the banking industry obtains more space for international business. Second, the internationalization of native enterprises and financial institutions will vigorously advance the export and overseas use of our home currency. Third, the internationalization of native enterprises calls for a more extensive financial demand and requires native banks to optimize international financial services so that the two complement each other.

Faced with the current changeable situation and reorganization of the international economic and trade order, China should focus more on its expansion of markets abroad, oriented more toward the global development that underscores both capital and product exports for the improved coordination and promotion of the internationalization of RMB, native enterprises, and banks. This is the core component of China's new strategy for open markets and the fundamental choice for China to export capital while exerting its impacts upon and strengthening global competitiveness. The establishment of the center provides an ideal platform for the effective integration of all three with multiple initiatives employed to form a new effective synergy.

Focus should be laid on promoting the export of the RMB under capital accounts. First, prompt native enterprises to go global, use the RMB for outward direct investment (ODI), and develop more RQDII and High-tech QDII. Second, allow non-residents to merge into the RMB through domestic onshore issuance of bonds, shares, and loans. Expand the scale of RMB panda bonds of their domestic onshore issuance. Duly introduce the shares of the "international board" that are oriented toward overseas offshore investors. Third, foster the overseas offshore demand for RMB, including promoting the transactions of RMB financial products and tools at offshore centers, the pricing of RMB in cross-border transactions on bulk commodities and the use thereof by third parties, and so on. Fourth, advance the foreign loans of RMB, including interest-free loans or assistance of RMB provided for developing countries.

Establish a cross-border investment and financing service system that supports the development of real economy and provides universal, diversified financial services for industrial transitions and upgrades. These services will be an important catalyst in helping enterprises to go global. First, provide services for the overseas transfer of traditional industries. Motivate backbone enterprises to leverage the center for the overseas transfer of traditional labor-intensive industries through setting up investment companies in the region of the center. Set up RMB private equity markets that are related to outward direct investment. Second, create RMB overseas investment funds and RMB export credit funds at the center to support the overseas operation and expansion of local enterprises. Third, promote the convenience of cross-border RMB financing. Allow local enterprises to raise RMB funds from overseas markets, such as Hong Kong, and use them mainly for overseas development. Support local enterprises in developing a bidirectional RMB cash pool within the group. Provide affiliated enterprises with cross-border lending. Support local banks in providing cross-border RMB syndicated loans with overseas banks to provide credit services for large transnational enterprises and transitional and upgrade. Carry out cross-border RMB trade financing.

Put extra effort into supporting the cross-border service trade. Combine the joint construction of the RMB offshore markets of Guangdong and Hong Kong with the liberalization of the service trade in those two places and the construction of Guangdong-Hong Kong-Macao Greater Bay Area. Build service trade concentration areas of IP, technology, and finance as well as cross-border service trade centers in the center. Optimize the service trade development environment. Promote the convenience of cross-border service trade. Prompt Guangdong and Hong Kong to strengthen cooperation in the service trade area for rapid development. Focus on developing modern service industries like finance, insurance, management consulting, laws, and accounting so as to accelerate their globalization and use of RMB for cross-border service trade and investment.

Set up a carbon spot and futures exchange with national standards to promote the formation of the "carbon emission right trading—RMB settlement" system. Currently, carbon trading has just started in Asia. As the world's largest carbon emission country and carbon credit supply country, China enjoys huge congenital advantages. Improvements should be made in China's carbon market system as soon as possible in order to obtain the Asian carbon trading pricing power. Explorations may be made in the establishment of a carbon spot and futures exchange with national standards at the center. The center may even become a carbon spot and a future Asian trading market, enabling the RMB to become the settlement currency for transactions thereof and making a breakthrough for the construction of the RMB currency area. On this basis, the "carbon emission right trading—RMB settlement" system will take shape as a strong addition to the "oil trading—USD settlement" system.

Encourage domestic banks in China to accelerate and enhance international competitiveness. As the major component of the domestic financial sector, the domestic commercial banks of China have the broadest customer base, organizational network, and RMB assets. They have the inherent advantages of taking part in the international financial market. Opportunities should be employed to quicken the steps of internationalization by first utilizing CIBF accounts for developing international banking business and enhancing operational service levels and internationalization in the competition and cooperation with overseas banks. Second, aggressively expand the overseas market, especially the markets in Hong Kong, Singapore, and London. Leverage the substantial accumulation of RMB, actively develop overseas RMB accounts, and expand the overseas use of the RMB. Third, increase services to those enterprises so that their business can go global. Accelerate the coverage of major economic and trade areas. Build a flexible, universal service chain so that the institutional setup and layout of financial resources can match the patterns of those enterprises going global.

4.4 Chinese Rules for Offshore-Onshore Connections

4.4.1 The Separation of CIBFs from Domestic Onshore RMB Account to Ensure Orderly Flow and Equal Rights

First, using the internal-external separation mode of the offshore financial market, the offshore accounts that CIBFs correspond to should be physically separated from domestic onshore RMB accounts and strictly managed separately. Only offshore RMB can be used for settlements at the center through CIBFs, which must correspond to actual quotations at the present stage, that is, rely on the background of real trade and investment. The offshore RMB held by non-residents and residents can be used for trade and investments through CIBFs in the region of the center. The center's reach can be expanded in the future as it fits. Offshore RMB may be freely converted to multiple foreign currencies through settlements. The funds in CIBF accounts are not included in the statistics of the domestic currency, but they are monitored in a timely manner for inclusion into currency statistics once they are transferred into a domestic account.

Second, CIBFs permit the free unilateral flow of RMB funds in domestic onshore accounts, which means that offshore RMB can be transferred from CIBF accounts into domestic accounts at any time without the need for corresponding actual quotations. However, once funds are transferred into a domestic RMB account, it will be impossible to reverse the operation and settlement at the center unless otherwise restricted by law, as in the case where regulations and existing laws take precedence over regulations according to FOREX supervision.

Third, the principle of equal rights should be strictly observed. The individuals that open CIBFs enjoy equal rights. If a non-resident holds a domestic onshore RMB account, then the transfer between CIBF accounts and domestic onshore RMB accounts enjoys the same treatment as that of residents. In addition, the offshore RMB used for trade and investments at the center enjoy the same rights as domestic RMB.

4.4.2 The Need to Accelerate the Amelioration of the Offshore Financial Legal System

The laws and regulations pertaining to the settlement center and CIBFs fall into offshore finance legislation, with offshore finance laws being formulated by the country where the market is formulated within the domain of international legislation. In a broad sense, the system of the laws on offshore finance generally includes or absorbs the applicable international treaties and practices for offshore financial business. For example, the rules for international financial regulations, with the Basel Accord at its core, can be deemed as the integration of domestic laws and international laws. There exist at present some defects in the system of laws and regulations on the offshore financial business in China. A series of regulations have been promulgated, such as *Measures for Management of Offshore Banking Business* (by the People's Bank of China), *Detailed Rules for Implementation of the Measures for Management of Offshore Banking Business* (by the State Administration of Exchange Control), *The Law of the People's Bank of China*, *The Commercial Laws*, *The Anti-Money Laundering Law*, *Regulations on Management of Foreign Exchange*, the *Management Measures for the International Commercial Loans Borrowed by Domestic Organizations*, and *Management Measures for External Guarantee of Domestic Institutions*. However, problems still exist, including a legal system to be improved, low legal effect ranking, fragmentary legal provisions, and a lot of other tasks to be undertaken. Since offshore finance is highly law-based internationalized business, there is a practical need for the formulation and improvement of laws and regulations being accelerated.

First, legislation should be promoted in incremental steps. At the national level, the People's Bank of China should issue relevant norms in the near future, approve the establishment of the center and CIBF accounts, clarify related systems and rules, connect with international laws to the greatest extent possible on the basis of domestic laws, and promote connections with overseas offshore market. In the meantime, it is imperative to amend the *Measures for Management of Offshore Banking Business*, the detailed rules for its implementation thereof and other relevant legal provisions. This will help us expand the business scope of the offshore market and place under standardized and unified administration the offshore business of Chinese banks and overseas banks in China. Conditions permitting, the National People's Congress should issue a law on offshore finance that meets the requirements of unified, complete, and international treaties and practices, including offshore financial subject law, foreign financial transaction law, and foreign financial regulation law. At the local level, provinces and municipalities where the center is located may, within the scope of local legislative authority, draw on international laws and rules and market experience to formulate specific standards and management systems for the center. The use of negative list management is strongly advisable. For example, Guangdong can use the NDF market of Hong Kong for reference, along with other relevant systems, in setting the management standards that suit the financial market in Hong Kong. Meanwhile, the region where the center is located may be authorized to emulate the practices of the Shanghai FTZ and halt the implementation of related administrative regulations and some provisions of the documents of the State Council according to the procedure.

Next come the key contents of legislation and law amendments in the close future. (a) Management of FOREX and interest rates. Although the free exchange of capital accounts has not yet been created for RMB, onshore FOREX regulations do not affect the operation of the offshore RMB market. It is proper to discuss the cancellation of FOREX regulations for the domestic onshore-offshore market, including CIBF's offshore RMB business so that the funds in CIBF accounts can be freely allocated and transferred. This will ensure the free flow and exchange of offshore funds. To this end, amendments and additions should be made to FOREX management regulations, management measures for the guarantee of domestic institutions, and other relevant regulations. As for interest rates, Article 22 of the *Measures for Management of Offshore Banking Business* provides that the interest rates of FOREX and loans of the offshore banking business can be set according to interest rates of the international financial market. However, offshore banks should maintain their transparency and announce, in real time, applicable interest rates.

(b) Regulation of operations. To reinforce the competitiveness of China's offshore financial business, it is necessary to loosen the controls over the operational activities of offshore banks to lower operational costs. Banks should be exempted from the reserves against the offshore deposits absorbed by banks. A provision concerning this in Article 23 of the *Measures for Management of Offshore Banking Business* should apply to CIBF accounts, and the future deposit insurance system layout should exempt deposit insurance for CIBF business. Future requirements may be relaxed appropriately for capital in cash and other additional capital for the offshore business of banks.

(c) Tax preferences. Low taxation is one of the important characteristics of offshore finance. It has become urgent to formulate the laws and regulations on offshore taxation that mesh with the national tax law system. This will ensure lower tax rates of offshore business than that of similar domestic businesses so that onshore business is relieved of its tax that used to be higher than that of neighboring offshore markets.

Therefore, China will have a competitive edge in carrying out offshore business. Before the related laws and regulations are issued, specific tax preferences may be first given to offshore businesses in the form of departmental regulations. Some of these regulations may include lowering the income tax rate, allowing exemption of business and stamp taxes according to international practices, and exempting CIBF accounts from interest withholding tax.

(d) Confidentiality obligations. Existing Chinese laws protect the private information of bank customers, such as the confidentiality obligation under Articles 29 and 30 of the *Law on Commercial Banks*. However, money laundering and corruption have been on the increase. If too much confidentiality is emphasized, the result will be loopholes that allow for the exploitation by criminals. Therefore, shortly after the center is established, laws and regulations should be formulated to identify the confidentiality obligations of financial institutions in pursuing offshore business according to the actual conditions of China. The relevant restrictive suggestions of international organizations must also be considered. Compromising confidentiality requirements may be adopted, which will be slightly more relaxed than the confidentiality obligations fulfilled by domestic commercial banks.

(e) Crackdown on international financial crimes. International organizations now fully cooperate in fighting financial crimes. Useful suggestions have been formulated to combat crimes in the fields of money laundering and tax evasion. China should formulate similar laws and regulations by using the guiding implications and codes of conduct of related international organizations as a reference. It should take an active part in the cross-border cooperation of fighting international financial crimes while promoting the healthy development of its offshore business.

4.4.3 Strengthen Risk Control

The biggest issue for developing the center is that, with deepened relevance in the internal and external finance of China and the weakening isolation program, offshore RMB may cause adverse impacts on the domestic onshore financial market. Therefore, the center should give top priority to risk control and take the following measures by strictly implementing the internal-external separation model.

(a) Restrict and dynamically adjust the offset quantity between the offshore and onshore positions of banks. After the offshore market is established, the interconnection between internal and external markets is mainly realized through the mutual offset between the positions of parent banks and their foreign banks. The internal position is offset externally as capital outflow or conversely as capital inflow. Under the "Detailed Rules for Implementation of the Measures for Management of Offshore Banking Business," the offset quantity of the internal and external positions of an offshore bank may not exceed 10% of the average monthly balance of the total offshore assets in the previous year. The opening degree of the domestic financial market is now higher to allow moderate enhancement of offset quantity. This is still restricted and may be adjusted dynamically in the future according to the permeation degree of internal and external markets, the changes in the situation, and the needs of development.

(b) Focus on control over the short-term capital flow. Short-term capital flow is a necessary inducement that causes international financial crises. The relevant experience of global offshore markets may be used as a reference to further increase the magnitude of the RMB exchange rate. Studies may be made to inhibit the entry and exit of short-term speculative arbitrage funds through such adjustment means as the Tobin tax. Under special circumstances, regulators may take temporary regulatory measures.

(c) Intensify anti-money laundering, anti-terrorist financing, and anti-tax evasion regulations. Promote the building of a monitoring system. Pay close attention to any abnormal cross-border flow of funds. Establish a regulation and law enforcement team composed of experts. The financial institutions and non-financial institutions in the region of the center should promptly, accurately, and ultimately submit balance sheets and related information to the national financial regulators. This information must be processed using the statistical declaration of the international balance of payment.

(d) Strengthen the collaboration between national and local financial regulations. National and local financial regulators will implement the regulations of local financial institutions and relevant businesses. They will strengthen collaboration according to their respective powers.

(e) Set up a comprehensive information regulation platform to implement monitoring, evaluation, and classified management of local non-financial institutions.

4.4.4 Strengthen the Appeal of Offshore RMB and Enhance Onshore Settlement Business Volume

Whether the center can take full advantage of its role depends upon whether a large quantity of offshore RMB is traded and settled there. Otherwise, no matter how ingenious the institutional design is, the center will wither for lack of transactions and eventually exist in name only. The increase of its settlement volume is contingent upon two factors. One is large enough stock and business demand of offshore RMB funds, which is an external factor, which presently has a good foundation. It is necessary to increase the supply of the offshore RMB market and enhance overseas demand now and in the future. The other is the enrichment of settlement functions, exchange quota, transaction currencies, investment tools, and market mechanisms of the center with a strong appeal for offshore RMB, which constitutes internal factors. The focuses should be laid on the following five aspects.

(a) Provide the center with flexible policies that go beyond existing regulations. A breakthrough should be made in the exchange of capital accounts. For example, the transactions under CIBF accounts should be free of the restrictions of quota and currencies for free allocation and transfer. Meanwhile, restrictions should be relaxed on relevant investment licensing and cross-border rights of properties, shares, and debts.

(b) Attract domestic and foreign financial institutions, intermediary service agencies, transnational corporations, high-tech enterprises, and incubators for the purpose of promoting the integrative development of industries, finance, science and technology within the region, as well as forming agglomeration effects and boosting market demands for cross-border trade and investment settled in RMB.

(c) Expand the RMB investment market oriented toward non-residents and develop diversified RMB financial products. In addition, more overseas RMB should be allowed to be invested in the domestic onshore real economy and capital markets through FDI or RQFII. Support should be provided to financial institutions in relying on CIBFs to expand offshore businesses, and overseas investors be provided with multiple RMB products. Investment tools that are needed must be supplied, including bonds, funds, ETFs, trust and wealth management products, and financial derivatives (introduced gradually). Financial derivatives would include forwards of the RMB exchange rate carbon futures, RMB life insurance provided to non-residents, accident insurance, and cross-border vehicle insurance.

(d) A cross-border factor trading platform should be created, and RMB be used as its pricing and settlement. Support must be provided to regions where the center is located by creating a factor trading platform or exchange for the cross-border transactions of property rights, stock rights, technology, financial assets, and bulk commodities. Introduction should be made of the transaction products and categories with prices listed in RMB and the use of RMB for the trading and transfer of overseas assets and factor resources.

(e) Gradual enhancement should be made in the service functions of the center. Service functions should include a provision for convenient payment and settlement services to form more market-oriented and expected RMB exchange rates. This will extend the functions of the trading system abroad, including quotation, the conclusion of transaction, liquidation, and information release.

4.4.5 Other Suggestions

Three additional recommendations should be made here.

The first recommendation is to set up the FTZ that connects with Hong Kong and Macao in the region where the center is established. Then, launch the experimentation of financial reform. In addition to major reform experiments, for example, the opening of RMB capital accounts, the market-oriented formation mechanism of the exchange rate and interest rate, and improvement of the architectural system of the financial market, consideration may also be given to the following explorations:

(a) Explore mixed business operations with integrated regulation. Break the boundaries of operations between banking, securities, and insurance industries. Set up financial markets with greater flexibility and open markets. Encourage cross-competition and cooperation between financial institutions and strengthen overall competitiveness.
(b) Explore the offshore business license management system of China's domestic banks. Management experience may be drawn on of Hong Kong in three-level banking licenses—full license, partial license, and deposit-taking companies. This should be done to substitute license management for current administrative limitations. Those banks with strong monetary strength, substantial international business, and a high level of risk control may register a full license with the center. Other commercial banks may register a partial license first and then gradually expand their scope of business with the accumulation of offshore experience to matching their offshore business and level of risk control.
(c) Explore the establishment of architectural regulation to stimulate the compatible financial regulation system. Scientifically divide national and local regulatory powers in the region of the center. Strengthen correspondence between authorities and responsibilities as well as rule-based, innovative, and inclusive regulation. For example, the access and regulatory powers of part of the business of offshore banks may be delegated to local regulators. This will give better performance to local initiatives while adding advantages, preventing risks, and promoting innovation. Additionally, we can boldly introduce the advanced systems, practices, and businesses of the international financial market into the center. This will be a catalyst for absorption, digestion, and re-innovation for domestic promotion after the success and further enhancement of the level of marketization, legalization, and internationalization of national finance.

The second is to push forward RMB internationalization under capital accounts and reforms in the opening of capital accounts. Related studies show that if capital accounts are late in launching, RMB internationalization can be accomplished by 10% at most, and that if RMB internationalization takes place only under trade, it will not be sustainable and is likely to fall into the "Triffin Dilemma." As the internationalization of RMB under capital accounts cannot take place independently of the reform of capital accounts convertibility, the two should go hand in hand and promote each other. For example, the restrictions can be simultaneously relaxed on the swap by enterprises and individuals and the regulation of RMB remittance. Simultaneous increase can be made in investment quotas and the QFII of overseas institutions for the inter-bank market of RMB. Meanwhile, non-residents may be permitted to conduct domestic onshore transactions to raise RMB and convert the raised RMB to FOREX for remittance. The opening of domestic onshore RMB investment markets to non-residents should be concomitant with the development of the offshore RMB investment market in Hong Kong and other locations.

The third is to coordinate the development positioning of the Shanghai FTZ and the center in Guangdong. Their development should be staggered, mutually complementary, and in a win-win interaction. They play an essential role in the internationalization of RMB. Since the principal task of the Shanghai FTZ in the financial field is to guide domestic financial development and focus on onshore financial innovation, these will turn Shanghai into an international financial center ranking side by side with New York, London, and Hong Kong. Guangdong has the potential to become a docking hub between RMB offshore and onshore markets and a bonding point of establishing the Hong Kong international financial center. Guangdong has endeavored to build a powerful province of finance, and the center in Guangdong shoulders the primary task of boosting the development of the RMB offshore financial market, advancing the construction of the RMB zone in Southeast Asia and providing international services for cross-border RMB trade and investment and for Chinese enterprises going global.

In the future, there will be both cooperation and a division of labor between the inter-bank FOREX trading market in Shanghai and the

Guangdong offshore RMB spot trading market. FOREX deals mainly in transactions of RMB and the US dollars. It is where the domestic onshore RMB exchange rate is priced. It reflects wholesale prices and is adjusted to certain extent, by the Central Bank. This market has typically shown relatively stable prices. The latter deals mainly in the transactions of multiple currencies, including RMB, HK dollars, and Singaporean dollars. It relies on acts of real trade and investments that are settled in RMB and other currencies to form an offshore RMB exchange rate. It reflects retail prices, and it is composed mainly of market transactions with great price fluctuations. However, the state will retain the final right of pricing.

In short, the offshore-onshore coordination of the Chinese financial market includes three levels—information exchange, partial coordination (also called discretion-based coordination), and full coordination (also called rule-based coordination). If full coordination is practiced, focus should be laid on the joint offshore-onshore coordination, that is, clearing and settlement system coordination, rule-based standard coordination, legal clause coordination, and regulatory system coordination. In the light of the actual need of China's development, the adoption and employment of different types and manners to drive the orderly coordination and interaction between the offshore and the onshore market will not only effectively accelerate RMB internationalization but also allow China to take part in the global financial governance and boost the stable development of global economic and financial markets.

5

The Settlement of "Carbon Emissions Trading" in RMB—Explorations in China's Pathway of "Overtaking on the Curve" in Finance

Before delving into the pathway and methods for China's financial sector to "overtake at the curve," it is imperative that we first gain an understanding of the Kyoto Protocol. If it be true that the General Agreement on Tariffs and Trade (GATT) has provided an international system for trade in tangible goods, then it is also true that the Kyoto Protocol has provided an international system for trade in intangible goods, enabling the formation of carbon commodities and the development of carbon markets to become new bright spots in global trade. The Protocol provides for joint implementation of greenhouse gas mitigation by all countries to achieve "stabilization of greenhouse gas concentrations in the atmosphere at a level that would prevent dangerous anthropogenic interference with the climate system." Thus, the Kyoto Protocol is reckoned as the third set of global rules after the Charter of the United Nations and the General Agreement on Tariffs and Trade.

5.1 The Kyoto Protocol

The Kyoto Protocol, otherwise known in full as the Kyoto Protocol to the United Nations Framework Convention on Climate Change, is a supplementary treaty to the United Nations Framework Convention on Climate Change (UNFCCC). It was adopted at the third session of the Conference of the Parties (COP3) in Kyoto, Japan, in December 1997. It entered into force on February 16, 2005, and by 2019, it had been ratified by 184 countries, which accounted for 61% of total global emissions. It is noteworthy that the United States signed the Kyoto Protocol without ratifying it, and later on withdrew from the treaty, with Canada following suit in December 2011. Its objective is to achieve "stabilization of greenhouse gas concentrations in the atmosphere at a level that would prevent dangerous anthropogenic interference with the climate system." The Protocol marked the first attempt in human history to place legally binding limits on greenhouse gas emissions (GHG emissions).

Under the Kyoto Protocol, four options are designed to assist state parties in meeting their emission reduction commitments:

- Emissions trading, which enables trade in emission units between two developed countries, meaning that a country with difficulties in emission objective compliance can buy surplus emission credits from another country that achieves a greater reduction than called for in the Kyoto Protocol.
- The "net approach," which calculates a country's GHG emissions on a net basis by subtracting the amount of CO_2 absorbed by forests from its actual human-induced CO_2 emissions.
- The employment of green development mechanisms for joint emissions reduction between developed and developing countries.
- The group compliance approach, whereby the EU, for example, is treated as an integral whole regarding emission reduction commitments, with emissions allowed to rise in some individual EU members and drop in others.

The Kyoto Protocol defines three "flexibility mechanisms" to assist parties in meeting their emission reduction commitments, namely International Emissions Trading (IET), Joint Implementation (JT) and the Clean Development Mechanism (CDM). These mechanisms allow developed countries to fulfill their emission reduction commitments in a flexible and cost-effective manner—such as through carbon emissions trading (otherwise known as "carbon market")—and developing countries to acquire technologies and funds needed to meet the costs of adaptation.

International Emissions Trading (IET) is one of the three flexible mechanisms incorporated into the Kyoto Protocol.

(a) Emissions trading. The mechanism, at its core, is designed to allow developed countries (Annex-I countries) to trade carbon emission credits among one another. Under emissions trading schemes, contracting parties to the Kyoto Protocol can, in a cost-effective manner, either transfer or acquire GHG emission permits through transactions or overseas cooperation. This helps mitigate the adverse economic impacts of emission reduction and optimize the cost-effectiveness of global emission control without jeopardizing the integrity of the global environment.

(b) Origin of IET. IET constitutes a flexible mechanism under the Kyoto Protocol that enables cooperation between developing and developed countries to mitigate greenhouse gas emissions. It allows investors from industrialized (Annex I) countries to launch and implement in developing countries projects that contribute to sustainable development and reduce the level of greenhouse gas emissions in destination countries, as a way of meeting Annex I countries' emission reduction and limitation obligations as agreed on under the Kyoto Protocol.

(c) Contracting parties. Under an IET scheme, the production of emission reductions generated by joint implementation (JT) projects can be used by contracting parties in meeting their emission reduction or limitation commitments. For developed countries, IET provides a flexible mechanism for fulfilling their commitments; for developing countries, through IET projects, they are able to acquire a fraction of financial assistance and cutting-edge technologies necessary for emission control. This makes IET one of the effective ways for global emission control and technology transfer.

Joint Implementation (JT) is a flexible mechanism defined in the Kyoto Protocol that provides for project-based cooperation between developed countries (Annex-I parties) to share the costs and credits of emissions reduction, under which a developed country can transfer its achieved (surplus) Emission Reduction Units (ERU) to another developed country in exchange for a deduction of a proportionate amount of its Assigned Amount Units (AUU). To put it in another way, JT, as set forth in the Kyoto Protocol, allows contracting parties of the Kyoto Protocol to certify, transfer, or receive emission reduction credits called Emission Reduction Units (ERU) under the supervision of the Joint Implementation Supervisory Committee.

The Clean Development Mechanism (CDM) is one of the three flexible mechanisms defined in the Kyoto Protocol, which is intended, at its core, to allow Annex-I parties (developed countries) to earn Certified Emission Reduction units (CERs) through investment and engagement in greenhouse gas emission reduction projects in developing countries (non-Annex-I parties).

(a) Origin of the CDM

The CDM is a flexible mechanism established under the Kyoto Protocol that provides for project-based cooperation between developed and developing countries in reducing greenhouse gas emissions. To put it in another way, it is a mechanism that, as stipulated in the United Nations Framework Convention on Climate Change, allows contracting parties to meet part of their emission reduction commitments under the Kyoto Protocol abroad. In specific terms, the CDM enables industrialized countries to organize and support projects that cut greenhouse gas emissions in developing countries—mainly through provision of financial resources and technologies—and then use the resulting emissions reduction credits toward their own reduction targets under the Kyoto Protocol.

(b) Participating parties

The Clean Development Mechanism allows countries to earn Certified Emission Reduction units (CER) by enabling emission-reducing projects or emission-mitigating projects based on carbon sequestration or storage in developing countries. CER units generated from implementation of such projects can be used by contracting parties to offset their emission reduction targets as agreed on under the Kyoto Protocol. A CDM project must meet the following requirements in order to gain eligibility to quality under the Kyoto Protocol: receive official approval from all countries involved in the project; contribute to sustainable development in the host country; generate real, measurable, and verifiable long-term results in GHG reduction and climate change abatement. Meanwhile, a CDM project must "provide emission reductions that are additional to what would otherwise have occurred."

A country must meet three basic eligibility requirements for participation in the CDM: undertake the CDM initiative voluntarily; establish a national CDM authority; ratify the Kyoto Protocol. Moreover, industrialized countries must meet several additional, more rigorous requirements: achieve their assigned emission reduction targets defined in the Kyoto Protocol; put in place a national system for GHG emission assessment; establish a national organization for CDM project registration; submit annual inventory reports; set up an account management system for trade in GHG emission allowances.

(c) Eligible projects

Potential CDM projects include, but are not limited to, the following areas: improving end-use energy efficiency; improving supply-side energy efficiency; renewable energy; alternative fuels; agriculture—reducing methane (CH_4) and nitrous oxide (N_2O) emissions; industrial processes—reducing emissions of carbon dioxide (CO_2), hydrochlorofluorocarbons (HCFCs), perfluorocarbons (PFCs), and sulfur hexafluoride (SF_6) in cement production and other industrial processes; carbon capture and sequestration—applicable to afforestation and reforestation projects only.

(d) Sectoral distribution of CDM projects

CDM projects cover a wide range of areas, such as energy (renewable/non-renewable energy), energy distribution, energy demand, manufacturing, chemical industry, construction, transportation, mining/mineral production, metals production, fugitive emissions from fuels (solid, oil, and gas), fugitive emissions from production and consumption of halocarbons and sulfur hexafluoride, utilization of solvents, waste disposal, afforestation and reforestation, and agriculture.

(e) GHG emission reduction

Greenhouse gases specified in the CDM rules include carbon dioxide (CO_2), methane (CH_4), nitrous oxide (N_2O), hydrofluorocarbons (HFCs), perfluorocarbons (PFCs), and sulfur hexafluoride (SF_6). As regards greenhouse effect generation, the emission of 1 ton of CH4 is equivalent to that of 21 tons of CO_2; the emission of 1 ton of N_2O is equivalent to that of 310 tons of CO_2; the emission of 1 ton of HFCs is equivalent to that of between 140 and 11,700 tons of CO_2.

(f) Prospect for the Clean Development Mechanism (CDM) in China

As of 2011, a total of 3105 CDM projects were approved in China. A total of 331 of them were in Yunnan, making it the country's leading province in terms of CDM project number, with Sichuan trailing behind with 292 projects. These approved CDM projects, as a whole, were estimated to generate annual emission reductions equivalent to 543 million metric tons of carbon dioxide (543 million tCO_2e). As regards the emission categories of the approved CDM projects, the lion's share of them were in new and renewable energy, accounting for 71.63%, with energy saving and efficiency being the second most popular category. As regards estimated emission reduction generation, new- and renewable-energy-related CDM projects were expected to fare best, producing 50.91% of annual total emission reductions, followed by those in energy saving and efficiency with 15.28%.

As of 2011, 1503 CDM projects were registered in China, 170 of which were in Yunnan, making it the top provincial-level destination for registered CDM projects, with Inner Mongolia coming in second. Together, they were estimated to produce emission reductions equivalent to 334 million metric tons of carbon dioxide (334 million tCO_2e) on a yearly basis. If divided based on emission categories, most of the registered CDM projects were in new energy and renewable energy, 80.73%, with energy saving and energy efficiency trailing behind as the second most popular category. In regard to estimated annual emission reductions, CDM projects in new and renewable energy were expected to fare best, able to produce 46.48% of estimated total emission reductions.

According to the official website of the National Development and Reform Commission of the People's Republic of China, 500 CDM projects were issued CERs in China as of 2011, 51 of them in Inner Mongolia and 49 in Yunnan Province. Together, they were projected to produce emission reductions equivalent to 186 million metric tons of carbon dioxide (186 million tCO_2e). When it comes to emission categories, new and renewable energy was the most favored emission category with 77.40% of the 500 CERs-issued projects, followed by energy saving and efficiency. Of these 500 CERs-issued projects, those intended for HFC-23 decomposition were expected to perform best in terms of estimated annual emission reductions, generating 35.84% of total annual estimated emission reductions; trailing behind in this regard are those related to new and renewable energy.

As the only internationally accepted carbon trade regime ever created, the Clean Development Mechanism is applicable, by and large, to emission reduction schemes across the world. With emission reduction becoming an international trend and with the advent of various regional-level voluntary emission reduction schemes, a promising future can be foretold for the CDM market, as indicated by the ongoing increase of carbon trading instruments. Given China's status as a major player in carbon trade, its CDM projects are in rhythmic tune with the changes of the international CDM market and thus blessed with endless possibilities.

5.2 Carbon, Carbon Emissions Rights, and Carbon Emissions Trading

5.2.1 Carbon

Carbon is a non-metal chemical element that belongs to group 14 of the periodic table of elements. "Carbon" as discussed in this chapter represents a shorthand for carbon dioxide (CO_2). Ever since the Industrial Revolution, there has been an explosive growth of greenhouse gases—primarily in the form of carbon dioxide, which, caused by the massive consumption of fossil fuels as vital sources of energy for anthropogenic activities, now culminate in what is known as global warming. "Carbon emissions reduction" refers broadly to the reduction of emissions of six man-made greenhouse gases identified in the Kyoto Protocol as causing climate change, namely carbon dioxide (CO_2), methane (CH_4), nitrous oxide (N_2O), hydrofluorocarbons (HFCs), perfluorocarbons (PFCs), and sulfur hexafluoride (SF_6).

5.2.2 Carbon Emissions Rights

Carbon emissions rights refer to the right or permit to emit greenhouse gases (carbon), with a cap set on the total amount of greenhouse gases produced to directly or indirectly support anthropogenic activities in human society. Carbon emissions rights constitute an asset that is at once significant in value and tradable as a commodity in the marketplace: a company having difficulty cutting its GHG emissions can purchase excess carbon emissions rights or permits from another company capable of reducing emissions with ease; the latter helps meet the former's obligation for reducing GHG emissions while gaining financial rewards. It is projected that carbon emissions rights are likely to overtake petroleum as the world's largest traded commodity.

5.2.3 Carbon Emissions Trading

The concept of controlling emissions via emissions trading (otherwise known as "cap and trade") was first proposed in 1968 by Canadian economist J. H. Dales. In an emissions trading system, an overall limit (or cap) is set on emissions through an inter-governmental or international agreement, and the legal rights to emit pollution—in the form of permits or allowances—are defined up to the level of the overall limit, so that environmental resources can be bought and sold like a commodity, thus resulting in the introduction of a variety of carbon commodities in international trade. To put it in another way, carbon emissions trading is an approach that harnesses market forces to reduce the emissions of greenhouse gases, primarily carbon dioxide, in a cost-effective manner. On May 9, 1992, arduous negotiations culminated in the adoption of the United Nations Framework Convention on Climate Change (UNFCCC) by the United Nations Intergovernmental Panel on Climate Change (IPCC) at the Earth Summit in Rio de Janeiro. In December 1997, the Kyoto Protocol was adopted as the first addition to the UNFCCC in Kyoto, Japan. The Kyoto Protocol established market-based mechanisms as a new approach to reducing effects on climate changes resulting from the increase of the concentration of greenhouse gases—primarily carbon dioxide—in the earth's atmosphere. The Protocol defined the rights to emit carbon dioxide as a tradable commodity, thus contributing to the emergence of trade in carbon dioxide emissions, known in short as carbon trading.

The basic principle behind carbon trading is as follows: one contracting party to a contract purchases from another contracting party GHG emission reduction credits that can be used to reduce the buyer's carbon footprint and meet its emission reduction targets. Since carbon dioxide (CO_2) has the highest concentration in the atmosphere among the six greenhouse gases identified for mitigation in the Kyoto Protocol, such emission reduction credits are calculated and traded in units of tons of carbon dioxide equivalent, expressed as tCO_2e. Trade in emission reduction credits is known as "carbon trading," and a market for such trade is called a "carbon market."

Let's take a moment to look at the basic economics behind carbon trading. Greenhouse gases (represented by CO_2) are in need of being addressed, but doing so causes disparity in costs among businesses; now that everyday exchange of commodities can be seen as an exchange of rights (property rights), then it stands to reason for the rights to emit GHGs to be exchanged; thus, the most cost-effective way to address pollution within a market economic framework is by use of carbon emissions trading. It is fair to say that carbon trading helps weave the scientific issue of climate change, the technical issue of carbon emission reduction, and the economic issue of sustainable development into an integral whole, thus harnessing the strengths of market-based mechanisms to unravel a multifaceted puzzle that interweaves the strands of science, technology, and economics. Carbon trading is, in essence, a financial activity where on the one hand, financial capital is used to finance, directly or indirectly, projects and enterprises that create carbon assets and on the other hand, carbon emission reductions produced by different projects and enterprises are traded in carbon financial markets and developed into standard financial instruments. With the carrying capacity of the environment considered, emissions of greenhouse gases—including carbon dioxide—should be checked and curbed, as provided for in the Kyoto Protocol, which will result in the increasing scarcity of carbon emissions rights and emission reduction credits (ERCs), enabling them to become a priceable product called "carbon asset." The three flexible mechanisms for carbon trading under the Kyoto Protocol of 1997—namely International Emissions Trading (IET), Joint Implementation (JT), and the Clean Development Mechanism (CDM)—allow carbon assets to be traded like a commodity and produce a raft of carbon commodities for international trade.

5.2.4 Formation of Carbon Commodities

With the implementation of the Kyoto Protocol, on the one hand, contracting countries to the Protocol have reached consensus on the types of emissions trading schemes to reduce carbon emissions and on the other, enterprises undertaking emissions reduction responsibilities have had the need to trade the rights to emit carbon dioxide among themselves. As such, the rights to emit carbon have in effect become a tradable, intangible asset of international significance. In many developed countries, carbon financial systems have taken shape under the support of a series of financial instruments, not the least of which include carbon allowance trading, direct investment and financing, bank lending, and carbon swaps. Meanwhile, derivatives based on carbon emissions trading have been mushrooming, such as carbon forwards, carbon options, and carbon futures. As things stand today, carbon emissions rights have evolved into a series of "carbon commodities" that are investment-worthy, fluid, and predicated on emissions allowance trading. Carbon commodities exhibit the following characteristics.

(a) As the primal form of carbon commodities, the right to emit carbon is essentially a government-created environmental policy instrument, for three reasons. First, in the light of the emission reduction targets required of it by the Kyoto Protocol, a country fulfilling its mandatory reduction responsibilities places a cap (limit) on the aggregate of greenhouse gases it is allowed to emit within a commitment period; the cap is then divided up and allocated to all companies covered by the emissions control scheme in the form of emission allowances; companies are allowed to sell their surplus emission permits or allowances to those exceeding their GHG emission limits. Such is the basic form of "cap and trade." Second, carbon trading markets and operating mechanisms are developed under the auspice of government. Third, the overall operation of carbon markets—including the generation of carbon assets, transfer of ownership, and contract compliance—depends on strong legal and regulatory protection provided by government.

(b) Carbon commodities are of the nature of global public goods, thus homogeneous in their features and having the attributes of a quasi-financial asset. Greenhouse gases and carbon-footprint-reduction-based commodities possess the nature of a global public good, as determined by greenhouse gases' intrinsic characteristics such as high mobility and long persistence. This means that it is difficult for any individual country to abate global warming single-handedly. A carbon commodity constitutes a contingent, intangible commodity, which means that it is in effect the rights to emit carbon that a buyer and seller trade with each other. The immediate scarcity of supply relative to demand in carbon markets is the primary determining factor for the prices of carbon commodities. Beyond that, global carbon emission rights and carbon commodities are homogeneous in nature, thus possessing the features of a quasi-currency, forward settlement and delivery, electronic registration, and zero holding costs. These features dictate the existence of an interweaving relationship between carbon spot trading and forward trading, which explains why a full-fledged carbon market system is one that aligns and combines carbon spots with carbon forwards.

(c) A carbon commodity market, by its very nature, is characteristic of alignment and unity among regions and between forwards and spots. Prime examples in this connection include the European Union Emission

Trading Scheme (EU ETS) and the Regional Greenhouse Gas Initiative (RGGI). As the most full-fledged and influential carbon trading market in the world, the European Union Emission Trading Scheme (EU ETS), since the date of its birth, has been a unified market that involves multiple state actors and allows for trade in carbon futures, carbon options, carbon funds, and other carbon-related derivatives. For this reason, the EU ETS is highly recognized as a multi-layered emissions trading scheme encompassing spots, futures, and options. Since being launched, RGGI has been designed in a way that prepares for its future linkage with other carbon markets and carbon derivatives markets. This has laid a solid foundation for the formation of an integrated carbon trading market.

5.2.5 Carbon Forwards

Having emerged in response to the need for hedging risks derived from spot transactions, carbon forwards refer to a customized contract between two parties to buy and sell a certain amount of carbon credits or units at a specified price at a specified time in the future. Certified emission reduction units (CERs) produced by CDM (Clean Development Mechanism) projects are usually traded in the form of forward contracts. Before the launch of a CDM project, both parties sign a contract that clearly specifies the price, amount, and time of transaction in the future. A carbon forward contract is non-standardized one where the price, time, and place of transaction are discussed and agreed on in an over-the-counter market. Default risk, as it should be, is high for CDM projects due to relaxed regulation.

5.2.6 Carbon Futures

As opposed to carbon spots, carbon futures are a form of carbon commodities based on the transaction experience in carbon markets, emerging in response to the need for coping with market risks. A carbon futures contract is a standardized forward contract that obligates a buyer to purchase a subject matter or a seller to sell a subject matter—in this case a predetermined amount of carbon dioxide to be emitted—at a predetermined price and on a predetermined future date. The delivery date for a carbon futures contract can be a week, a month, three months, or even a year away from the date of contract conclusion. A place where transactions of carbon futures take place is called a carbon futures market. An investor is entitled to invest or speculate in carbon futures. Given that carbon futures trading is a type of contract-based transactions conducted openly for the forward sale and purchase of carbon dioxide, the transactional process is in itself a comprehensive indicator of both supply and demand parties' expectations regarding the price trends and fluctuations of supply and demand at a specified future time. For this reason, information of prices in carbon futures markets is consistent, open, prescient, and, if used well, conducive to increasing market transparency and boosting efficiency of resource allocation.

5.2.7 Carbon Options

Carbon options represent a financial derivative which, after the conversion of the rights to GHG emission into a commodity via the delimitation of property rights among countries, offers the buyer the right, but not the obligation, to buy or sell the underlying asset—in this case carbon emission rights or allowances—at an agreed-upon price during a certain period of time or on a specific future date. Carbon options contracts give buyers the option to call or put on carbon trading, which means that they can profit in a rising carbon market or a falling carbon market.

5.2.8 Carbon Funds

Countries across the world can set up dedicated funds for financing, controlling, or intervening in carbon emissions trading to support energy-saving and emission-reduction projects, via public offering, private placement, crowdfunding, and other sources of fundraising. A snapshot of the world's carbon fund landscape reveals that there are currently about 50 funds and procurement organizations that acquire Certified Emission Reduction units (CERs) internationally, most of them launched and managed under one of these models: (a) wholly launched and managed by government (with examples found mainly in Finland and Austria); (b) jointly launched by international organizations and governments and managed by international organizations (most such funds are made possible by cooperation between the World Bank and national governments); (c) established by governments and operated as a corporation (with prime examples including carbon funds in the UK and Japan); (d) jointly established by governments and enterprises and managed as a corporation (with typical examples found in Germany and Japan); (e) financed by enterprises and managed as a corporation (primarily serving as intermediaries in CERs transactions). These types of carbon funds vary by establishment objective, source of funding, size of financing, operating time limit, operating model as well as function, efficacy, and influence when it comes to promoting energy conservation, emission mitigation, and CDM development in different countries around the world. As judged from the real-life results and effects they produce, nevertheless, these funds have contributed, to varying degrees, to their home countries' efforts in combating climate change, cutting energy consumption, and reducing emissions.

5.2.9 Carbon Markets

A carbon market is an international marketplace that is artificially defined and created for trading carbon emissions. The supply side of a carbon market consists of project developers, emitters with low emission-reduction costs, international financial institutions, carbon funds, banks, consultancy firms, technology transferors, and so on. The demand side comprises of contractually obligated buyers—including emitters with high emission-reduction costs, and voluntary buyers—including CSR-motivated (corporate social responsibility) enterprises as well as enterprises, governments, NGOs, and individuals primed for compliance-based carbon trading. Beyond their role on the supply side, financial institutions—including brokerage houses, exchanges, trading platforms, banks, insurance companies, hedge funds, and so on—assume concurrently the role of an intermediary once entering a carbon market. Carbon trading is the buying and selling of the rights to emit greenhouse gases—calculated in units of tons of carbon dioxide equivalent or tCO_2e—in accordance with international laws.

By legal basis of establishment, carbon markets can be divided into mandatory carbon markets and voluntary carbon markets. A mandatory carbon market is an inter-enterprise or inter-governmental market to buy and sell the rights to emit carbon for the sake of meeting legally binding emission reduction targets; it comes into being when a government sets a cap on the total amount of greenhouse gas emissions permitted from its jurisdiction, divides the cap up, and allocates it in the form of specific emission allowances to enterprises covered by the emission-reducing scheme. A voluntary carbon market is one established by certain enterprises via internal protocols based on such considerations as social responsibility fulfillment, brand development, and protection against future changes of environmental policies and geared toward regulating emission surpluses and deficits through allowance trading.

By transaction object, carbon markets can be divided into allowance-based transaction markets and project-based transaction markets. The former deals with transactions—usually in physical form—of emission reduction units generated under total emission control, with its transaction object being the allowances initially allocated to enterprises (installations) by policy makers, such as Assigned Amount Units (AAU) under the Kyoto Protocol and European Union Allowances (EUA) under the European Union Emission Trading Scheme (EU ETS). The latter deals with transactions—usually in the form of futures—of emission reduction units generated due to the implementation of emission reduction projects, with its transaction object being emission reduction certificates acquired through project-based reduction of greenhouse gas emissions, such as Certified Emission Reduction (CER) produced under Clean Development Mechanism (CDM) projects and Emission Reduction Units (ERU) produced under Joint Implementation (JT) mechanisms.

By organizational form, carbon markets can be divided into exchange-traded markets and over-the-counter markets. Initially, carbon emissions were primarily traded over the counter. As time passed, exchange-traded

Table 5.1 Levels of carbon markets

Level	Transaction object	Participants	Functions
Initial carbon allowances market	Initial carbon allowances	Governments and emission control enterprises (new installations included)	To create carbon allowances
Carbon spots market	Carbon allowances spots	Emission control enterprises and other qualified investors	To discover basic prices and circulate resources
Carbon derivatives market	Carbon futures, carbon options, and other carbon derivatives	Emission control enterprises, financial institutions, and other qualified investors	To discover prices, hedge, and diffuse risks

platforms were put in place in succession along with the development of carbon trading. As things stand today, over 20 carbon trading platforms have been established globally, covering Europe, North America, South America, and Asia. Europe has the most exchange-traded platforms for carbon transactions, with two prime examples being European Climate Exchange (ECX) and BlueNext Environment Exchange (BlueNext).

By transaction market level, carbon markets can be divided into initial carbon allowances markets, carbon spots markets, carbon derivatives markets. Transaction markets at different levels vary in transaction objects, participants, and functions, as shown in Table 5.1.

5.3 The Status Quo of World Carbon Market Development

Today, the world's carbon trading landscape is dominated by four carbon markets, namely European Union Greenhouse Gas Emission Trading Scheme (EU ETS), UK Emissions Trading Group (ETG), Chicago Climate Exchange (CCX), and National Trust of Australia (NSW). Of these four carbon markets, only the European Union's EU ETS and the UK's ETG are international in their scopes of services, given that neither the United States nor Australia is a contracting party to the Kyoto Protocol. America's and Australia's carbon markets have more of a symbolic, commercial value.

5.3.1 European Union

Over the better part of the twentieth century, climate change action has evolved from its infancy as an environmental movement into a global political consensus under the United Nations framework. The European Union stepped into the leading role in the international actions on climate change in 2001 when the United States officially announced its withdrawal from the Kyoto Protocol. Carbon emissions trading has since become an indispensable policy instrument of the EU for combating climate change and the most critical method for EU members to meet their emission reduction commitments. The EU has undertaken two key measures to build its core competitiveness in global carbon-constrained markets: first, establishing an integrated market for emissions trading within the EU to enhance intra-union liquidity of emission reduction allowances; second, fostering compatibility of its emissions trading system with those in developing countries through the CDM to lower its own emission reduction costs.

Officially launched in January 2005, the EU ETS was and still remains the world's biggest greenhouse gas emissions trading market. From 2005 to 2012, the annual volume of carbon emissions transactions skyrocketed from US$ 10 billion to US$ 150 billion, which translated into a whopping average yearly increase of 47%. The EU controls the pricing power in carbon emissions trading, accounting for 99.3% of total emission allowances traded globally in 2012. Divided into three distinct phases, the EU ETS has now entered its third phase (from 2013 to 2020), during which its coverage is expanded to include sectors such as petroleum and chemicals. In Phase III of the scheme, the cap on the total emission allowances is required to decrease by a linear reduction factor (LRF) of 1.74% per annum, which enables reaching the target of cutting the EU's GHG emissions by at least 20% compared with 1990 levels. In Phase III, over

50% of total carbon allowances are allocated by auctioning, and the share of auctioned allowances is expected to reach 100% by 2027.

The EU ETS scheme offers spot transactions of European Union Allowance (EUA) credits and Certified Emission Reduction (CER) units, along with transactions relating to carbon derivative contracts such as CER futures contracts, EUA futures contracts, CER options contracts, and EUA options contracts. Beyond that, the EU announced the establishment of linkages between European and Australian carbon markets in August 2012, with both sides reaching agreements on the monitoring, reporting, verification, certification, and regulation of carbon emissions. Under this first cross-continental carbon emissions trading system, a one-way link was set up in 2015 to allow EUAs into the Australian scheme and will be expanded into a two-way link to allow Australian Issued International Units (AIIUs) into the EU ETS by July 2018.

It can be concluded from above that the European Union is at the world's forefront of carbon emission trading in every possible way, from the introduction of carbon spot trading to the launch of carbon futures trading and to the establishment of a cross-continental emissions trading system. Meanwhile, the EU's vibrant carbon trading market has helped boost the development of its carbon financial sector. As the EU strengthens the commodity property of carbon emission rights and develops its carbon market toward maturity, a succession of financial institutions—including investment banks, hedge funds, private equity funds, and securities firms—are plunging into the field of carbon emissions trading, thus making carbon emissions management the fastest-growing business in Europe's financial services sector. With a constant stream of financial institutions and private investors entering carbon trading business, the EU's carbon market is continuously growing in capacity, liquidity, and transparency and, in turn, is drawing more enterprises and financial institutions into it. Along the way, Europe's financial industry has seen its competitiveness significantly enhanced.

5.3.2 The United States

Despite its withdrawal from the Kyoto Protocol, the United States remains a vibrant actor in global carbon markets, with two highly recognized trading schemes—the Regional Greenhouse Gas Initiative (RGGI) and the voluntary, legally binding Chicago Climate Exchange (CCX).

The Regional Greenhouse Gas Initiative (RGGI) is the first mandatory market-based program in the United States to reduce greenhouse gas emissions. Incepted in 2005, RGGI represents a cooperative effort among nine US states—Connecticut, Delaware, Maine, New Hampshire, New York, Vermont, Massachusetts, Rhode Island, and Maryland—to cap and reduce carbon dioxide (CO_2) from fossil-fueled power plants. In 2007, Regional Greenhouse Gas Initiative, Inc. (RGGI, Inc.) was created as RGGI's non-profit legal entity. RGGI, Inc.'s legal entity responsibilities include: recording and monitoring data from emissions sources subject to RGGI; tracking CO_2 emission allowances; maintaining the auction and trading of CO_2 allowances in both primary and secondary markets; providing technical assistance to the participating states in applying for offset projects and reviewing project benefits. The RGGI cap is established to limit the emission of carbon dioxide (CO_2) only, and the RGGI compliance obligations apply to fossil-fueled power plants 25 MW and larger—as measured in the post-2005 period—within the nine-state region. RGGI is structured to operate in two phases: in Phase I, which ran from 2009 to 2014, the goal was to keep unchanged the total amounts of CO_2 emissions within the RGGI region and in each participating state; in Phase II, which began in 2015, the RGGI cap will be cut by 2.5% per annum for a total reduction of 10% by 2018 on the 2005 levels. The RGGI program has made remarkable contribution to environmental protection over the past years.

The Chicago Climate Exchange (CCX), founded in 2003, constitutes the world's first legally binding, international-rules-based system for the registration, reduction, and trading of greenhouse gas emissions. The exchange has nearly 200 members from a dozen sectors such as aviation, automobile, electric power, environment, and transportation. The membership of the exchange can be divided into two groups: corporations, municipalities, and other GHG-emitting installations as one group—which are required to meet their emission reduction commitments—and CCX participants as the other. The exchange trades in emissions of six greenhouse gases: carbon dioxide (CO_2), methane (CH_4), nitrous oxide (N_2O), hydrofluorocarbons (HFCs), perfluorocarbons (PFCs), and sulfur hexafluoride (SF_6). All members of the CCX can choose to purchase carbon offsets on a voluntary basis. The CCX represents a bid to fight the greenhouse effect, an ever-growing social challenge, by leveraging market mechanisms. The exchange once controlled the pricing of Verified Emission Reduction (VER), a type of carbon offsets exchanged in a voluntary, legally binding market.

In January 2013, California officially kickstarted its first-ever statewide carbon trading program, a move that immediately catapulted the state to become the world's second largest carbon market at the time, as measured by the total amount of capped emissions. In January 2014, California's emissions trading system was officially linked to Québec's Cap-and-Trade System for GHG Emissions Allowances, making it the first-ever transnational carbon trading system in the Americas. California allows its emission control enterprises to meet their compliance obligations by purchasing verified carbon credits from US-based emission reduction projects. Beyond that, the state also signed memorandums of understanding with governments in Mexico and Québec to help its emission control enterprises fulfill their obligations in the California market through investment in emission reduction projects in Mexico and Québec.

5.3.3 Asia

Some countries in Asia have established or are in the process of establishing their own carbon markets. Japan is the first Asian country to have done so, whose carbon market has undergone two important stages of development. The first stage of development is marked by the introduction of the Japanese Voluntary Emissions Trading Scheme (JVETS) in 2005, a voluntary cap-and-trade system essentially designed to support GHG emissions reduction activities by Japanese companies. The second stage is marked by the inception of the Tokyo Cap-and-Trade Program

(Tokyo ETS) in 2010, known as the world's first urban cap-and-trade program to cover office buildings. This mandatory program covers approximately 1400 GHG-emitting facilities in the industrial, commercial, and public sectors.

Carbon credits began to be traded in India in 2008, making it the first developing country to have adopted a domestic market-based mechanism for carbon trade. In 2012, the Bureau of Energy Efficiency (BEE) launched the Perform Achieve Trade Scheme (PAT Scheme), a mandatory program to reduce the energy consumption and GHG emissions from Indian enterprises in cement, steel, and other energy-intensive sectors. EUA (European Union Allowance) futures are also tradable in India's carbon market, along with five other types of certified allowance futures.

As the seventh largest GHG emitter in the world, the Republic of Korea (ROK) meets over 90% of its total energy demand through imports. In 2012, the country started to take incremental steps to build a comprehensive emissions target management system. In 2015, the ROK launched the Korean Emissions Trading System, otherwise known as the KETS. As the ROK's first nationwide cap-and-trade program, the KETS covers many large GHG-emitting installations in power generation, manufacturing, transportation, and domestic aviation. The KETS sets a cap on the total amount of six major greenhouse gases allowed to be emitted into the atmosphere, requiring mandatory reduction of emissions from covered installations through transactions of pre-allocated allowances.

5.3.4 China

China is the world's second largest emitter of greenhouse gases. With a growing number of Chinese enterprises actively engaged in carbon trading, China is hailed by many as the most promising market in the world for emissions reduction.

In 2011, the National Development and Reform Commission designated five cities (Beijing, Tianjin, Shanghai, Shenzhen, and Chongqing) and two provinces (Guangdong and Hubei) as destinations for ETS (emission trading scheme) pilot programs. The bulk of preparatory work for launching these ETS pilot programs in the designated cities and provinces occurred in 2012. On June 18th, 2013, Shenzhen opened a carbon trading market, with Shanghai and Beijing following suit to launch their own carbon markets on November 26th and 28th respectively in the same year. On December 20th, 2013, the carbon market of Guangdong opened for business, followed by its equivalent in Tianjin six days later. Hubei's and Chongqing's carbon markets went into operation the following year.

The 2015 China Carbon Price Survey, jointly conducted by China Carbon Forum (CCF) and International Consulting Company (ICF), was released on September 8th, 2015. According to the survey, China's carbon emissions will peak in 2030; at the same time, as time goes by, the future carbon price will gradually bid farewell to its current low level. China's efforts to "speed up the development of a national carbon market" can be loosely divided into three phases:

(a) The preliminary (preparatory) phase, lasting from 2014 to 2016, which marks a crucial stage for the development of China's carbon market.
(b) The launching phase, running from 2016 to 2019, during which tasks related to all building blocks of a carbon market are launched in full swing to test how the carbon market "apparatus" works; the framework of a national emissions trading scheme (ETS) had been put in place by the end of 2017, an intermediate achievement toward completion of the phased mission.
(c) The high-speed operating phase, beginning after 2019, during which the carbon market will be catapulted into a "high-speed operating mode," playing a central role in GHG emission reduction and mitigation.

Given the above, it stands to reason to say that carbon spot trading has been officially initiated in China. A look at the pilot carbon spot trading markets in China shows that all of them are mandatory, as opposed to voluntary, which means that all are "cap-and-trade" markets for carbon emission quotas (allowances). All of them use three methods—Historical Emission Method, Industry Benchmark Method, and Historical Intensity

Method—to define and appraise the total amounts of quotas, but they differ when it comes to quota allocation: in Beijing and Shanghai, carbon emission quotas are allocated for free, while in Guangdong, Tianjin, and Shenzhen, they are allocated "generally for free and partially for compensation" as a way of stabilizing and suppressing price fluctuations in secondary markets. The pilot carbon markets are dominated by emission control enterprises (installations) and supplemented by institutional investors—individual investors who meet eligibility requirements are allowed into the markets in Guangdong, Tianjin, and Shenzhen. Table 5.2 shows an institutional comparison of carbon trading markets in Beijing, Shanghai, Tianjin, Shenzhen, and Guangdong.

From what is stated above, it can be concluded that on the one hand, China is the world's second largest GHG emitter with the most promising market for emissions reduction and on the other hand, China's emissions trading scheme is a work-in-progress, with market operational mechanisms still being improved, carbon futures and forwards markets still being nurtured and product development and a carbon futures exchange yet to be established.

5.4 The Settlement of "Carbon Emissions Trading" in RMB

Given the above, China should go all out to explore the possibility of binding "RMB settlement" with "carbon emissions trading" as a way to "overtake on the curve" in the international financial architecture. The next decade constitutes a crucial period for China to reduce its carbon emissions.

The United States and their developed counterparts in Europe have, in recent years, hyped the importance of levying carbon taxes and tariffs. The year, as reported, will be 2020, which will coincide with the time when China's carbon emissions reach their peak levels. Once carbon tariffs are levied and tariff rates are set as per American and European standards, Chinese exports will inevitably encounter trade barriers in the form of high carbon tariffs, especially given China's huge carbon

Table 5.2 An institutional comparison of carbon markets in five designated regions

Contents	Guangdong	Shanghai	Tianjin	Beijing	Shenzhen
Total quota amount in 2018	4.22 million tons of CO_2	1.58 million tons of CO_2	1.1 million tons of CO_2	0.5 million tons of CO_2	0.32 million tons of CO_2
Quota allocation	Generally for free and partially for compensation	For free	Generally for free and partially for compensation	For free	Generally for free and partially for compensation
Methods for quota appraisal and definition	Historical Emission Method and Industry Benchmark Method	Historical Emission Method and Industry Benchmark Method	Historical Emission Method, Historical Intensity Method, and Industry Benchmark Method	Historical Emission Method, Historical Intensity Method, and Industry Benchmark Method	Historical Emission Method and Industry Benchmark Method
Actors in carbon spot trading	Emission control enterprises and institutional investors	Emission control enterprises, institutional investors, and eligible individual investors	Emission control enterprises, institutional investors, and eligible individual investors	Emission control enterprises and institutional investors	Emission control enterprises, institutional investors, and eligible individual investors

emissions. To put it in another way, the next five to ten years will represent a crucial period for the development and restructuring of Chinese enterprises. Should this period go by without proper action being taken, odds are that Chinese enterprises will not only face exorbitant costs of carbon emission quotas but also suffer high-emission-induced setbacks in exports.

As such, it is of critical importance for China to find ways to expedite the development of a carbon market—one that is full-fledged enough to encompass both carbon spot trading and carbon futures trading, in the sense that doing so will give an impetus to the establishment of deterrent mechanisms against carbon emissions, thus forcing enterprises to speed up their transition toward greener business models. Meanwhile, it is equally important to encourage and steer, by use of industry and taxation policies, Chinese enterprises toward adopting low-carbon technologies, providing green environmentally friendly services, and producing low-carbon-footprint products, because doing so will comprehensively enhance their positions in the global industrial chain and upgrade China's foreign trade toward greener growth.

5.4.1 Carbon Emissions Trading as an Institutional Arrangement for Optimizing Regional Distribution of Industries in China

A review of domestic and international practices shows that carbon emissions trading is a more efficient way than carbon taxation and mandatory emission reduction to tackle a multifaceted conundrum surrounding climate and energy within a market economic framework. Carbon trade is, by definition, an institutional arrangement designed to control carbon pollution and optimize the distribution of carbon resources on a global scale by using market-based mechanisms to address the negative externalities of carbon emissions and internalizing such external costs into the internal costs of emitters. As a market-based approach, carbon trade enables the conversion of emission reduction costs into carbon rewards and tilts financial resources toward low-carbon economic sectors, thus ultimately resulting in the minimization of emission reduction costs in society as a whole. This explains why carbon trade can give tremendous boost to the efforts of countries around the world in restructuring and upgrading their industries and transforming their economic growth patterns.

Given its vast territory and unequal regional economic development, some local governments in China have attached undue importance to the pursuit of GDP growth in the process of development. Due to the constraints of natural environment and the necessity for ecological protection, conditions for developing high-intensity manufacturing are simply non-existent in China's mid-west and other underdeveloped regions. The development of an emissions trading scheme is able to effect the transformation of the existing unequal development model into a market-based, ecologically harmonious one for better coordinated development among regions and for optimization of regional distribution of industries. This is because with a full-fledged emissions trading scheme, underdeveloped regions will be encouraged to achieve quantification of carbon emission reduction by protecting their eco-environments and by implementing carbon capture and storage in forests, while economically developed regions with high carbon footprint will provide financial support to underdeveloped regions through procurement of carbon reduction credits.

5.4.2 The Development of a Standardized Carbon Market as a Financial Launch Pad for China's Twenty-First Century Maritime Silk Road Initiative

As regards carbon trade in Asia, it is conducted merely in Japan and India, but on a small scale; the ten ASEAN countries have yet to make exploratory attempts in this field. In sum, carbon trade based on mandatory emission reduction is still in its infancy in Asia. Against this backdrop, it is strategically important for China to develop a full-fledged emission trading scheme and ultimately expand it into one of regional scale that covers ASEAN countries and other Asian economies along the Belt and Road corridors. Such an ETS can serve as a financial launch pad for the implementation of China's twenty-first Century Maritime Silk Road initiative. Furthermore, it also delivers benefits in three ways: demonstrating China's sincerity and commitment to, in Chinese President Xi Jinping's words, "share opportunities, meet challenges head on and achieve common development and prosperity" with its neighboring countries and regions, enabling the formation of a financial system for low-carbon economic development in China and ASEAN countries and increasing the reach and influence of China's financial market.

5.4.3 "RMB Settlement" for "Carbon Emissions Trading"—A New Pathway Towards "Overtaking on the Curve" for RMB Internationalization

(a) A currency must fulfill three fundamental conditions to become a global currency: serving as a medium of settlement and payment in international trade, being accepted as a reserve currency (a store of value) by monetary authorities outside its country or region of issue, being held in significant quantities as an anchor currency by monetary authorities outside its country or region of issue. The basic pathway for a national currency to evolve into a global and even key global currency is a currency of account and payment—a reserve currency—an anchor currency. Beyond that, it has to be accepted by the majority of countries under the international monetary system and display high cross-border mobility. Under the current international monetary system, major global currencies include the US dollar, the euro, the Japanese yen, and the Great Britain pound, with the US dollar as the dominant global currency.

(b) A review of history shows that energy binding can, more often than not, catapult a country onto a rising trajectory and go a long way toward propelling a national currency into a global one. This is because energy trade accounts for a large proportion of global trade. Two historical snapshots tell this story.

- Right before and in the wake of World War I, coal-dominated energy trade skyrocketed, enabling coal to eventually overtake wheat as the world's second largest traded commodity behind cotton.
- In the post-World-War-II period, the US dollar represents as much as 64.51% weight of Goldman Sachs Commodities Index (now known as the S&P GSCI), which currently comprises 24 commodities including Crude Oil, Brent Crude Oil, Gasoline RBOB, Heating Oil, Gas Oil, and Natural Gas.

Two takeaways can be drawn from these two examples: first, the stature of a country's currency in international trade and finance rises and falls in proportion to how integrated the country's economic activities are with energy trade; second, a national currency begins its rise when it establishes itself as a currency of account and payment for international merchandise trade—energy trade in particular—or when it is bound with energy trade.

(c) Prior to the Industrial Revolution which began in Britain in the late 1700s, the binding relationship between energy and currencies was yet to be defined and established. In the sixteenth century, the gravity center of international trade shifted from the Mediterranean and Italy to Belgium and the Netherlands in Northwestern Europe. The Netherlands dominated global commerce in the century that followed, resulting in the Dutch guilder becoming a key currency in international trade. Global commerce at the time, however, revolved around the transactions of timber, fish, grains, furs, spices, cotton textiles, silk, and porcelain, commodities that came out of manual workshops, the production of which required low quantities of energy. It is for this reason that no binding relationship between energy and currency came into existence at that time.

(d) The bundling of the pound sterling (GBP) with coal trade. In the last quarter of the eighteenth century, Great Britain overtook the Netherlands as the world's dominant trading power, as a consequence of which London replaced Amsterdam as the world's premier financial center. The invention of the steam engine set in motion a chain of technological revolutions, which collectively culminated in a great leap forward from manual labor to machine production. Coal thus became a pillar of industrial production in modern times. The rolling Industrial Revolution, coupled with the emergence and development of mechanized industries, ignited a spike in demand for energy. In 1840, Britain became the first country to complete the Industrial Revolution, which led to its transformation into the earliest consumer of coal-based energy in recent history. By the mid-nineteenth century, Britain had accounted for roughly two-thirds of the world's coal output, making itself a primary supplier and predominant player in the global coal market. By binding its national currency with coal trade, Britain managed to turn British Pound Sterling into a pivotal currency in global trade, one that figured prominently under the Gold Standard, chosen by many central banks over gold as a store of value. At that time, 90% of international transactions were settled in British pounds.

(e) The binding of the US dollar with petroleum trade. The pound sterling eventually lost to the US dollar its position as the dominant international currency, which was a natural outgrowth of the substitution of petroleum for coal as the world's preeminent energy source—an energy revolution brought about by the two world wars. The invention of the internal combustion engine during the second half of the nineteenth century propelled petroleum to become the new "life blood" of the Industrial Revolution. The 1920s witnessed a sudden surge in demand for petroleum, facilitated in large part by the popularization of internal combustion engines, as a result of which trade in this highly coveted commodity went through the roof. During World War II, the United States became the primary supplier of energy (petroleum) for its allies. When the ashes of war finally settled, the United States had controlled nearly two-thirds of the world's crude oil production. In the 1970s, Uncle Sam struck up a series of secret deals with Saudi Arabia to establish the US dollar as the one and only petrocurrency in the world—otherwise known as the US dollar denomination of oil. The top two oil futures exchanges in the world—the Chicago Mercantile Exchange (CME) and the International Petroleum Exchange (IPE)—used the US dollar as the currency for denomination, settlement, and payment of oil futures contracts. In this way, the United States succeeded in establishing and securing its international pricing power of oil commodities by wielding the US dollar as a financial weapon, thus enabling the formation of an international monetary system dominated by the US dollar as the standard unit of currency or, as some economists call it, the "numeraire currency."

(f) Robert Mundell's "Three Islands of Stability" hypothesis—a trinity of currencies (dollar-euro-yuan). In 2001 and on many other occasions during the following years, Robert Mundell—a world-renowned financial economist and the 1999 Nobel Prize winner in economics—put forth his bold hypothesis of "Three Islands of Stability," stating that three currency areas respectively dominated by the dollar, the euro, and the yuan would serve as three stabilizing factors in the global monetary system. Based on this claim, Mundell further proposed establishing a new international monetary system with a "supranational currency area" comprising of the dollar, the euro, and the yuan, under which the exchange rate among the three major currencies is fixed at between 1:1.2 and 1:1.4, while other currencies are allowed to float against the "supranational currency" as a whole. Such a system, Mundell contended, could contribute to improving international monetary stability and introducing greater flexibility into international settlement and payment relations. Robert Mundell's proposition drew attention to and inspired reflection on the existing international pyramid of currencies. In this connection, it is worth noting that on the one hand, the international monetary system with the US dollar at its center is in immediate need of reform and on the other, some new subjects have emerged to intrigue and captivate academic minds in both China and abroad—that is, how can other currencies, as best represented by the RMB, ascend to the top of the existing international pyramid of currencies, or what is the way for the RMB to pull off the feat of "overtaking on the curve" and become an international currency and even a key currency?

(g) The settlement of carbon trade in RMB. The rise of the pound sterling and the US dollar through their binding respectively with coal and petroleum trade helps shed light on a simple and yet clear evolutionary route of the status of currencies. First, with the low-carbon economic system set to be adopted as the predominant growth model throughout the world, new breakthroughs, new applications, and new combinations are sure to emerge in the clean energy technology sector, driving up the use and trade of low-carbon, new energy sources. Against this backdrop, a boom of carbon credits, carbon commodities, and carbon emissions transactions can be expected to be on the horizon. Second, China is at once the world's second largest GHG emitter and, as recognized by the international community, the most promising market for emissions trading, with an ever-growing number of its enterprises engaging in carbon trade. Third, global carbon trade, according to the World Bank's estimates, is expected to total US$ 3.5 trillion in value by 2020, thus enabling carbon to overtake petroleum as the world's largest traded commodity. With the international monetary system having undergone two periods of development characterized respectively by the "coal-pound" and "petroleum-dollar" binding relationships, now is the time for China to push for the settlement of carbon transactions in RMB and establish with ASEAN and other countries a financial system in favor of low-carbon economic development. Herein lies a new path for China to achieve "overtaking on the curve" with respect to RMB internationalization in energy trade.

5.5 Accelerating the Development of China's Carbon Market

5.5.1 Establishing and Perfecting China's Carbon Market System

China is steadily advancing the development of its carbon market system by adopting the traditional bottom-up approach—"introducing pilot ETS programs in designated areas before rolling out a nationwide, full-fledged ETS program and launching carbon spot and futures trading in different time frames," which is a clear departure from the EU's top-down approach to developing a cross-member-state, unified ETS featuring synchronized launch of spot and futures trading. As it stands today, China's National Development and Reform Commission is taking a leadership role in building national integrated systems for carbon trade registration and GHG emission statistical accounting, with plans to expand carbon trading from pilot localities to the entire country in a step-by-step fashion within the next two years. Despite these actions and plans, major obstacles still exist for the development of a national ETS in China.

Obstacle 1: In the absence of a unified platform for carbon trade, the segmentation of markets is blurred and mobility is lacking, as a result of which a mechanism for price discovery has yet to take shape. Firstly, China's carbon market is still in its primitive stage with a lack of nationwide carbon trading venues. Pilot provinces and municipalities differ greatly in core institutional designs ranging from carbon emissions monitoring, reporting, and certification to carbon quota registration and trading rules, without integrated standards in place in these aspects. Secondly, the regional pilot programs, during the preliminary phase of their implementation, merely cover a small number of emission control enterprises showing only reluctant interest in emissions trading; this situation is exacerbated by a low level of engagement in emissions trading by financial institutions and non-emission-control enterprises; the pilot markets are widely plagued by lukewarm participation, limited transaction volumes, and inadequate liquidity. Meanwhile, competent authorities in one or two pilot areas place lopsided emphasis on achieving mandatory emission reduction targets through allowance allocation and commitment compliance, thus disregarding the importance of spot trading market development. Moreover, the functions of China's carbon market are subdued and suppressed owing to the unavailability of carbon futures, options and other derivatives for enterprises to hedge risks and manage prices.

Obstacle 2: Financial institutions have shown a lukewarm engagement in emissions trading, which is compounded by a lack of carbon finance-related professionals. Support from the financial sector is indispensable if carbon trade is to grow in size, with high liquidity and in a way that becomes an economic activity of national and even international proportion with derivative transactions. Support in this regard, however, is currently insufficient for the following reasons: a shortage of carbon finance-related organizations, institutions, and professionals; inadequate investment in project development and operational modes related to carbon financial instruments and carbon products; a lack of systemic and well-devised policies and documents for guiding carbon financial services; the unavailability of financial derivative instruments such as carbon funds, carbon futures, and carbon options; and the absence of mechanisms for risk sharing and benefit compensation.

Obstacle 3: Due to the low level of its emissions trading scheme, China has almost no say in the global carbon market. Some emissions trading schemes—whether provincial (state-level), national, or continental—have established, through external linking mechanisms, one-way or two-way links with other emissions trading markets, especially those in developing countries, in their efforts to secure institutional dominance, gain a bigger say, and acquire pricing power in the future of carbon trade. Prime examples in this connection include the European Union Emission Trading Scheme (EU ETS), America's Regional Greenhouse Gas Initiative (RGGI), California's emissions trading system, and Québec's Cap-and-Trade System for GHG Emissions Allowances. As it stands today, institutional setups are basically non-existent in China for linking the pilot ETSs in its seven designated provinces and municipalities with external carbon markets. Beyond that, China has almost no say under the Kyoto Protocol's existing CDM mechanism. Given their unfamiliarity with the rules, regulations, and operational patterns pertaining to the transactions of carbon financial products, Chinese enterprises have largely been commissioning international carbon financial institutions to sell their CDM credits, the prices of which are controlled by international financial institutions and denominated in euros rather than in RMB. The result is that China, though the largest seller in the CDM market, is disadvantageously at the lowest end of the CDM industrial chain.

5.5.2 Creating a Unified National Carbon Futures Exchange

China's carbon market system is established for the following objectives: to incorporate carbon trade into a unitary nationwide emissions trading market in a way that combines international voluntary reduction with domestic mandatory reduction; to create and perfect a carbon market system that encompasses spot and futures transactions; to build national and world-class platforms for emissions trading; to strengthen exchanges and cooperation with carbon markets around the world; to strive for a strong say and pricing power over carbon trade globally, in Asia in particular.

As dictated by the attributes of carbon markets and indicated by international experience, the effective pathway toward the development of a carbon market system is to unify transactions and launch both carbon spot and carbon futures markets in a synchronic way. As such, it is imperative for China to undertake the following three steps based on existing carbon spot markets in pilot provinces and cities: first, expediting in full swing the establishment of a unified national carbon spot market; second, launching a carbon futures exchange simultaneously; third, building and perfecting a system of pluralistic services for carbon finance-related organizations.

What follows is the framework of a unified national carbon market system, as shown in Chart 5.1.

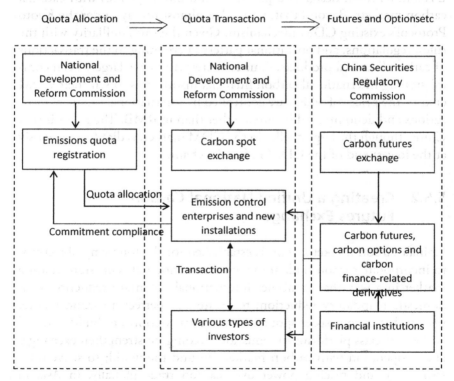

Chart 5.1 The framework of a unified national carbon market system

5.5.3 Striving for a Decisive Say in Asia's Carbon Futures Market with Standardization Development as a Point of Departure

This will require China to work on two fronts: devising full-fledged emissions standards and basic trading mechanisms; designing well-based standards and mechanisms for carbon futures trading.

On the first front, China must endeavor to achieve the following objectives. (a) Controlling total emissions and standardizing targets with respect to total emissions control based on emission intensity. Under the principle of common but differentiated responsibilities, China has voluntarily made a promise to cut the intensity of carbon emissions per unit of GDP by 40% to 45% by 2020 from the 2005 base level. Accordingly, China can adopt this relative emissions control target—the reduction of carbon emissions intensity by 40% to 45%—as the carbon emissions control target for the transitional period of the development of its carbon market.

The hypothesized method of action is to use the following formula for calculating "carbon emissions intensity": carbon emissions divided by GDP aggregate. Specifically, targets with respect to emissions intensity reduction per GDP unit are set for each year leading up to 2020 based on the overall 2020 target of reducing emissions intensity per GDP unit (carbon emissions/GDP); the target of emissions control is calculated based on GDP growth forecast and desired reduction of emissions intensity per GDP unit for a following year. The calculation equation is as follows: emissions control target = emissions intensity reduction target × GDP growth forecast. The increment of carbon emissions allowances is defined and set based on the difference between one year's emissions aggregate and next year's total emissions control target; emissions aggregate or emissions increment is incorporated into an annual reduction plan as a mandatory target.

(b) Standardizing the mechanism for initial emission allowance allocation. At the core of every carbon trading system is a mechanism for initial emissions allowance allocation, for two reasons: the allocation of emission allowances is tantamount to that of property interests; how validly and reasonably emission allowances are allocated can determine the practical fairness and operational effectiveness of a carbon trading system. During the preliminary stage of China's carbon market, emission allowances can be allocated mostly for free in accordance with a principle similar to the grandfather-clause principle adopted by the European Union, which means that the lion's share of emission allowances is allocated to existing emitters for free, with only a small part allocated for compensation. Given that most emission allowances (credits) are allocated free of charge, any participating emitter, should it reduce more emissions than it is required to, can sell its surplus allowances (credits) in exchange for financial rewards. In this way, more enterprises will be incentivized to engage in emissions trading, thus resulting in the expansion of China's carbon market in size and scope.

After the carbon market develops in depth and breadth, China can allocate its emission allowances (credits) in a way that combines free-of-charge allocation with compensatory allocation, with specific procedures illustrated as follows: the government adjusts through macroeconomic regulation and control the proportion of paid (compensatory) emission allowances in a timely and appropriate manner; the government then takes an evolutionary, sector-based approach to decrease the proportion of free-of-charge allowances while increasing the proportion of paid (compensatory) allowances on a year-by-year basis in selected high-emissions sectors such as electricity, steel, and coal; next, earnings generated from auctioning paid (compensatory) allowances are used to set up a carbon fund that provides financial support for the development of low-carbon, environmentally friendly technologies and industries in the form of subsidies; finally, emission allowances are allocated largely on an auctioning basis, leading to the formation of a fair, efficient, and market-based system for emission allowance allocation.

(c) Standardizing the emission permit mechanism. Firstly, it is imperative for China to set up a greenhouse gas emission permit mechanism similar to EU ETS Directive, under which each economic entity that emits greenhouse gases is required to possess an emission permit issued by a competent authority. To put it in another way, every installation included into the emission permit mechanism is required to apply for a GHG emission permit from the competent authority of its jurisdiction.

Secondly, it is necessary to clearly define the contents to be filled in an emission permit application form. Such contents normally involve (1) emission source, emission installation, and relevant activities, including the technology (technologies) being used; (2) raw materials and auxiliary materials being used that are likely to produce GHG emissions; (3) guidelines and measures to be adopted for monitoring and reporting.

Thirdly, it is of critical importance to define the preconditions for emission permit issuance and formulate standards governing the monitoring and reporting of GHG emissions. An emitter will not be granted a GHG emission permit until, and only until, its GHG emissions monitoring and reporting reach the standards that satisfy the competent authority of its jurisdiction.

Fourthly, it is essential to formulate clear and detailed contents of emission permits, which should include descriptions of emission installations and related activities, requirements for monitoring, and detailed descriptions of monitoring methods and requirements for reporting.

(d) Standardizing the mechanism for emissions trading registration. It is imperative that China establish a national emissions trading registration system under which every emissions trader is required to set up an account for registering all emissions data and transactions. All data pertaining to GHG emissions by enterprises and to the issuance, possession, transfer, acquisition, cancellation, and retrieval of emission permits can be input and collated in this standardized database. Given that China's emissions trading system is bound to be linked with the international carbon market, this registration system must be constructed in a way that meets the technical standards formulated by the parties to the United Nations Framework Convention on Climate Change, especially in terms of its structure and data formats. Only in this way can it be guaranteed that this registration system can exchange data with the Kyoto Protocol's CDM registration system and carbon trading registration systems in various countries in an accurate, transparent, and effective manner.

(e) Standardizing the monitoring and certification mechanism. When it comes to emissions trading, a monitoring and certification mechanism represents a verification and certification system designed to authenticate emission reduction performances by emitters engaged in emission allowances trading. China needs to establish a third-party body—independent of both emitters and administrators—and charge it with inspecting, monitoring, and verifying emission reduction data collected from emitters in order to ensure data accuracy.

There are three things to note in this context. First, it is of critical importance to develop organizations and train professional talents in the field of emission certification, which should be coupled with establishing qualification standards for certification organizations and personnel. Such certification organizations are required to have a good command of specialized techniques regarding things like baseline determination and emissions monitoring, in addition to methodologies for emission reduction accounting.

Second, to monitor the amounts of carbon emissions and ascertain the accuracy of related data, it is imperative for China to set up a standardized national carbon emissions accounting system and a standardized methodology for emissions calculation. In this connection, China can learn from the example of the European Union that employs this equation for emissions calculation:

$$\text{GHG Emissions} = \text{Activity Data} \times \text{Emission Factor} \times \text{Oxidation Factor}$$

Herein, Activity Data include the amount of fuel used, productivity, and so on; Emission Factor refers to the ratio between the amount of emissions generated and the amount of a given raw material processed, typically expressed in units of mass per gallon of fuel; Oxidation Factor measures the percentage of carbon that is actually oxidized when combustion occurs, expressed in terms of the ratio of oxidized carbon.

Third, certification reporting should be linked to the mechanism for emission allowances transfer and trading for the sake of ensuring the necessity of emitters being subjected to certification.

On the second front, China must design well-based standards and mechanisms for carbon futures trading. These include (a) Underlying asset. A carbon futures contract represents a standardized futures contract traded with carbon emission rights—measured based on tons of carbon dioxide equivalent—as the underlying asset.

(b) Trading unit and quotation price unit. The value of a carbon futures contract is equivalent to the trading unit multiplied by the contract's market price. If the trading unit is set too high, it will hamper the liquidity of carbon futures contracts; if the trading unit is set too low, it will dampen the incentive of investors to enter the carbon futures market for risk hedging. For this reason, the trading unit can be set in reference to that adopted in the international carbon futures market—that is, 1000 tons of CO_2 equivalent per 1000 shares. The quotation price unit is used to reflect the quotation prices of carbon futures contracts during open bidding and can be set as "RMB yuan per ton."

(c) Tick size. A "tick" represents the standardized minimum price movement of a futures contract. Every price quoted by either a buyer or a seller in futures trading must be an integral multiple of the tick value. It is as advisable as it is suitable to set the tick size of a carbon futures contract at the range of RMB 0.01 yuan to RMB 0.05 yuan per ton and the tick size of 1000 carbon futures contracts at the range of RMB 10 to RMB 50 yuan per 1000 tons accordingly.

(d) Price limit and margin. Given that carbon emissions vary from season to season and from time to time, carbon spot prices fluctuate typically with high frequency and in wide ranges, a fact that calls for setting a wider price limit for carbon futures than for other commodity futures as a way of encouraging and enlivening carbon futures trading. Meanwhile, the margin for carbon futures should be set at a higher level than those for other commodity futures in order to effectively manage the spectrum of risks resulting from wild price fluctuations. As it stands today, the price limits for most contracts in China's commodity futures market range between 3% and 7% of the settlement price of the previous trading day, and the initial margin requirements for most contracts are set at 5% to 10% of the contract value (with brokerage agencies allowed to impose on their clients an extra margin equivalent to a minimum of 3% of the contract value). It is advisable to set the price limit for carbon futures contracts at around 8% of the settlement price of the previous trading day, and the initial minimum margin requirement at no less than 10% of the contract value. A price limit system and a margin system so designed are conducive to risk management, especially when it comes to neutralizing risks from trading halts.

(e) Delivery. There are three aspects to this: (1) Standard commodity for delivery: Carbon emission reductions or increments—calculated in units of tons of carbon dioxide equivalent or tCO$_2$e—that are approved, certified, and registered by competent national authorities; (2) Delivery method: Given that carbon allowances constitute as much a right as a special commodity and that all trading firms thereof are registered and put on records at competent national authorities, the delivery of carbon allowance futures contracts should be assigned by competent national authorities (undertaken by registration and trustee agencies certified by competent national authorities in real practice) and settled in cash; (3) Delivery day: In line with the practices in the international carbon futures market, the last Monday of every contract month can be designated as a delivery day for carbon allowance futures contracts (a delivery day will be postponed if it coincides with a statutory national holiday); (4) Delivery settlement price: The settlement price of the last trading day is taken as the final settlement price.

(f) Contract month. Every month of the year should be a contract month, for two main reasons. First, carbon is emitted in all twelve months of the year, though specific amounts of emissions vary depending on climatic conditions. Second, carbon capture and storage is an ongoing, never-ending process. The preliminary design of China's carbon futures contract is shown in Table 5.3.

(g) Trading mechanism. A full-fledged trading mechanism is necessary for the effective operation of a carbon futures market, coupled with two equally full-fledged mechanisms for settlement and risk management. The specifics can be summarized as follows.

Table 5.3 Design of China's carbon futures contract

Terms of contract	Contents
Trading unit	1000 tons of CO$_2$ equivalent per 1000 shares
Quotation price unit	RMB yuan per ton
Minimum price movement	RMB 0.01 yuan to RMB 0.05 yuan per ton or RMB 10 yuan to RMB 50 yuan per contract
Price limit	±8% of the settlement price of the previous trading day
Minimum margin	Equivalent to 10% of the contract value
Delivery day	The last Monday of every contract month, postponed if it coincides with a statutory national holiday
Last trading day	The day prior to the delivery day
Contract month	From January to December (delivered on a monthly basis)

First, it is imperative to establish full-fledged mechanisms for trading and settlement, which should cover aspects such as market entities, delivery rules, price formation systems, and so on. Among them, the establishment and orderly operation of a carbon futures exchange constitute a systematic project which can be done in a way that draws lessons from existing futures exchanges, whether in terms of hard facility preparation or configuration of software programs and qualified personnel.

Second, it is imperative to establish an effective mechanism for risk management that consists of a margin system, a price limit system, a position limit system, a large holder position reporting system, a forced liquidation system, a forced underweight system, a settlement margin system and a risk alert system, all operating with effectiveness and efficiency. As regards the risk alert system, a computer-based risk warning system—one that monitors risks in real time—should be included into it in order for it to achieve three basic functions:

- Determining the level of risks in the carbon futures market through real-time detection and reporting of abnormal conditions regarding such single indices as capital, positions, prices, among others and through comprehensive analysis of all single indices. This computer-based risk warning system can be used to track and monitor the operation of the carbon futures market, detect potential risks in time, and ultimately achieve effective early risk warning and risk management.
- Speedily locating the causes of risks and getting to the heart of problems by use of inquiry systems and relevant tools, thus preparing the groundwork for the adoption of effective risk prevention precautions.
- Processing multiple contracts comprehensively and simultaneously. When multiple contracts are linked together or traded in reverse in the carbon futures market, this system must be capable of holistically handling the conditions of multiple contract traders.

5.5.4 Strengthening Legal Frameworks and Binding Carbon Futures Trading with RMB International Settlement to Boost RMB's International Standing

5.5.4.1 Devising Full-Fledged Laws to Protect Carbon Property Rights

The experience of developed countries shows that the most important institutional prerequisite for establishing a carbon market is to legally define carbon allowances as a right and allocate rights and responsibilities based on the legal definition thereof. In this sense, it stands to reason that China can promote the orderly development of its carbon market through carbon property rights protection legislation. To this end, China must lose no time in promulgating national higher laws for its carbon market system and refining system designs around seven operating mechanisms relating to carbon trading—namely, an emissions cap and allocation mechanism, a property rights incentive mechanism, a compliance mechanism, a transaction guarantee mechanism, a mechanism for emissions reduction facilitation and violation punishment, a relief mechanism and a mechanism for external linkages and cooperation. These efforts must be coupled with clearly defining the responsibilities of various competent organizations and unifying the pilot carbon markets into an integral whole.

First, promulgating forceful higher laws to protect carbon property rights. At the national level, such laws can provide legal basis and guarantee for the operation of the carbon market by making clear definitions and specifications for the total control, permission, allocation, transaction, and management relating to CO_2 emissions and for the rights, obligations, and legal responsibilities of both sellers and buyers.

Second, developing national standardized methodologies. As of today, China's National Development and Reform Commission has made public *The List of Voluntary Greenhouse Gas Emissions Reduction Methodologies* and has set unified standards for China's voluntary emissions reduction projects. These standards, however, have yet to be matched with national standardized methodologies for carbon allowances. For this reason, it is necessary to develop a set of scientifically sound, easy-to-operate, and standardized methodologies based on practice and match them with an objective accountability system and an objective assessment system with respect to emissions reduction, with a view to ensuring the carbon market's predictability, fairness, and equity. Equally necessary is the need to reduce disputes regarding allowance allocation and transaction outcomes by harnessing the strengths of examination systems and methodologies, so as to eradicate, once and for all, carbon leakages arising from inter-regional disparity in emissions reduction standards.

Third, formulating and perfecting laws and regulations governing carbon futures trading. China learns from the European Union cutting-edge practices regarding how to develop carbon futures-related laws and regulations. Meanwhile, by reviewing and revisiting the experience and lessons accumulated over the years on the development of traditional futures laws and regulations, China can devise a scientifically sound legal framework for carbon futures trading, which should include regulations, measures, and codes of conduct in these respects: *Regulations on the Administration of Carbon Futures Trading, Measures on the Administration of the Carbon Futures Exchange, Provisional Measures on the Administration of the Carbon Futures Investor Protection Fund, Measures on the Administration of Carbon Futures Practitioners, Codes of Conduct Concerning the Practice of Carbon Futures Practitioners.*

5.5.4.2 Incorporating Asia-Pacific Countries and Regions Into China's Carbon Futures Market and Prompting the RMB to Become a Major Denomination Currency for the Settlement of Carbon Futures Contracts

A look at Asia Pacific's carbon trading landscape reveals that carbon spot trading is conducted merely in Japan and India, but on a small scale, while the ten ASEAN countries have yet to make exploratory attempts in this field. Carbon trade based on mandatory emissions reduction is still in its infancy in Asia Pacific and has yet to extend into the realm of carbon futures. Despite the fact that the euro is dominating, for the time being, the global landscape of carbon trade as the preeminent denomination currency, there has not yet existed a solid, unbreakable binding relationship between the euro and carbon trading. This makes it all the more imperative for China to expedite the development of its own carbon futures exchange, one that incorporates a wide range of Asia-Pacific countries and regions. Once becoming a major currency for settling carbon futures transactions, the RMB can facilitate the formation of a financial system for low-carbon economic development in China and ASEAN countries, achieve "overtaking on the curve" toward internationalization, and further enhance China's standing in international finance.

5.5.4.3 Formulating National (International) Regulatory Norms on Carbon Futures Markets

By learning the full spectrum of advanced experience from the EU and America regarding carbon futures market development, China should put in place a three-level regulatory regime that comprises China Securities Regulatory Commission, China Carbon Futures Exchange, and China Carbon Futures Association, while at the same time strengthening cooperation with overseas carbon futures markets and regulatory bodies. It is necessary for China to institute an internationalized trading regime and match it with equally internationalized trading rules and regulatory cooperation norms, so as to ensure openness, fairness, and justice; give full play to the functions of its carbon futures market; and protect the rights and interests of emitters and investors from home and abroad. Meanwhile, in order to guard against risks and keep the carbon futures market in good order, China must adopt internationally accepted precautionary measures and mechanisms, including margin requirements and price limits, time-limited liquidation, forced liquidation, "Circuit Breaker Trigger," trading halts and closing.

6

The Present and Future of China's Internet Finance—The Trend of FinTech Innovation in China

Internet finance, is it a bright angel or a dark trap?

6.1 An Overview of the Development of Online Banking

6.1.1 Definition of Online Banking

Definitions of online baking vary from country to country and from one international organization to another. Two striking definitions come to mind, one from the Basel Committee on Banking Supervision and the other from the Federal Reserve. The Basel Committee on Banking Supervision defines online banking as the provision of financial services to customers through electronic channels, including retail and wholesale banking services. According to the Federal Reserve, online banking is a system that allows banks or other financial institutions to deliver products, services, and information to retail customers and corporate clients via the Internet. It is reasonable to conclude from these two definitions that the "Internet" and "banking services" constitute the two pillars of the online banking system.

Technically, an online bank is a virtual bank that operates from start to finish all in the online space by harnessing information technologies; in reality, however, its business must be conducted all in physical space. From this standpoint, it seems that the "virtual" side of an online bank exists only in the sense of operational practices.

6.1.2 Types of Online Banks

Online banks are divided into two types, pure online banks and electronic banking branches. The former type refers to "one-site" banks that as a rule operate with only one office and without physical branches or physical operations, conducting their business all via the Internet. Such banks are "virtual" in every sense of the word. The latter type refers to online services that traditional commercial banks deliver to individual customers or corporate clients through online banking sites or Internet-based client applications.

6.1.3 An Overview of Online Banking Abroad

In 1995, Security First Network Bank (SFNB) was founded in the United States as the world's first pure Internet bank that had neither physical branches nor vaults, with its operation purely reliant on the Internet. SFNB claimed to provide customers with a variety of accessible, affordable, and secure banking services, anytime, anywhere, and anyhow—the so-called 3A services. Following the founding of SFNB, a succession of other banks and financial institutions in America launched their online banking business. Later on, this trend of online banking crossed American borders and spread to Japan and European countries like Britain, Germany, and France, causing the number of online banks to grow exponentially on a yearly basis.

Starting off with US$ 1 million, SFNB underwent a period of rapid development before gradually sinking into financial distress, which soon metastasized into a massive deficit and ultimately resulted in its acquisition by Canada's RBC Royal Bank for over US$ 20 million in 1998. As a review of SFNB's experience reveals, it is only natural that in the absence of mature financial technologies, full-fledged online credit inquiry systems, and well-designed regulatory frameworks, pure online banks are held back by many bottlenecks in their developmental processes, including:

- Limited channels for capital flows. Due to their having no physical branch and operating with a small number of employees, pure Internet banks have distinct advantages over traditional banks when it comes to cost economization. However, the flip side is that given the current level of technology, pure Internet banks pale starkly in comparison to traditional international banks in terms of the ability to gain profits in international financial markets by flexible use of various financial instruments.
- Huge operational risks. Pure online banks face daunting risks from (1) underdeveloped laws and regulations governing online transactions, (2) technical uncertainties regarding cyber security, and (3) imbalanced development of online credit inquiry systems.
- Clear inability to verify the authenticity of customer information. Given their entirely Internet-dependent business model, it is difficult for pure online banks to effectively verify customer-submitted information regarding personal descriptions, credit records, and loan repayment capacity.
- High regulatory difficulties. Globally, pure online banking has yet to become the mainstream trend in the banking sector.

6.1.4 An Overview of Online Banking in China

It was in 1996 that traditional banking business began to expand into the Internet in China. As it stands today, practically every large- and medium-sized commercial bank in China has launched its own online branch or established its own homepage and website. By now, however, there has not yet been a pure Internet bank in China. As of this point, there are no such things as pure Internet banks in China, but only electronic banking branches. Recent newcomers on the scene of Internet finance—including

Renrendai (a peer-to-peer lending platform), Alibaba's Yu'eBao (a value-added banking service), and Tencent's WeBank (China's first online bank)—amount to nothing but the embryonic forms of Internet banks and Internet-based money market funds. This situation is largely attributable to two factors: first, unclear legal frameworks and regulatory mechanisms governing Internet banking; second, a lack of infrastructural conditions for the existence and development of pure Internet banks—which, in specific terms, means that a full-fledged online credit inquiry system is yet to take shape and efficient, reliable infrastructures for Internet finance are still in the process of being developed.

6.1.4.1 Services of Online Branches of Commercial Banks in China

So far, services provided by online branches of commercial banks in China cover a broad range of products, as categorized below:

- Information services, including news information, internal banking information and business briefings, online navigation of banking branches, foreign exchange quotation, deposit and lending rates, stock index quotation, and net asset value.
- Personal banking services, including account inquiry and management (transfer of funds between passbooks and bank cards, mutual transfer of current deposits and time deposits, interest calculation, etc.), loss reporting of passbooks and bank cards, agent payment, foreign exchange trading services, personal electronic remittance services, micro-lending on securities, buying and selling of treasury bonds, and so on.
- Corporate banking services, including account inquiry, inter-company money transfer, balance of account, agent payment, intra-city settlement, off-site remittance, international settlement services, and so on.
- Bank-securities transfer, which refers to real-time transfer of funds between bank deposit accounts and securities margin accounts.
- Online payment, including business-to-customer (B to C) payment and business-to-business (B to B) payment.

- Investment and wealth management, including wealth management products, escrow management, bank-futures and bank-securities business, trading relating to equities, insurance, and gold.

Of the above services, the buying and selling of equities, bonds, and funds are now available online through practically every electronic banking branch. After over two decades of development, there have been remarkable improvements in the level of services provided by electronic banking branches in China, but problems still remain, which can be summarized from two perspectives: in terms of breadth, a narrow range of service coverage and in terms of depth, a lack of customized services.

6.1.4.2 The Development Stage of Online Banking in China

Based on a comparison of online banking in China and abroad and a review of the evolution of online banking services, it seems reasonable to split online banking development into four stages:

First, the stage of networked banking, in which online banks are treated more as an online showcase for brick-and-mortar ones, with their business restricted to account inquiry and other information services.

Second, the stage of Internet-assisted banking, in which commercial banks transplant their existing licensed business activities onto the Internet, taking the Internet as an online distribution channel for their services and a vehicle for boosting working efficiency, reducing operating costs, and enhancing service quality.

Third, the stage of customized banking. Driven by Big Data and the third Industrial Revolution, online banks make the transition from providing product-oriented services to providing demand-oriented services, truly putting customers at the center of their business, injecting innovation into their financial service systems, and on the basis of service standardization, customizing products to meet specific needs.

Fourth, the stage of online banking trusts, in which Internet trust corporations are formed, whose business not only revolves around online banking services but also encompasses insurance, securities, futures, and other financial areas as well as commerce, industry, and related sectors.

Based on this analysis, it is fair to say that China's online banking sector is in the process of transitioning from the third to the fourth stage of development.

6.2 An Overview of Electronic Currency

6.2.1 The Concept of Electronic Currency

Throughout the recorded history of mankind, money has found its expression primarily in several forms: material money, cold hard metals, paper, credit currency, and electronic currency. Electronic currency, otherwise known by many other names including electronic cash, electronic wallet, digital currency, and digital money, is a type of currency available in digital form, transferred and circulated through the Internet and can be used to make payments. It has advantages over physical money in the sense that it enables anonymous, untraceable transactions; reduces the costs of transactions and transfers; exhibits low holding risks; offers payment flexibility and convenience and is replication-proof and thereby counterfeit-proof. It possesses five monetary functions: a measure of value, a medium of exchange, a unit of account, a store of value, and global currency.

6.2.2 Types of Electronic Currencies

By means of payment, electronic currencies can be divided into five categories:

- Electronic currencies for storage of value, mainly in the form of stored-value cards.
- Electronic currencies for payment and credit, such as credit cards.
- Electronic currencies for use of deposits, including debit cards and E-cheques which, by definition, constitute a form of electronic payment by wiring deposit money on the Internet using computers or mobile applications.
- Cash-like electronic currencies.

- Electronic bill submission and payment, which represents a method for consumers to receive and pay bills on the Internet and consists of two parts—electronic bill payment and electronic bill submission. In real-life practice, for example, a bill is delivered in electronic form to a consumer through the Internet; the consumer pays the bill online upon receiving it.

Underpinned by electronic computer technologies, electronic currencies can be used extensively for value storage, payment and circulation in the processes of production, exchange, distribution, and consumption. They integrate the functions of saving, lending, and non-cash settlement and exhibit distinctive features such as user-friendliness, security, speediness, and reliability. As things stand today, electronic currencies exist, in most instances, in the medium of bank cards like magnetic cards and smart cards.

6.2.3 Electronic Currency and Virtual Currency

(a) Connections and differences. Electronic currency and virtual currency are connected in the sense that virtual currency is a form of electronic money, whereas electronic currency cannot be totally equated with virtual currency. As alternatives to electronic currency, digital gold currency (DGC) and cryptocurrency are both a form of digital currency that exists much more for real-life transactions of commodities and services than for virtual community activities like online gaming. As a deeper form of expression for electronic currency, digital currency (also known as virtual currency) is divided into two types, digital legal tender and private digital currency. Although there is often ambiguity between electronic currency and virtual currency in conceptual respect, the differences between them are in effect as stark as day and night. An electronic currency represents the electronic form of a legal tender currency and can be used as a medium of exchange in the place of paper banknotes. Virtual currency, in contrast, is a digital unit of value, which is either generated based on an online software system or issued by its online operators. Usually referred to as "private digital currency," virtual currency adopts neither the designation nor unit of legal tender.

(b) Digital legal tender. Digital legal tender, otherwise called "central bank digital currency," can compete to replace paper banknotes as a medium of exchange, help central governments secure control of monetary sovereignty, and work in the interests of currency issuance and monetary policy. Beyond that, it also performs four distinct functions:

- Boosting the effectiveness of the interest rate transmission mechanism of monetary policy. Technologies derived from digital legal tender can be harnessed to increase liquidity—both between financial markets and within individual markets—and reduce the overall interest rates of financial systems, thus bringing a higher level of smoothness to the term structure of interest rates and enabling the interest rate transmission mechanism to work with greater ease and efficiency.
- Improving the accuracy of monetary indicators. Big Data systems and information advantages that come with digital legal tender can be fully exploited to increase the measurability of the velocity of money and facilitate the calculation of monetary aggregates and the analysis of monetary structures, thus leading to the enrichment and enhancement of the accuracy of monetary indicators.
- Assisting regulatory authorities in tracking money flows when and where necessary. By setting up a controllable, anonymous mechanism, monetary regulatory authorities can keep track of how a digital legal tender is being used. Such a mechanism acts as a valuable supplement to existing regulatory systems, assisting regulatory authorities in cracking down on money laundering, tax evasion, capital control avoidance, and other illicit behaviors, something that is impossible to do with private digital currencies.
- Enhancing the precision of monitoring and risk assessment. The very existence of digital legal tender can force central banks to develop financial infrastructures; perfect payment systems; increase the ease, efficiency, and transparency of settlement, thus enabling regulatory authorities to monitor, assess, and guard against financial risks based on complete, real-time, and authentic transaction ledgers of different institutions and at different frequencies.

Given the above functions, there have been attempts around the world to explore the possibility of issuing digital legal tenders. Three examples immediately come to mind: the US Congress's proposal for the federal government to devise national policies that emphasize the use of digital legal tenders; the British government's consideration regarding the launch of a crypto legal tender by the Bank of England; the designation by the European Commission of cryptocurrency development as a priority.

Recent years have witnessed a boom of the Internet in China. Statistics show that as of June 2019, the number of Internet users in China reached 854 million—roughly the size of the population in Europe, with a penetration rate of 61.2%, which was 7.1 percentage higher than the world's average and 2.8 percentage higher than the average in the Asian-Pacific region. Given a large Internet population and the rapid development of mobile payment solutions, there have been favorable infrastructural conditions in China for the issuance of a digital legal tender, which will, in turn, promote the modernization of China's financial architecture and expand the RMB's international reach and influence. (c) Private digital currency. In general, there are two forms of representation of private digital currencies: virtual currencies and media of exchange for online services. Virtual currencies are best represented by Bitcoin. Virtual currencies include Bitcoin, Ethereum, Ripple, Litecoin, Monero, Dash, Ethereum Classic, MaidSafeCoin (MAID), NEM, Augur, and so on, as shown in Table 6.1.

Note that as of March 24, 2018, there have been some changes in the rankings of the world's top 10 cryptocurrencies.

Statistics show that as of July 2016, there had been over 740 private digital currencies in the world, more than 710 of which were tradable online. As of January 2017, 26 private digital currencies had crossed the mark of US$10 million in total market value. Bitcoin is arguably the most popular cryptocurrency among investors worldwide, known as the first decentralized, tradable virtual currency ever created in the world. Bitcoin is programmed such that the number of bitcoins in existence does not exceed 21 million, all of which are projected to have been mined by 2140. The generation, circulation, and management of bitcoins are not the responsibility of any one person, organization, company, or country. Bitcoin is a true Internet currency in every sense of the word and

Table 6.1 Ten major virtual currencies (as of March 24, 2018)

序号	Name	Market cap	Price	Volume (24 h)	Circulating supply	Change (24 h)
1	Bitcoin	$151,592,966,656	$8950.70	$6,252,030,000	16,936,437 BTC	5.68%
2	Ethereum	$53,340,505,443	$542.18	$1,458,950,000	98,381,181 ETH	4.38%
3	Ripple	$25,831,627,971	$0.660753	$479,377,000	39,094,227,299 XRP	4.08%
4	Bitcoin cash	$17,289,564,486	$1014.96	$286,143,000	17,034,725 BCH	3.92%
5	Litecoin	$9,278,745,131	$166.39	$322,765,000	55,764,706 LTC	4.75%
6	EOS	$5,268,660,772	$7.04	$672,396,000	748,301,091 EOS	7.13%
7	Cardano	$4,935,295,658	$0.190353	$155,305,000	25,927,070,538 ADA	0.03%
8	NEO	$4,478,981,000	$68.91	$128,689,000	65,000,000 NEO	5.45%
9	Stellar	$4,470,072,199	$0.240988	$51,660,400	18,548,941,024 XLM	6.12%
10	IOTA	$3,842,394,868	$1.38	$29,673,100	2,779,530,283 MIOTA	8.97%

Source: coinmarketcap.com

represents the first attempt in human history to decentralize the monetary system that has long been dependent solely on central issuing authorities around the world.

The world's first Bitcoin AMT machine has opened in Canada, which allows users to freely exchange their credits of the digital currency into cash in Canadian dollars. Although whether Bitcoin is able to become a mainstream currency in the foreseeable future remains a subject of debate, the idea of "decentralization" and "peer-to-peer transaction" is set to give rise to a global virtual currency with powerful features and universal acceptance. On the one hand, as a key building block of a possible non-sovereign monetary system, Bitcoin has enjoyed some acceptance and recognition in certain sectors of the money market.

On the other hand, the assertion that "Bitcoin technologies will take the center stage of the financial industry" has grabbed the attention of governments worldwide. At the national level, it is necessary for governments to face squarely and seriously the existence of Bitcoin and act preemptively by pondering whether there is a need to mobilize national computing power to amass as many bitcoins as possible. Another issue worth consideration is whether it is necessary to facilitate the establishment of a possible non-sovereign monetary system, so as to enrich the means of international settlement by use of new international settlement currencies and enable the international financial system to develop in a more harmonious, steady fashion.

Media of exchange for online services are best represented by QQ Coin, with other examples including Baidu Coin, Weibo Coin, and online gaming points. QQ Coin was originally designed by Tencent as an instrument for QQ (an instant messaging software) users to buy online gaming services, obtainable by purchase at the rate of one RMB for one coin. Under normal circumstances, QQ Coin could be considered analogous in nature to point cards or gaming cards created by other online gaming or virtual services providers, in the sense that they are all accessorial tools for online virtual services.

Due to a boom in Tencent users—derived primarily from the company's efforts to expand and integrate its online services—QQ Coin is gradually becoming accepted by online vendors as a medium of exchange for online services and real merchandise. With QQ Coin increasingly incorporated into facets of everyday life, its monetary function is growing in importance. Recent years have even seen the acceptance of QQ Coin as a payment instrument by Internet platforms and companies outside of Tencent's sphere of business. As a virtual, Internet-based currency, QQ Coin is growing in popularity and reach in the virtual world. As things stand today, there is a lack of regulation over QQ Coin, including regarding its issuance and circulation, a problem compounded by unclear allocation of responsibilities between regulatory bodies in this respect. By original design, the flow of QQ coins is a one-way process—that is, real money (in the form of online banking deposits) is exchanged for QQ coins which can then be used to purchase virtual services (i.e., accessorial services or chips in online games, accessorial functions of instant messaging tools, etc.). As regards online shopping (business to customer), the institutional design is such that it is not yet possible for QQ coins to be converted back into real money. QQ Coin, as generally held, is by its very nature a delivery instrument in digital form and without two-way convertibility with real money; QQ Coin is very unlikely in theory to cause any shockwave across existing currency issuing systems.

In reality, however, adaptations exist when it comes to the use of QQ coins, with striking examples including secretive deals between consumers, online transfer of payment in QQ coins, conversion of QQ coins into real cash offline, and so on. In these ways, QQ Coin is turned into a semi-currency. As virtual currencies like QQ Coin grow in reach and coalesce to form a unitary market, free exchange and conversion between them will become achievable, possibly resulting in the elevation of virtual currencies from a semi-currency status to a currency status within certain domains. This will mean the emergence of a new form of currency and payment as an addition to existing legal tenders and payment instruments. That being said, the very existence of virtual currencies threatens to plunge financial systems into chaos if issuing companies violate rules and abuse them as a new financing instrument. Given the absence of related legislation and the deficiency of regulation over virtual money, it is imperative that virtual currencies like QQ Coin be well included into the sphere of currency regulation and control at the national level, especially with respect to issuance, security indicators, and risk prevention.

6.3 The Development Trends of Internet Finance

Two judgments can be made on the basis of the above analysis. First, electronic banking branches—whether in China or other parts of the world—haven't yet been able to disrupt existing banking systems in fundamental ways. Second, electronic and virtual currencies—be them in China or other parts of the world—haven't yet developed to the point of having concrete implications for currency issuing systems and monetary regulatory policies at the national level.

There are, however, three trends of Internet finance that deserve close attention.

6.3.1 The Trend of Business Integration in Internet Finance

Two factors act as key drivers for this trend. The first is technological preparedness. The uninterrupted development of information technologies has brought about a tidal wave of changes, most notably the remarkable improvements of basic transmission networks in both transmission range and speed, the higher integration of large-scale integrated circuits, the quantum leaps in supercomputing, and the emergence of cloud computing and storage platforms. Given all these changes, it is now possible for business affairs that were otherwise unable to be handled at the same time and place before to be collectively done on an integrated online platform. Nowadays, the operating platforms of online banks are fully capable of processing multiple business affairs simultaneously.

The second is pressure from external sources. The robust development of Internet finance—as evidenced by Ant Financial (Internet microlending), Renrendai (P2P lending), and third-party payment methods—has been squeezing the market share and profit margins of commercial banks (including those with online branches). Under such circumstances, commercial banks are striving for innovation and integration of services as a way out of this dilemma.

6.3.2 The Trend of Financialization of Online Platforms

(a) Internet-enabled networking platforms are being used as a channel for financial services. Given their gigantic user bases, Weibo, WeChat, and other social media platforms, if harnessed for the delivery of financial services, will empower platform-based Internet finance to shake traditional financial institutions to their cores. Moreover, Internet financial technologies have the power to transcend the barriers of time and space. For this reason, traditional financial institutions—which operate primarily under a branch-based, hierarchical structure—will likely lose their advantages and worse still, face the threat of being phased out in this Internet age where easy-to-use, efficient, and popular online platforms are being financialized.

(b) Scenario-based finance is becoming a focal point of future study on Internet finance. Scenario-based finance, also called "embedded finance," refers to the integration of financial activities into existing scenario-based services via the use of Internet-powered FinTech. Scenario-based finance is designed to fuel an explosion in the application of financial services, in a way that benefits online vendors and users and enables economic activities to be carried out more efficiently. This new financial trend involves both Internet companies and financial institutions.

- Scenario-based financial services by Internet companies, with prominent examples including: (a) WeChat Red Envelope; (b) Uber and Didi Chuxing; (c) O_2O (Online-to-Offline). The characteristics of such scenario-based financial services can be encapsulated in one sentence: "Financial services are readily available whenever and wherever you need them in your daily life." Under this kind of scenario-based finance, financial institutions' electronic channels are integrated with their users' usage scenarios in a way that downplays the presence of finance while heightening user experience. Scenario-based finance has acted as a catalyst for the emergence of mass shopping sprees on e-commerce third-party online payment platforms—that is, Alibaba's Singles' Day shopping festival where online shoppers pay through Alipay, Alibaba's third-party online payment platform, without ever realizing how much money is leaving their pockets.
- Scenario-based financial services by financial institutions. Real-life examples in this regard include aviation insurance, life insurance and property insurance, and other insurances which come about through the combination of insurance services with common travel scenarios; potentially promising strategic cooperation between Internet companies and licensed banking institutions such as village and township banks (VTB), rural commercial banks, and urban commercial banks.

In sum, compared with traditional finance, scenario-based finance is more attuned to the rhythms of real life, the pulse of the market, and the unique needs of different customer segments. Embedding easy-to-use, speedy financial services into real-life scenarios can help improve the quality of financial services and convert consumer demand into purchases. Thus, embedded finance has become a revolutionary agent for the transformation of Internet finance. Derivative services from embedded finance include embedded lending, embedded insurance, embedded claim settlement, and embedded futures.

(c) Supply chain finance (hereinafter referred to as "SCF") brings the Internet, finance, and industrial chains into a triad relationship. SCF is a series of technology-empowered processes that allow a financial institution to serve a core client in financing, settlement, and wealth management while providing a diversity of flexible financial products and services to the client's suppliers and distributors at both upstream and downstream ends. A supply chain is a system that moves a product from its points of origin to its end destination by controlling logistics, capital flows, and information flows. Typically comprising of raw material purchases, intermediary product production, end product output, and delivery to consumers through a sales network, a supply chain manages to link suppliers, manufacturers, distributors, vendors, and end users together in an integral networked chain. Based on supply chain ecosystem, SCF is a model in which the Internet, finance, and industrial chains are integrated to form a triad for unifying the flows of information, capital, and logistics.

SCF is a vehicle for financial institutions to optimize supply chain processes, manage working capital, and improve operating cash flow by harnessing technologies relating to financing and risk alleviation, thus enabling businesses to fulfil their commercial needs. SCF services are primarily grouped under two categories: accounts-receivable financing and lending-based financing. By and large, the former can be sub-grouped into accounts-receivable discount, forfeiting, factoring, and accounts-payable financing. SCF service solutions can be tailor-made for different real-economy enterprises to suit their supply chain operating processes. This explains why SCF has given rise to a diversity of derivative services and products. As such, the following requirements should be met in order to fully tap the potential of SCF: possession of professional industry knowledge by financial institutions, integration of information collection technologies, electronic transmission of financial data, online transactions of financial products, standardization of norms for SCF processes, and SCF-related legal and regulatory support.

6.3.3 Challenges Facing Internet Financial Regulation

6.3.3.1 Impacts of Internet Financial Products on Financial Regulation

China's Internet financial products can be divided into three types. Online payment products cover online banking payment, third-party payment based on third party, independent organizations' transaction and payment platforms, mobile payment—based on mobile terminals—for services and digital or hard goods. Online credit services are primarily represented by those from Alibaba's Ant Financial and P2P lending platforms. Third-party online wealth management products include those from Alibaba's Yu'ebao, Baidu's Baifa, Tencent's WeBank, and so on. Yu'ebao and its like have received from the People's Bank of China third-party payment licenses, which translate into approval of their entry into the third-party payment market. Regulation of their business, however, still falls short of what is needed. As regards P2P lending platforms like Renrendai, there seem to be a lot of grey areas, both in terms of market access and business regulation. Nevertheless, the emergence of these new forms of Internet finance has left the existing model of financial regulation in a dilemma while posing some notable challenges for electronic banking branches derived from traditional commercial banks. As echoed by media analyses from both home and abroad, this flurry of Internet financial products, if left unregulated, will threaten China's financial security.

6.3.3.2 Impacts of Block Chain on Financial Regulation

Block chain, originally block chain, is an important concept that comes with the rise of Bitcoin. Block chain is the underlying technology and fundamental framework on which cryptocurrencies like Bitcoin work. Generally speaking, there are four things to note about this new promising technology.

- A block chain is a chain of data blocks generated through cryptographic methods. Each block stores information called a hash value, which indicates a Bitcoin network transaction and can be used to verify the validity of data and generate the next block.
- Like a distributed ledger, a block chain stores data in a distributed, decentralized fashion across a large number of storage nodes, with each node having a full copy of the entire block chain.
- A block chain is designed such that no single node can record the ledger data unilaterally, thus preventing user data from being tampered with. In this way, all nodes in a block chain can act as validators of transactions.
- A block chain is a decentralized network in which every participant is equal to any other in terms of rights and obligations.

As such, a block chain typically has the following characteristics: decentralized, distributed data storage; data integrity protection; data irrevocability; transaction traceability; digitalization.

Block chain technology can be applied to optimize financial payment systems and build efficient, secure FinTech systems. Let's look in details at the use of this innovative technology in the financial industry, sector by sector.

- Banking. With inter-bank competition intensifying due to interest rate marketization, there exists the possibility of profit-driven breaches of financial regulations. Block chain technology has the promise to enable transparent cross-border payments between banks, companies, individuals, or settlement institutions in the commercial paper market, because each and every node in a block chain network can verify the legitimacy of transactions in the commercial paper market or cross-border payment market by tracing transaction records. Given this distinct feature of block chain, the use of this transformative technology will go a long way toward streamlining banking procedures, maintaining financial order, and guard against financial risks.
- Securities. The application of block chain technology can be extended to various processes in the securities market, including the registration, issuance, clearing and settlement of securities, thus boosting transac-

tional efficiency in two respects: enabling remarkable simplifications of transactional procedures and intermediary links and making possible the achievement of real-time, $T+0$ settlement.
- Insurance and other sectors of the financial industry. Block chain technology has the potential and promise to reshape currency markets, payment systems, financial transactions, and services while transforming economic production modes and people's ways of living.

The development of block chain applications can be split into three stages. Block chain 1.0 is marked by the applications of cryptocurrencies for money transfer, remittance, and digital payment. Block chain 2.0 focuses on using block chain technology to undertake a broad range of "smart contracts" for a whole slate of economic, market, and financial applications. Block chain 3.0 is characterized by block chain applications well beyond currency, finance, and market—particularly in the realms of government, health, science, culture, and art. Block chain 3.0 platforms based on distributed ledger technology are projected to become a driver for the development of the on-demand economy and sharing economy.

On the one hand, block chain-related innovations and applications have been garnering attention and recognition worldwide. Take just a few for example. The United States Department of Homeland Security (DHS) and the National Science Foundation (NSF) have given many rounds of subsidies and financial support to block chain projects. The British government is endeavoring to tap the immense potential of block chain applications in traditional finance as well as in public and private service sectors. The Federal Financial Supervisory Authority, better known by its abbreviation BaFin, is exploring the possibility of using block chain technology in the areas of cross-border payment, inter-bank transfer, transaction data storage, and so on. In its 2016 white paper titled *The Blockchain Technology and Application Development White Paper*, China's Ministry of Industry and Information Technology analyzed in depth a variety of block chain application scenarios and envisaged a roadmap for block chain technology development in China. In October 2016, block chain was written, for the first time ever, into the "13th Five-Year Plan for National Informatization."

As shown in the above examples, the ever-advancing information technology has played an important role in finance worldwide over the past few years. With the growing penetration of cloud computing and Big Data in traditional finance, the entities and models of financial services are gaining a breadth of diversity in their development, thus causing shockwaves across the global financial system in business and technological paradigms. In this sense, there is no doubt that block chain technology, more powerful in functionality than cloud computing and Big Data, is bound to fuel a new round of revolution for the global economic and financial systems.

On the other hand, though, not a single country is ready for the mass use of block chain technology in finance. Finance-related block chain applications come with risks attached, which can be broadly classified under five categories.

- Risks regarding the security and stability of peer-to-peer networks. A block chain is based on a peer-to-peer network consisting of equal peer nodes, and every node can join or leave freely at any time without any impact on the entire network operation. For this reason, a block chain-enabled system is susceptible to attacks in the form of address spoofing, route deception, and algorithm cracking, any one of which can cause volatility of consensus algorithm results.
- Risks regarding transaction rollback of consensus mechanism operation. Given the decentralized, distributed storage model of block chains, a same data block on a block chain can reach different nodes at different times, making it difficult to maintain consistency between different nodes regarding their consensus algorithms. This can cause block chain forks when the nodes are in the process of achieving a transaction consensus, resulting in the emergence of transaction rollback.
- Risks regarding information security of transaction data. In the absence of the use of hardware-based encryption, nodes on a block chain network are allowed to attach custom messages to data blocks, which, once added, become immutable as part of the block chain protocol. Should there be any viruses or trojans embedded in the added custom

messages, they will immediately spread across the entire network to carry out malicious attacks.
- Risks regarding technical endorsement for data trustworthiness. Given block chain's high dependence on cryptographic algorithms and consensus mechanisms, transaction data on a block chain network will lose their trustworthiness once the underlying cryptography is cracked or the cipher code is stolen.
- Risks regarding extensibility security loopholes. Given block chain's programmable extensibility, any backdoor or security loophole on a block chain network's loaded extended applications can pose an immense potential threat to transaction security.

From the perspective of financial operation and regulation, China has yet to devise a concrete action plan for formulating technical and legal rules regarding the mass application of block chain technology in finance. In this connection, China faces outstanding challenges in finance-related block chain application and regulation.

6.3.3.3 Impacts of Monetary Policy and Monetary Regulation

News reports about financial frauds, scams, and crimes have now become a regular fact of life. Just to list a few headlines: Financial pyramid schemes lurking on WeChat Moments; Pyramid selling organizations issued RMB 350 million worth of virtual currencies; A Ponzi scheme in the making with Bitcoin as a bait; Time to crack down on terrorism-related financing. These unceasing streams of financial frauds, scams, and crimes threaten to cause direct disruptions to currency issuance, currency circulation, monetary policy implementation, monetary regulation, and financial stability at national levels.

The following observations can be made from the above analysis.

- Digital currencies and digital legal tenders are set to play a bigger role in finance. New technologies like Big Data, cloud computing, the Internet of Things (IoT), artificial intelligence, and block chain have been developing without interruption. All of these new technologies, coupled with the digitally connected population, smart phone users, e-commerce, Internet penetration, and extended working space in China, will enable increasingly efficient and low-cost applications of digital currencies, digital legal tenders, mobile and cross-border payment solutions, eventually resulting in the generation of new growth points for China's economy and finance.

- Block chain has the promise to become a new driver for global economic and financial development. Block chain is the basic underlying technology of Bitcoin, featuring decentralization, high transparency, tamper-proof ability, and NSPF (no single point of failure) design. Block chain is also a collection of some of the most basic computer technologies including distributed data storage, peer-to-peer transmission, consensus mechanism, and cryptographic algorithm. For these reasons, it is fair to say that block chain has the potential to directly impact the future of Internet finance and reshape practically every facet of finance, not the least of which are the monetary market, payment systems, financial services, and financial modalities. To put it in another way, block chain constitutes a key technological agent for change in Internet finance and is set to inject new vitality into China's economy and financial industry.
- Embedded finance (scenario-based finance) and supply chain finance will be important points of departure for the financial industry to serve the real economy. These new forms of finance hold the promise of improving financial institutions' abilities to serve the real economy, for two reasons: first, they enable more effective integration of financial solutions—financing, payment, settlement, and wealth management—into the real economy; second, by harnessing the financialization of Internet platforms and the emergence of Internet financial technologies, they can transcend the barriers of time and space and make it possible to provide efficient, affordable, and secure "3A services" (Anytime, Anywhere, Anyhow) to real-economy entities (small- and medium-sized enterprises included).
- FinTech is changing the way financial services are provided in China. The application of FinTech enables effective solutions to the "last-mile" bottleneck problem hindering the development of inclusive

finance, namely the lack of credit reporting infrastructure. The combination of financial data and information technology is bringing forth a variety of financial products with the potential to alter Chinese people's habits of production and consumption. AI and block chain are converging to form a powerful force that hastens the rise of intelligent finance; revamps modern financial, monetary, clearing, and settlement systems; and revolutionizes global finance in a seemingly imperceptible and yet consequential manner.
- There exist some outstanding challenges facing Internet finance in China. To begin with, Internet finance-related products, platforms, and organizations, if left unregulated, can threaten financial security at the national level. Second, incidents of violent debt collection by online lenders crop up constantly, constituting a menace to social stability. Third, the lack of laws, regulations, and standards for e-commerce makes it difficult for online shoppers to protect their rights and interests. Fourth, it is imperative that regulatory rules be formulated to curb the rampancy of private digital currencies.

When it comes to finance, the overriding theme is always the need to ensure security, liquidity, and profitability. For any economic entity that dives into Internet finance, what it pursues by doing so is nothing more than risk aversion, liquidity, and profitability. The problem is, however, that these three objectives are often contradictory to one another. This is especially true with respect to profitability and risk aversion, which are sometimes inclusive and other times exclusive to each other. If this risk-profitability correspondence relationship teaches us anything, it is that profits come from managing risks. In real life, this translates into two choices for navigating risks: you either replace the uncertainties of risks with certainties or exclude unfavorable risks while keeping favorable risks. In China's case, it is important for China's central bank to promote the development of Internet finance; it is more important, or even paramount, to guard against and substitute risks with certainties. In other words, the first and foremost choice for China in this connection must be to have a clear understanding of and take strict precautions against the unique risks of Internet finance.

6.4 The Unique Risks of Internet Finance

Hereby, the unique risks of Internet finance refer to system operating risks caused by the use of information technologies and associated business risks derived from Internet-based financial services.

6.4.1 System Operating Risks

System operating risks can be grouped into security risks, management risks, authentication risks, and outsourcing risks.

6.4.1.1 Security Risks

Security risks include both endogenous and exogenous risks. In the case of Internet finance, endogenous risks refer to the type of risks that are caused by the inherent defects of networks and computers (in respect of both software and hardware) or by technological immaturity. Typical examples include shutdown, stoppage, malfunction, breakdown, and so on, and exogenous risks refer to the type of risks from man-made damage of computers and networks. Endogenous variables and exogenous variables are among the most frequently discussed concepts in finance. For example: Is money supply more a question of endogenous variables than exogenous variables or vice versa? This question, in essence, is one about the endogeneity and exogeneity of money supply. The endogeneity-exogeneity dichotomy offers us an approach to problem analysis. We can thus take this dichotomous relationship as a point of departure for analyzing the security risks of Internet finance.

Damages from exogenous risks are usually inflicted by attacking computers, servers, and domain name resolution systems with viruses, trojans, and hacks and finds its expression in many forms—that is, software and hardware destruction, computer and network breakdown, information leakage, information theft, information tampering, and so on. Cyber-attack perpetrators are diverse and complex in their motivations and behaviors, including both organized hacker groups and lone-wolf hackers. The most common financial cyber-attacks include deleting or revising online banks' service procedures and stealing client information. There are worse cases where hackers, by revising the operational procedures of master servers and databases through electronic orders, transfer into their personal accounts portions of commercial bank customers' interest income on deposits, or conduct illegal direct transfer of funds electronically.

One of the most recent examples of cyber-attacks is CTB-Locker, a ransomware that has gone viral since early 2015. It encrypts files present in a victimized user's computer and requires the victim to pay a ransom in bitcoins in order to recover them. Specifically, ten minutes after infecting a computer, CTB-Locker begins encrypting files stored in it, making them inoperable via custom access methods. The ransomware, it turns out, has the power to encrypt 110 types of stored files (e.g. docx, pdf, xlss, jpg, etc.), which means practically every file type one can think of. Although CTB-Locker can be removed by use of an anti-virus software, the encrypted files, nevertheless, remain resolutely encrypted. Upon infection, a virus screen will appear, displaying a timer stating that if the ransom is not paid within the next 96 hours, and all the encrypted files will be deleted permanently.

The ransomware encrypts target files using RSA 4096, an encryption algorithm so complicated that it takes, by some estimates, hundreds of thousands of years for a normal computer to solve it. Even with a supercomputer, the algorithm cannot be broken without years of computation. Given that no single organization or individual, whether in China or abroad, is currently capable of cracking the ransomware, paying the ransom seems the only plausible option for any victim who wants recovery of his or her encrypted files. As this malicious virus uses an anonymous network and demands Bitcoin-enabled anonymous payments, it is impossible to track and locate its originator. As it stands today, the hacker behind this malware is still at large.

As reported by Reuters, the No.1 suspected originator of CTB-Locker is Evgeniy Mikhailovich Bogachev, a Russian known for having orchestrated a scheme to install a malware on over one million computers without authorization. This man lurking online in the dark is currently in the second place on the FBI's Cyber's Most Wanted List. This Russian hacker is so badly wanted by the FBI that the agency has offered US$ 3 million as reward for information leading to his arrest and/or conviction, the highest bounty ever posted by US authorities for a suspected cybercriminal.

When it comes to cyber-attacks, two more problems are worthy of urgent attention. The first is the threat of state-sponsored hacking, which constitutes a politically driven attack against sovereignty. State-sponsored hacking differs from normal hacking in the fundamental sense that it is typically supported with national-level computing power, carried out by a hacking group whose membership includes top-tier experts in mathematics, system control, and other related fields and aimed at launching systemic attacks that cause total paralysis of networked systems and other devastating consequences.

The second problem is the threat of information leakage. As things stand today, core components of servers and networked equipment that Chinese banks procure and install are mostly manufactured elsewhere outside China. This is especially true when it comes to computer system chips, whose core technologies and intellectual property are all in the hands of foreign companies. Given such circumstances, Chinese commercial banks are incapable, in a technical sense, of holding these foreign companies accountable for guaranteeing information security. All they can do is to resort to soft approaches like contractual stipulations and legal restraints. Should there be any backdoor embedded in an online bank's system, all its information—including user information, transaction information, and encryption information—will be laid bare for nefarious eyes to see, subject to potential extraction, exploitation, and even tampering at any time. This threat of information leakage exists at all times like a sword of Damocles over the head of Chinese commercial banks.

6.4.1.2 Management Risks

Management risks include technical and ethical risks. The former refers to risks that threaten the reliability, stability, and security of Internet financial systems as a result of system-related poor technical design, bad selection, malfunction, and ill-management. Common examples include risks derived from communication breakdown, system paralysis, data distortion, and operational malfunction. The latter refers to risks associated with the ethics or illegal profit-seeking activities of individuals responsible for the management of networks, computers, and databases. Such risks find their expression in the concrete form of account password compromise, data theft, data tampering, and so on.

6.4.1.3 Authentication Risks

Security assurance—with respect to customer authentication and personal information transmission—represents a key building block for conducting services electronically in the Internet financial sector. An authentication system is responsible primarily for the generation, issuance, and management of digital certificates. Analogously, an authentication system serves as an online notary and trustworthy third party to verify the identity and regulate the behaviors of both parties in an electronic transaction. Simply put, it is a guardian of the order across electronic transactional processes.

An authentication system, however, faces technical risks in user certificate issuance, certificate management, internal security, and other respects. Should anything go awry, these technical risks can result in massive losses. For example, a customer is vulnerable to financial identity theft that leads to money losses when using personal information—such as regarding bank accounts, credit accounts, and passwords—via an insecure electronic transmission channel.

6.4.1.4 Outsourcing Risks

Information technology outsourcing has become a major trend in Internet finance. Nowadays, large banks—out of the consideration to pool available resources to develop core business—as well as small- and medium-sized banks—out of financial pressure—have outsourced much of their technical work to third-party companies. The problem is, however, that companies commissioned to do such technical work are mostly young in the market. For this reason, it is difficult for financial institutions to make accurate judgments regarding their level of credit worthiness. Worse still, given that a technical company is oftentimes a service provider for multiple financial institutions concurrently, a flaw in its technologies can cause a chain reaction across the highly networked financial sector. Another issue worth consideration is how to prevent a third-party contractor from leaking information relating to financial institutions and their clients.

6.4.2 Business Risks

Business risks are grouped into strategic risks, reputation risks, legal and regulatory risks, and monetary policy risks.

6.4.2.1 Strategic Risks

Strategic risks refer to the negative impacts on an online financial institution's earnings and capital, as derived from the institution's decision-making mistakes or defective execution of decisions. For the administrators of a financial institution, it is incumbent upon them to stay cool-headed in a complex, ever-changing market environment; catch the pulse of the market with foresight; keep abreast of the changes in market demand; and make quick, smart adaptational decisions at any time in terms of product positioning, design, technical support, and business innovation. Equally necessary is the need to appropriately plan, manage, and supervise the configuration of tangible (computer hardware, software, transmission networks, etc.) and intangible (managerial expertise) resources to improve products, services, processes, and transmission channels. Otherwise, the application of information technologies will end up posing severe strategic risks to the financial institution.

6.4.2.2 Reputation Risks

There are many factors that can impact the reputation of an Internet financial institution, not the least of which are security, information accuracy, timely and appropriate risk reporting, in-time response to customer enquiry, protection of customer privacy, and so on. Factors like these, if ill-managed and poorly handled, will cause negative impacts on the brand image and reputation of an Internet financial institution.

6.4.2.3 Legal and Regulatory Risks

The risks in this category result from the fact that existing finance-related laws and regulations fall well behind the ever-evolving advancement of innovation in Internet finance.

- Risks from the exercise of existing laws and regulations. Problems exist regarding the applicability of existing laws and regulations in Internet finance, particularly for defining whether a specific Internet financial behavior is legal or illegal.
- Risks from the void of new laws and regulations. New laws and regulations on Internet finance have yet to be formulated, which makes it difficult to define and determine whether a specific Internet financial behavior is legal or illegal.

6.4.2.4 Monetary Policy Risks

Electronic and virtual currencies are typically characterized by the following features: disparate issuing entities, high liquidity online, technical complexity, high anti-counterfeiting costs. If left unchecked and unregulated, electronic and virtual money can bring about monetary policy risks in the following forms.

- Issuing entity risks, which mean that electronic and virtual money can be issued by virtually every type of institutions one can think of—commercial banks, non-bank financial institutions, and non-financial

institutions as well. The diversity and complexity of issuing entities can lead to increased risk coefficients in the digital currency sector and even the financial industry as a whole, because, for example, the mismanagement of an issuing entity is liable to turn into insolvency or trigger a run on the digital money market, thus causing negative ripple effects across the entire financial system.
- Currency circulation risks. As a result of the rise of electronic and virtual currencies, there has been a constant flurry of Internet financial modalities that can act as both transactional and investment vehicles. This is liable to cause strong volatility of money supply across the entire money market, simply because demand for investment money is shifted by a congruence of factors in both interest-rate and exchange-rate markets. Payment in electronic or digital currencies is likely to lead to a huge increase in the velocity at which money circulates. Higher money velocity, coupled with the ease with which electronic or digital money can be liquidated, will increasingly blur the lines of division between M0, M1, M2, and M3, eventually making it more difficult for central banks to control and monitor money supply. Virtual currencies, if overissued, have huge potential to cause "virtual inflation," which is liable to spill over into the physical money market and directly impact the level of inflation in real life.
- Counterfeiting and money laundering risks. Electronic and virtual currencies exhibit a high level of dependence on new and high technologies, the very existence of which makes fraudulent and tampered payment instructions more deceptive, undetectable, and unidentifiable to ordinary users. This translates into higher anti-counterfeiting costs and difficulties with respect to non-physical money. Meanwhile, given a lack of regulation on the virtual money market, it is highly possible for electronic or virtual currencies to be abused by evildoers as money-laundering channels.

Beyond all the above, Internet finance also faces risks similar to those confronting its traditional counterpart, such as credit risks, country risks, market risks, interest rate risks, and foreign exchange risks. All these are unique risks that China cannot afford to overlook when developing its Internet finance. Thus, taking precautions against them must be a top priority for China in this regard.

6.5 The Necessity of China's Promoting Steady Development of Internet Finance

This author holds the view that China needs to integrate the development of Internet finance into its national strategic plan for the sake of ensuring sovereign security and taking the preemptive opportunities brought about by this emerging financial segment. Specifically, this requires China to focus on two fronts.

On the one hand, it is necessary to change the national mindset. Thanks to the dazzling development of information technologies and to the ever-evolving innovations in Big Data and cloud computing, the Internet has been able to meet finance in a marriage that induced a tectonic change in mindset regarding socioeconomic development. This has forced China to face a dilemma head-on, which is how to handle the collision between the traditional corporate mindset of fragmented, hierarchical management and the Internet mindset of integrated, flat management.

Internet technologies are breaking down the barriers of time and space, gradually bringing together services from different sectors and segments, services that would otherwise remain in separate management domains. Take, for example, smart IC cards. Although the One Card System—an integrated suite of productivity tools and processes—is now mature technically, implementing it will be practically difficult if national ministries and commissions or intra-company departments cannot get over the throw-it-over-the-wall mentality, still holding tightly onto their own sets of standards and strategic objectives without making any concession to one another. This example is cited here to emphasize the importance of coordination at the national level. The integration of such services as the One Card System will become as inevitable as it is imperative, provided that there is a clear strategic mindset and a unified, coordinated roadmap at the national level.

On the other hand, it is equally necessary to undertake top-level planning and strive for standardization across all areas of Internet finance, giving full consideration to the overall development of the financial industry. In specific terms, it is imperative for China to practice unified planning and management regarding the development of Internet finance and increase the intensity of planning, coordination, and regulation in the areas of market access, technological security, product development, business innovation, and project management. To this end, China needs to establish an Internet finance development and coordination commission and task it with these responsibilities: devising development strategies for Internet finance, coordinating and integrating resources from various related sectors, setting unified standards, and synergizing the efforts of competent authorities for effective implementation of development strategies.

6.5.1 Establishing an Effective Payment and Clearing System for Internet Finance

Stepping up security efforts for key information infrastructure is the top priority toward protecting against Internet financial risks. Key information infrastructure constitutes the nerve center of Internet finance. A highly effective payment and clearing system is one of the infrastructural cornerstones for underpinning, in a broad sense, the development of national economy and finance and, in a narrow sense, the development of Internet finance as well. In order to be effective, a payment and clearing system must encompass the following elements: running efficiency, systemic stability, operational safety, business inclusion, wide-ranging services, full preparedness for emergency situations, and so on.

As things stand today, China's central bank, the People's Bank of China (PBOC), has put in place a second-generation modern payment system with a full-fledged architecture, which consists of the Settlement Account Processing System (SAPS) at its core, a series of payment service application systems—including the High-Value Payment System (HVPS), the Bulk Electronic Payment System (BEPS), the Cheque Image System (CIS), the Online Payment Interbank Clearing System (OPICS), the Electronic Commercial Draft System (ECDS), and the Domestic Foreign Currency Payment System (DFCPS)—and the Payment Management Information System (PMIS). On the basis of the PBOC's modern payment system, a payment and clearing system for Internet finance can be established through efforts in the following three respects. First, electronic banking branches should serve as online extensions of brick-and-mortar commercial banks. This requires that electronic banking business—whether on websites, app platforms, or ATM machines—should be able to be operated through direct, remote connections to banks' service terminals via client gateway access so that instructions are issued and received the same way as they would be at bank counters. The objective is to synchronize back-office management with front-office management. Interbank and cross-regional clearing of payments can be realized by enabling commercial banks to access the PBOC's modern payment system through special communication links.

Flexible diverse options for access and clearing are now available under the PBOC's second-generation payment system. In other words, the model of multi-point access for multi-point clearing has now been changed into one of single-point access for single-point clearing or multi-point access for single-point clearing. In specific terms, this means Chinese commercial banks need to steadily achieve single-account clearing, with each establishing at the China National Clearing Centre (the PBOC's settlements and clearing arm) but one account through which to process all clearing and settlement instructions. When that is realized, municipal-level clearing centers will only provide acquiring and region-based data backup services, thus resulting in a gradual drop in the number of clearing accounts by commercial banks or their banking branches. Furthermore, it is necessary to merge decentralized clearing systems into a centralized, integrated one based on the PBOC's six payment systems. This will go a long way toward enhancing clearing systems' working efficiency and resolving the dilemma of high risks and low efficiency associated with multi-account clearing.

Second, it is necessary to strengthen security supervision of pure online banks—if any appears on the banking scene in the future—under the principle of prudential supervision. The objective in this regard is to progressively allow pure online banks to access the PBOC's modern payment system, but under the precondition of implementing rigorous approval processes. This objective, though, should be realized in two steps.

Step 1: When pure online banks are still in their infancy, they can be allowed to link up to the payment systems of large commercial banks that have clearing accounts in the PBOC's China National Clearing Centre, in a way similar to how the Clearing House Interbank Payments System

(CHIPS) in New York operates. The pure online banks can entrust the commercial banks to undertake, on a commission basis, interbank clearing of payments via their clearing accounts within the PBOC system. This modest first step is conducive to stability maintenance and risk prevention in the financial market.

Step 2: When pure online banks develop to the point where their security and stability are guaranteed, those that meet eligibility requirements can be allowed to directly access the PBOC's modern payment system and enjoy single-point access for single-point clearing. Strict requirements, however, must be imposed on those pure online banks with access to the PBOC's payment system, especially in respect of capital adequacy ratio, reserve requirements, clearing provisions, and system security technologies. Only by granting pure online banks access to the national clearing network can they be enabled to play out their strengths and unique roles. Doing so also makes it possible and easy for the central bank (PBOC) to exercise real-time, effective supervision of pure online banks.

Third, importance must be attached to two more issues with respect to Internet financial clearing and settlement.

- One is system security control. When an Internet financial payment and clearing system is linked with an external system, prudential isolation precautions should be adopted and matched with rigorous visit control tactics. Development and training activities in the production system should be forbidden, and utilization of non-system-specific storage media should be banned. Particular efforts should be made with respect to protection and monitoring of Internet edge devices (such as firewalls), system intrusion detection and virus prevention.
- The other is disaster recovery. Today, the PBOC's system is underpinned by a disaster recovery architecture that consists of a production and operation center in Beijing, an intra-city backup center in Beijing and a long-distance backup center in Shanghai. The disaster recovery architecture is designed to achieve synchronized backup and automatic switchover in case of system failure. Based on the PBOC's disaster recovery architecture, all clearing participants must strengthen capacity building in respect of emergency response and develop their own data disaster recovery centers.

6.5.2 Establishing a Multi-Layered Legal Regulatory System for Internet Finance

In China, the development of legislation falls relatively behind the development of computing technologies and the Internet. This problem of discrepancy between legislation and real-life developments is even more pronounced in the field of finance. Just to list a few examples to illustrate this point.

- The *Law of the People's Republic of China on Commercial Banks* and the *Law of the People's Republic of China on the People's Bank of China* were adopted to regulate the activities of traditional banks, but there is nothing about Internet finance in either of them.
- The *Law of the People's Republic of China on Electronic Signature* was formulated and designed as a technical law in response to the development of e-commerce, yet covering only a small fraction of Internet financial services.
- In 2001, the People's Bank of China formulated the *Interim Measures for the Control of Online Banking Operations*, in which principled requirements are made relating to the qualification of banks intending to open online banking operations. When it comes to regulation of Internet financial activities, though, this legal document does not go any further beyond the realm of regulatory approval. As a result of this, financial institutions face the dilemma of lacking legal basis for resolving potential disputes with customers.
- In 2006, China Banking Regulatory Commission promulgated the *Measures for the Administration of Electronic Banking*, in which principled requirements are made regarding market access, risk aversion, and regulation in Internet finance. The implementation of these measures, however, is not underpinned by any detailed, follow-up instruction. Nor do these measures touch upon newly emerging organizational forms and business modalities in Internet finance. The result is that many regulatory defects still exist in respect of the operation of Internet finance. Beyond that, given their distinctly low status at the legislative level, these measures fall well behind the real-life developments of Internet finance.

- As of July 2015, a series of policies were issued by governing and regulatory bodies to consolidate financial supervision and monitoring, such as the *Guide to Promoting the Healthy Development of Internet Finance* promulgated by the People's Bank of China along with nine other ministries. They have played their due role in facilitating the normative development of China's Internet finance.

As shown from the above examples, more measures are needed for establishing a full-fledged legal framework for the development of Internet finance. What should be done first is consolidate top-level design for the Internet financial legal framework. There are four key building blocks of Internet financial legislation: establishment and improvement of a credit inquiry system, an information disclosure system, and a statistical platform for Internet finance; formulation of regulatory models and standards on Internet financial institutions, markets, products, technologies, and high-tech professional teams; development of a "regulatory sandbox" that offers tools such as restricted authorization, individual guidance, waivers, and "no enforcement action letters" (NALs); and protection from hacking and information theft.

As such, the top level of China's Internet financial legal framework can be designed in two steps or, rather, by use of one of two possible methods in accordance with the developments of and regulatory needs of Internet finance and electronic currencies.

Method 1: revising existing legal and regulatory systems. Specific measures include adding the definitions of online banking branches and pure Internet banks into the *Law of the People's Republic of China on Commercial Banks* and the *Law of the People's Republic of China on the People's Bank of China*; making further, detailed clarifications on the access criteria, approval requirements, and business scopes for these two types of Internet banks; making clear the PBOC's legal status as the regulatory body for electronic and virtual currencies and matching it with regulatory policies and measures; setting up a mechanism of regular, prudential regulation on digital currencies.

Method 2: formulating a law on Internet banks or on Internet finance. From the legislative perspective, this means that on the one hand, a clear-cut legal framework must be established for the orderly development of

Internet finance and electronic currencies and on the other hand, efforts must be made to strengthen overall, legislative-level regulation on Internet finance, electronic currencies, and digital currencies. As a new addition to China's legal infrastructures, this Internet finance law should be designed in a way that makes it distinguishable from laws and regulations governing traditional banks. It must encompass the following elements: legal entity, access requirement, business approval, regulatory objective, regulatory measure, exit mechanism, rights and obligations of all parties concerned, legal responsibility for violation of relevant rules and regulations, and so on. It should be formulated with vision and foresight in order to accommodate new developments or whatever new developments that may occur in the future—that is, new developments with respect to the aforementioned four key building blocks of Internet financial legislation.

What should be done next is to supplement the Internet finance law with detailed rules and regulations. On the basis of the above-mentioned legal system adjustment, continued efforts must be exerted to prescribe and refine corresponding rules and regulations that specify clear and feasible norms relating to the management of Internet financial service contracts, Internet financial risk control, codes of business conduct, electronic payment methods and tools. Meanwhile, initiatives must be taken to realize "seamless regulation" in the real sense of the term by intensifying regulation on various Internet finance-related respects. It is imperative that the People's Bank of China promulgate the *Measures for the Administration of Electronic Currencies* to incorporate electronic and virtual currencies into its regulatory ambit and standardize the issuance, use, and circulation of these newcomers on the currency scene. Filing-on-record and reserve requirements should also be applied to the issuing entities of electronic and virtual currencies, so that they pay reserve funds to the PBOC at a certain ratio.

Third, it is imperative to enhance existing laws and regulations to strengthen their interconnectivity. For the sake of legal system integrity, it is imperative to adjust and improve the provisions relating to the rights, duties, and obligations of all concerned parties involved in Internet finance, such as those included in the *Criminal Law of the PRC*, the *Criminal Procedure Law of the PRC*, *General Principles of the Civil Law of the PRC*, and the *Civil Procedure Law of the PRC*, so that clear, unequivocal provisions are available for handling Internet financial crimes and settling Internet financial civil disputes—that is, whether or not electronic contracts are legally binding and whether or not electronic records can be used as credible evidence. Given the many contradictions between existing financial regulatory legal systems, especially regarding the relationships between competent regulatory bodies, it is necessary—under the precondition of ensuring the scientific development of Internet finance and protecting the rights and interests of customers—to comb through existing provisions and rules, so as to guarantee the inner coherence of all regulatory legal systems and the interconnectivity of supplementary implementation measures. This is a boon for improving the efficacy and effectiveness of Internet financial regulatory provisions.

6.5.3 Building a Three-Level Internet Financial Risk Control System

In order to effectively control and regulate Internet financial risks, it is imperative to manage and defuse risks at the national, industrial, and corporate levels.

6.5.3.1 Risk Prevention and Control at the National and Macro Level

The priority is to foster favorable environment and platforms for the healthy development of Internet finance and provide financial security protection at the sovereign level. To this end, measures have to be taken at both technical and institutional levels.

(a) At the technical level, the first thing is to develop and apply indigenously patented information technologies—both hardware and software—to build all-rounded network security systems or Big Data security protection nets. However, indigenously branded information technologies from Chinese IT providers—that is, Lenovo, Huawei, and ZTE—are only technically fit to be installed in the branch-level and subbranch-level servers of Chinese commercial banks. The highest level servers of these banks are installed with information technologies from foreign IT corporations. The reason, in the final analysis, lies in the fact that domestic IT companies are well behind their foreign counterparts in the production of large-scale-integrated (LSI) chips, particularly when it comes to meeting the demand for mass production of LSI chips. This has to do with a core bottleneck problem—the technology for manufacturing arithmetic chips. To fundamentally manage the endogenous risks facing its Internet financial system, China needs to strive for breakthroughs and crack the chip bottleneck by launching a project of developing "indigenously patented" computer chips for the servers of Chinese commercial banks.

Second, it is necessary to work toward the establishment of a regulatory model featuring "whole-process prevention and control against internal and external threats." To this end, efforts must be focused on the following five respects.

- Adopting multi-server technology based on the principle of physical separation to ensure the security of control center host computers and intranets, so that when one server is under attack and runs in an unsafe mode, there is another server available to work as a substitute.
- Upgrading firewall technologies to build national safety protection nets. Although there should not be any hierarchy when it comes to the development of the Internet industry, there has to be hierarchy in the area of Internet security protection. In this sense, it is imperative to protect the security of Internet financial systems by preventing hacking and virus attacks through proper employment of firewall technologies.
- Monitoring entire systems on a daily basis by employing measures relating to internal intrusion detection and vulnerability scanning. Specifically, entry points that are susceptible to intrusion must be scanned daily to ensure that security problems are detected in time.
- Promoting the use of smart router technologies. Security protection applications must be infused into routers located at network nodes. Also important is the need to intensify security scanning and screening

during network transmission in order to prevent information from being stolen and tampered with during transmission.
- Implementing data backup and insulation blocking. Reliable failure recovery mechanisms should be implemented to achieve hierarchical management of databases. This should be matched with efforts to strengthen capacity building in disaster recovery management.

(b) At the institutional level, efforts must be focused on perfecting the legal framework for Internet finance with specific measures in this connection being elaborated in previous texts and incorporating Internet credits into the work-in-progress social credit system in China, which requires efforts on three fronts:

- Fostering a social credit mentality and giving "credibility and integrity" an institutional guarantee by establishing objective, fair corporate, and individual credit assessment systems and an e-commerce identity authentication system.
- The PBOC's credit inquiry system should include Internet credit information that is based on records of behavioral patterns and recognize such information as an important component. With networked applications developing ever so fast, individual behaviors will increasingly shift from the real world to the virtual world. Against this backdrop, the adoption of Big Data mindsets and approaches to record, classify, analyze, and utilize these behaviors will become one of the foundations underpinning the sound and steady development of Internet finance. Meanwhile, the PBOC's credit inquiry system should, under the precondition of ensuring full privacy protection, remain as open and open-sourced as possible in order to maximize its social impact.
- Strengthening financial institutional infrastructure. Limiting the types and numbers of electronic or digital currencies is necessary for effectively managing liquidity risks.

6.5.3.2 Risk Prevention and Control at the Industrial and Mezzo Level

First, an Internet financial alliance should be built to beef up risk management from the perspectives of industrial development and self-regulation. This Internet financial alliance needs to work on two fronts.

- On the one hand, the alliance should pool available resources together, establish relevant mechanisms, and lead the efforts in the study of technological conundrums common to all Internet financial entities. By encouraging and empowering Internet financial entities to jointly crack technological conundrums and share technological achievements, the alliance can help reduce the costs and resource waste associated with uncoordinated R&D efforts and promote the integration of industry and technical standards.
- On the other hand, the alliance needs to keep track of the developments of cutting-edge ideas and technologies, so as to provide analytical, consultative, and instructional services that facilitate technology selection and business improvement in the industry. Doing so is a boon for avoiding industry-wide risks associated with technology selection. This is pretty much like creating a technology roadmap. Furthermore, by harnessing industry-wide synergy to beef up management of domestic Internet financial certification systems, the alliance can help end at an early date the dilemma of different financial institutions going their own way, thus putting in place a truly unified financial certification center in China.

Second, an Internet financial arbitration system should be established. Key business formats of Internet finance include online payment, online lending, crowdfunding, fund sales, Internet insurance, Internet trust, Internet consumer finance, and so on. Internet financial arbitration refers to a mechanism for arbitration institutions to resolve disputes that arise from financial investment. The process of Internet financial arbitration goes as follows: two disputing parties, upon reaching an agreement for arbitration on voluntary basis, submit a request to a third-party arbitrator from a non-judiciary institution for making a legally binding ruling on a matter in dispute between them. Given its features of voluntarism, professionalism, flexibility, and efficiency, the development of Internet financial arbitration meets the need for innovation in Internet finance. A well-developed Internet financial arbitration system can be a crucial supplement to the industry's legal rights protection system and regulatory coordination system.

6.5.3.3 Risk Prevention and Control at the Corporate and Micro Level

The following three approaches should be adopted in this connection. (a) Implementing strict operational procedures and rigorous internal management systems, by following these principles: segregation of duties, many taking joint responsibility for one particular task, each taking responsibility for his or her own particular task, nobody going beyond his or her own sphere of jurisdiction. (b) Beefing up efforts in personnel training. The objective is to constantly inject talented, new blood into Internet finance. (c) Improving financial institutions' technological capabilities to protect themselves from risks and attacks. Initiatives should be taken to transform and upgrade firewalls, networked user password access technologies (including soft keyboard password inputs, one-time passwords, USB-KEY, public-key cryptography, private-key cryptography), intrusion detection systems, network security transport protocols, and network security trading technology, so that a favorable internal environment is in place for the healthy development of Internet finance.

6.5.4 Promoting Intellectual Property Protection and Standardization in Internet Finance

Beyond the above-mentioned national initiatives to promote the development of core hardware technologies, the strategy to protect Internet financial intellectual property should also include a standardization approach that covers a broad range of things introduced by financial institutions, such as online services, financial trading products, financial equipment, and software platforms. The Chinese government must strive for a greater say over the formulation of international Internet financial standards, particularly with respect to product, technical, industrial, and security standards, as a way of promoting intellectual property protection and standardization in Internet finance.

6.5.5 Strengthening International Cooperation for the Steady Development of Internet Finance

In the US, the security problem is considered a primary potential threat to the steady development of Internet finance. In the UK, the world's first regulatory sandbox was launched in 2015. In the European Union, initiatives are being taken to develop global FinTech centers.

China can advocate strengthened international cooperation for promoting the steady development of Internet finance and the global economy at large. Feasible proposals may include the establishment of an Internet financial information sharing mechanism and the creation of an Internet financial pluralistic dialogue mechanism and an Internet financial security cooperative control mechanism. Proposals such as these are in the interest of creating international synergy and globally accepted rules for the sound, steady development of Internet finance across the world.

7

The Prevention and Diffusion of Systematic or Regional Financial Risks—The Methodology for China to Resolve Financial Crises

7.1 Meaning and Types of Financial Crises

In finance, the term "financial crisis" is usually discussed in association with "financial fragility."

7.1.1 Meaning of Financial Crises

A financial crisis is defined in *The New Palgrave Dictionary of Economics* (Palgrave Macmillan, 2008) as "a sharp, brief, ultra-cyclical deterioration of all or most of a group of financial indicators: short-term interest rates, asset (stock, real estate, land) prices, commercial insolvencies and failures of financial institutions" and is defined by Kindleberger (2007) as a shock or sudden and rapid changes on all or most financial indicators (such as short-term interest rates, stock prices, and real estate prices) and the collapse of financial institutions.

7.1.2 Systematic Risk

In *Guidance to Assess the Systemic Importance of Financial Institutions, Markets and Instruments: Initial Considerations* (a report prepared by the International Monetary Fund, the Bank for International Settlements, and the Secretariat of the Financial Stability Board in 2009), a systematic risk is defined as "a risk of disruption to financial services that is (1) caused by an impairment of all or parts of the financial system and (2) has the potential to have serious negative consequences for the real economy."

7.1.3 Conventional Types of Financial Crises

Five conventional types of financial crises can be identified as follows:

- Banking crisis. Normally considered as a typical example of a financial crisis, a banking crisis refers to a systemic crisis of the banking sector which occurs when failure in one bank or a group of banks spreads to others in the system.
- Currency crisis. A currency crisis is one relating to currency circulation, purchasing power, and exchange rates.
- Debt crisis. A debt crisis is a situation in which a country is unable to pay back its external debts, including sovereign and private external debts.
- Stock market crisis. A stock market crisis refers to a crash in the stock market.
- Concurrent crisis.

7.1.4 New Characteristics of Financial Crises at the Present Stage

Today, financial crises are characterized as follows:

- Vicious cycles of risk are exacerbated by procyclical behaviors and institutional factors—a cross-temporal dimension.

- Systemically important financial institutions are playing a crucial role—a cross-sectoral dimension.
- Financial market integration is accelerating crisis transmission—the links between financial systems.
- The ever-evolving financial innovation is creating a growing number of crisis transmission chains—varieties of financial derivatives.
- The interaction between financial systems and the real economy is growing tighter.

7.2 A Review of Major Financial Crises in the World History

7.2.1 The Great Depression from 1929 to 1933

During the 1930s when the Great Depression ravaged the American economy, more than 11,000 banks either went bankrupt or had to merge, as a result of which the total number of banks in the country dropped significantly from over 25,000 to about 14,000. In 1930, the number of bank failures exceeded four digits, amounting to 1350 and representing 5.29% of total banks. This number went up further to 2293, accounting for 9.87% of total banks. The trend peaked in 1933 with over 4000 bankruptcies in the year alone, about 20% of total banks. The Great Depression plunged the US economy and finance into a full-blown recession.

7.2.2 The Eruption of the 1997 Asian Financial Crisis

The financial crisis that gripped much of East Asia in 1997 started with the collapse of the Thai baht, which was quickly followed by the sharp devaluation of the Indonesian rupiah, the Philippine peso, and the Malaysian ringgit. The crisis later spilled over to Singapore, Taiwan (China), Hong Kong (China), and eventually reached the shores of the Republic of Korea and Japan in Northeast Asia. After this wave of currency meltdowns swept all countries in East Asia except China, Russia and Brazil also began to experience severe financial shocks.

The Asian financial crisis emanated from unusual, wild swings in the foreign exchange markets. The fluctuations were so drastic that they soon triggered a currency crisis that plunged the currency and stock markets into disarray, eventually producing massive impacts on the real economy.

7.2.3 The International Financial Crisis of 2007–2008

Serious consequences are discernible after the international financial crisis of 2007–2008.

- Financial institutions suffered devastating losses. According to IMF estimates, the total losses of financial institutions worldwide could have reached as much as US$ 4 trillion.
- Financial markets went into a wild tailspin. In 2008, the Dow Jones Industrial Average fell by 33.8%, and the EURO STOXX 50 and the Nikkei Stock Average by 44.3% and 42.1%, respectively.
- Market confidence dived to a record low. As some large financial institutions plunged toward insolvency, counterparty risk rose to unprecedented levels, creating a sense of heightened panic, dampening investors' appetite for risk and causing an acute liquidity shortage. In September 2008, Lehman Brothers went bust in what is now remembered as the biggest bankruptcy ever in American history.
- The real economy was dealt a catastrophic blow. The financial crisis jolted the American, Eurozone, and Japanese economies into recession and dramatically slowed down the growth of emerging and developing economies.
- The European Union fell into a debt crisis, also regarded as a continuation of the 2008 financial crisis.

Four noteworthy things are to be gleaned from what is described above. First, the mechanism in which financial fragility evolves into a financial crisis is usually triggered by a payment crisis. This, broadly speaking, takes place within four steps:

- The balance sheets of financial institutions worsen, culminating in a run on banks;
- The financial institutions have to sell their assets as a desperate attempt to acquire liquidity for meeting payment requests;
- With the financial institutions in a rush to sell their assets, asset prices take a nosedive;
- Plummeting asset prices further worsen the private sector's balance sheets.

Second, a financial crisis often comes with a credit crunch, producing a vicious cycle that devastates the real economy, resulting in a slumping economy, rising bankruptcies, and plunging confidence. In the end, the central bank becomes the last source of credit supply. As efforts to diffuse the financial risks intensify, the central bank becomes a major actor—but not the only one—for tackling the crisis.

Third, the globalization of finance can aggravate, either directly or indirectly, the cross-border spread of a financial crisis in two ways: (1) trade ties, which make bad balances of payments contagious among countries, and (2) financial ties, which enable countries to influence one another when there are changes in direct investment and credit is tightened.

Finally, a financial crisis is highly destructive in the following ways: pushing financial institutions to the brink of insolvency; increasing the fiscal burdens of national governments as governments are usually forced to bail out troubled institutions; eroding the efficiency of monetary policies; producing debt-deflation spirals; and seriously denting economic growth.

7.3 The US Response to the 2008 International Financial Crisis

Two clarifications need to be made here. First, there is no detailed or in-depth analysis in this chapter of what causes a financial crisis and how to prevent it from occurring again. Rather, this chapter is focused on exploring ways for dealing with a national systemic or regional financial crisis, for two reasons: the first reason is that there have been countless books that delve into cause analysis of financial crises and offer suggestions regarding preventive measures; the second, more important reason is that when a country gets into or faces a financial crisis, oftentimes its government either finds itself unable to meet the challenge head-on or acts with vacillation, bogged down over policy debates, thus resulting in ineffective coping tactics, untimely response, indecisive actions, and higher losses. In this chapter, the US response to the 2008 financial crisis—a subject this author delved into during his study trip to Yale University in 2012—is listed as an example to illustrate how to address a financial crisis at the national level. As far as any national government is concerned, it is a substantive, practical, and replicable example of how to handle a daunting emergency or a grave financial crisis. As such, the focal point of this chapter is to discuss the methods, steps, tactics, and measures for responding to and addressing a financial crisis.

Second, when it comes to discussing how to address a financial crisis at the national level, it is important that we return to the concept of "Big Finance" mentioned in Chap. 1. If the "Big Finance" concept has taught us anything, it is that when learning, discussing, and using finance, we should not limit ourselves to studying merely a central bank's monetary policy goals, tool selection, and policy outcomes, but instead should take a multi-pronged, holistic, and interactive approach by combining monetary policies with fiscal, exchange rate, and regulatory policies. This is the approach for monetary policy makers to take if they want their policies to deliver desired policy outcomes, particularly in a crisis situation when the stability of a financial system is at stake. This is also the approach for a national government to take in order to achieve financial stability and sustainability and to successfully address a financial crisis.

7.3.1 An Overview of the US Response to the 2008 Financial Crisis

Primary participants in dealing with the 2008 financial crisis include the Federal Reserve, the Department of the Treasury, the Federal Deposit Insurance Corporation (FDIC), the US Securities and Exchange

Commission (SEC), and the US Congress. Secondary participants include other executive departments and agencies of the US Federal Government—that is, the Department of Housing and Urban Development.

- The Federal Reserve. As an organization insulated from the transfer of federal executive power and partisan disputes, the Federal Reserve is charged with implementing monetary policies. It played a central role in the 2008 market-based response to tackling the financial crisis and stabilizing financial markets, with a tactic that combined traditional, aggressive monetary policies with unconventional, non-traditional ones.
- The United States Department of the Treasury. After the Federal Reserve's monetary policies proved unable to contain the broad, ever-worsening financial crisis, the Bush administration decided just in time to intervene. The Federal Government's intervention efforts culminated in the enactment of the Troubled Asset Relief Program (TARP), which was spearheaded by the Treasury Department and designed to inject investment and liquidity into major financial institutions and certain large corporations by purchasing toxic assets from them.
- The Obama administration. After being sworn into office, Barrack Obama, in addition to continuing his predecessor's relief program, also introduced a series of regulatory proposals and financial stabilization policies, including massive, quick tax cuts and expanded deficit spending to stimulate the economy. Although the virulence of the financial crisis spanned two administrations, the Obama administration—whether judged from its bailout plan, massive tax cuts, or deficit spending—largely maintained continuity with the previous administration in terms of how to weather the financial storm.
- The US Congress. Through timely legislation, the Senate and the House of Representatives provided a legal environment favorable for addressing the crisis, stabilizing the financial sector and revitalizing the economy.
- Through coordination with Congress, the Bush and Obama administrations signed into law a flurry of acts, most notably the *Emergency Economic Stabilization Act of 2008*, the *Economic Stimulus Act of 2008*, the *American Recovery and Reinvestment Act of 2009*, and the *Dodd-*

Frank Wall Street Reform and Consumer Protection Act (known as the most important piece of financial regulatory legislation since the Great Depression).

In sum, the United States went all out to tame the raging beast of the 2008 financial crisis, by introducing a stimulus package that encompassed monetary policies, fiscal policies, regulatory policies, economic recovery plans, and legislative guarantee. With the benefit of hindsight, it is fair to say that the stimulus package produced concrete, tangible effects in stabilizing and revitalizing the financial markets.

7.3.2 The US Tactics and Measures for the 2008 International Financial Crisis

The financial crisis began on February 27, 2007, when the Federal Home Loan Mortgage Corporation—a government-sponsored enterprise listed on the New York Stock Exchange and otherwise known in brief as Freddie Mac—declared its intention to stop purchasing the riskiest subprime mortgages and mortgage-related securities. Within the several months that followed, a succession of key participants in subprime mortgage lending either filed for bankruptcy protection or sank into financial distress, including New Century Finance, Countrywide Financial, Freddie Mac, and the Bear Stearns Companies. The credit rating agencies Standard & Poor's and Moody's constantly downgraded the credit ratings of subprime mortgage bonds. The 12 members of the Federal Open Market Committee (FOMC) voted in favor of keeping its target for the Federal Funds Rate unchanged at 5.25% at the two meetings held respectively on June 28 and August 10.

It was not until August 17, 2007, that the Federal Reserve started to lower its key discount rate—the interest rate a Federal Reserve bank charges for lending to depositories (such as banks and credit unions) to meet temporary cash shortages—by half a percentage point from 6.25% to 5.75%. On September 18, the Fed lowered the Federal Funds Rate by 50 basis points to 4.75%. And thus began the Federal Reserve's aggressive monetary policies, which brought the Federal Funds Rate from 5.25% in

August 2007 to zero at the end of 2008. Meanwhile, through open market operations, the Fed was able to stem lending to individual companies during an increase in reserve requirements or liquidity supply in the whole banking system. Its top priority was to ensure the supply of funding to banks and non-bank financial institutions. As the financial crisis escalated, the Fed undertook the following three coping tactics: providing emergency loans to crisis-afflicted, non-bank institutions, lowering the Federal Funds Rate to zero, and, ultimately, purchasing a lot of treasury bonds as well as bonds and CMOs (collateralized mortgage obligations) issued or guaranteed by agencies and instrumentalities of the US government.

7.3.2.1 Three Monetary Policies by the Federal Reserve

Both conventional and non-conventional monetary policies were enforced to cope with the crisis.

(a) Conventional monetary policy (A): boosting liquidity by use of aggressive traditional monetary policy tools, namely, increasing open market operations, massively reducing the discount rate and changing reserve requirements. In October 2008, the US Congress passed the Emergency Economic Stabilization Act of 2008, which allowed the Federal Reserve to pay depository institutions interest on both their reserve and excess reserve balances with a view to increasing liquidity and restoring financial stability. As a result, the Fed cut the Federal Funds Rate all the way down to zero, thus causing a substantial drop in the interbank rates. This directly led to higher liquidity and indirectly to stronger personal purchasing power, lower corporate operational costs, more consumption, and less unemployment.

(b) Conventional monetary policy (B): boosting liquidity by making more use of existing liquidity instruments, primarily the discount window and central bank swap lines. The discount window is a tool of monetary policy that allows eligible institutions to borrow directly from the Federal Reserve—usually on a short-term basis—to meet temporary shortages of liquidity. The term finds its origin from the practice of sending a representative to the teller window of a federal reserve bank when a bank or other financial institution needed to apply for a loan. The discount window constitutes one of the three traditional monetary policy tools that the Fed can employ to provide short-term liquidity to the markets as a last-resort lender. This monetary policy tool was seldom used prior to the outbreak of the 2008 financial crisis, except for a short period in the wake of the September 11 attacks in 2001 as a temporary approach to release liquidity into the tightening short-term credit market. There are basically three reasons for the reluctance of banks to use the discount window: first, the Federal Funds Rate is usually higher than the interest rate in the interbank lending market; second, a financial institution could be perceived by the market as being weak if it borrows from a Federal Reserve bank; third, the Fed's discount window is commonly treated as a backup to other interbank lending instruments. After the outburst of the financial crisis or more specifically, since December 2007, the discount window has been transformed from a backup tool for providing short-term liquidity into a regular, daily tool for liquidity injection. Through the discount window, the Fed launched a monetary policy program called Term Auction Facility (TAF), which was aimed at providing short-term loans to financial institutions in need of liquidity, with terms ranging from 28 to 84 days. At the end of 2008 when the financial crisis reached a fever pitch, outstanding TAF loans amounted to about US$ 900 billion, nearly equivalent to the value of the Fed's total assets.

In March 1962, the Federal Reserve established its first swap line with the Bank of France and later expanded its swap network to include central banks in the UK, Germany, and other European countries. A swap line works in one of two ways: a central bank sells a specified amount of its currency to the Fed in exchange for dollars at the current spot exchange rate or the Fed gives dollars to a country's central bank in exchange for a specified amount of the country's currency. Central bank swap lines help tackle bottlenecks in the international distribution of liquidity, thus enabling financial institutions to obtain badly needed liquidity. Following the outbreak of the financial crisis in 2007, the Fed set up temporary swap lines with 14 central banks, including the European Central Bank, the Bank of England, and the Bank of Canada. At the end of 2008, short-term loans provided via this lending facility totaled US$ 500 billion in value. All these swap lines offered to and by the Fed expired in February

2010 and ceased to be in use. In May 2010, however, the Fed reinstated its US dollar-denominated swap lines with certain central banks in response to a short-term liquidity disruption in the US financial market. In November of the same year, the Fed announced the reintroduction of its foreign currency swap line system, under which the Fed would give US dollars to five central banks—the European Central Bank and the central banks of Japan, Canada, the UK, and Switzerland—in exchange for their currencies. The foreign money acquired via this lending system was provided to financial institutions that needed to settle transactions in non-US dollar currencies, so as to boost the short-term non-US dollar liquidity.

(c) Non-conventional monetary policy: providing emergency loans through rapid expansion of non-traditional lending programs to inject liquidity into the markets and restore market confidence. The legal authority for the Fed to use this diverse spectrum of non-traditional programs comes from Section 13(3) of the Federal Reserve Act (passed by Congress in 1913), which enshrines a clause that has long remained obscure from public knowledge. The clause unequivocally states: "In unusual and exigent circumstances, the Board of Governors of the Federal Reserve System, by the affirmative vote of not less than five members, may authorize any Federal Reserve Bank to discount for any individual, partnership, or corporation, notes, drafts, and bills of exchange: Provided, that such entity is unable to secure adequate credit accommodations from other banking institutions."

In the midst of the financial crisis, the Federal Reserve harnessed the power of non-conventional monetary policy and, through coordination with the Treasury Department, acted promptly to provide direct lending to liquidity-strapped financial institutions. Thanks to the Fed's timely employment of non-traditional lending programs, stability was restored in the financial and capital markets. What follow are four striking cases of how the Fed used non-traditional monetary policy to resolve conundrums during the crisis period.

Case One: In March 2008, the Fed extended an emergency loan of roughly US$ 29 billion to JP Morgan Chase to facilitate its acquisition of Bear Stearns, then America's fifth largest investment bank, which was on the brink of collapse due to heavy involvement in the burst subprime mortgage bubble. This exemplifies how in the middle of the crisis the Fed managed to stabilize securities organizations that directly engaged in capital market operations.

Case Two: On the morning of September 15, 2008, Americans woke to the news that Lehman Brothers, then the world's fourth largest investment bank—then the world's fourth biggest investment bank—had filed for bankruptcy protection, which still holds the record for the largest bankruptcy in US history to date. On September 16, one day after the collapse of Lehman Brothers, the Federal Reserve announced its decision to grant an 85-billion-dollar loan to American International Group (AIG), which was then teetering on the brink of insolvency. The Fed's bailout lending to AIG, which eventually totaled US$ 122 billion on a cumulative basis, enabled the world's largest insurance company to survive the financial tsunami. With the benefit of hindsight, it is fair to say that the Fed's liquidity injection measures, such as emergency lending to AIG, proved effective in stabilizing financial markets and restoring the confidence of investors at a time of severe liquidity shortages. An example of such effectiveness is the gradual return of the Dow Jones Industrial Average, a barometer of the American economy and stock markets worldwide, from the bottom to the pre-crisis level (prior to February 2007) in early September 2012. On September 1, 2012, the Dow Jones Industrial Average closed at 13,090.

Case Three: In October 2008, the Federal Reserve provided a liquidity backstop to US issuers of commercial paper.

Case Four: In October 2008, the Fed provided lending to money market mutual funds with a view to boosting liquidity among capital investment agencies. From August 2007 to December 2008—a period when the financial crisis was in full swing, the Fed saw its assets swell by 100% to a record level of around US$ 2 trillion after implementing a combination of aggressive traditional and non-traditional monetary policies. To put it in another way, the Fed injected US$ 1 trillion into the financial market during this period, which translated into a huge increase in market liquidity.

7.3.2.2 Five Fiscal Policies by the US Government

To cope with the aftereffects of the 2008 international financial crisis, the US government put into effect the following fiscal policies.

(a) The Troubled Asset Relief Program (TARP). On October 3, 2008, President George W. Bush signed the Emergency Economic Stabilization Act of 2008 into law within hours of its enactment by US Congress, an act that created the TARP program to address the subprime mortgage crisis. Thus, the Bush administration began implementing the TARP program, which originally authorized expenditures of US$ 700 billion. The TARP includes two key components:

- Providing much needed funding and support through the Federal Reserve to Freddie Mac and Fannie Mae.
- Authorizing the Treasury Department to purchase preferred shares, stocks, and warrants of major banks and large corporations—Citigroup, Bank of America, J.P. Morgan Chase, Goldman Sachs, American International Group (AIG), General Motors, Chrysler Corporation, and so on, including bank equity shares through the Capital Purchase Program, preferred shares of AIG through the program for Systemically Significant Failing Institutions, and capital injections to automakers and their financing arms through the Automotive Industry Financing Program.

By June 30, 2012, the Treasury Department had bought equity shares and warrants from 709 commercial banks and investment banks. On March 28, 2012, the Congressional Budget Office (CBO) released a report stating that total TARP disbursements would be reduced to US$ 431 billion, less than 1% of America's annual GDP. In terms of percentage to GDP, the disbursement amount of the TARP (less than 1% of annual GDP) is much smaller than that of the bailout program (as much as 3.2% of annual GDP) implemented under the Reagan and Bush administrations to deal with the economic crisis during the 1980s.

Under the TARP program, the Federal Government would take over Fannie Mae and Freddie Mac through direct capital injection. On

September 7th, 2008, the newly established Federal Housing Finance Agency (FHFA) announced its decision to place Fannie Mae and Freddie Mac into conservatorship of the government-sponsored enterprises (GSEs). On the same day, the Treasury Department declared its plan to inject capital into the two teetering mortgage giants. Meanwhile, the Federal Government's competent regulatory agencies were tasked with managing the regular business of and appointing new directors' boards to the two mortgage finance companies. It is noteworthy that though as listed companies, Fannie Mae and Freddie Mac, since the days of their founding, have existed as government-sponsored enterprises with missions to promote the development of the property market on the Federal Government's behalf by offering low-interest mortgage loans and mortgage-backed securities services.

Furthermore, the TARP program also authorized the Treasury to provide bailout funding to automobile manufacturers by purchasing troubled assets from them. For example, on January 16th, 2009, the Treasury offered a bailout loan of US$ 1.5 billion to Chrysler Corporation, one of the "Big Three" automakers in the United States. This represented the first loan from the TARP program to the automobile industry after the outbreak of the financial crisis. On March 19th, 2009, the Treasury released a plan to grant bailout money worth US$ 5 billion to auto parts suppliers.

(b) Massive tax cuts. In October 2010, an $858 billion tax cut plan, proposed by the Obama administration, was approved by US Congress. The plan was focused on three key respects: extending the Bush tax cuts by US$ 350 billion, extending unemployment benefits by US$ 56 billion, and reducing workers' payroll taxes by US$ 120 billion. Beyond that, businesses also received tax cuts worth US$140 billion for capital improvements, along with R&D tax credits worth US$80 billion. The estate tax was exempted, and there were additional credits for college tuition and children.

(c) Continuation and expansion of deficit spending. In 2009, President Obama continued his predecessor's course of economic stimulus policies. As a result, the US federal budget deficit for fiscal year 2009 broke the US$ one-trillion mark for first time in US fiscal history, reaching as much as US$ 1.4 trillion. In 2010, the Federal Government spent roughly US$

3.8 trillion and reported a US$ 1.6 trillion budget deficit. In 2011, the Federal Government spent some US$ 3.8 trillion and registered a budget deficit of US$ 1.3 trillion. In 2012, the Federal Government spent US$ 3.7 trillion and reported a deficit of US$ 1.1 trillion.

(d) Issuing short-term treasury bonds to add supplementary liquidity to the Federal Reserve. On September 17th, 2008, the Treasury created a new supplementary financing program to supply the Fed with liquidity generated from the issuance of short-term treasury bonds. Moreover, the Treasury announced two days later that it would provide a short-term guarantee of US$ 50 billion to help money market mutual funds meet their obligations.

(f) Boosting employment, consumption, and investment. Following the outbreak of the financial crisis, the US fiscal policies became focused on three main targets. The first is using the federal budget from a long-term and socially relevant perspective to restore economic stability and growth. For several consecutive fiscal years, the federal budget deficit has remained hovering at around 9% of America's annual GDP. In fiscal year 2017, the deficit, though down somewhat, was still high at around 5% of GDP. Here comes a dilemma: if the Federal Government continues down the path of excessive borrowing and deficit spending, this will spell trouble for the country's future economic prospects; if the Federal Government adopts austerity measures simply to reduce and avoid fiscal deficits, this will dampen the recovery of the US economy. All things considered, it seems that only with the implementation of balanced fiscal policies that are at once appropriately relaxed and conducive to cutting deficits can the Federal Reserve be able to keep interest rates down, boost investors' confidence, incentivize household spending and business growth, and ultimately facilitate economic recovery. The second is boosting medium- and long-term economic growth with taxation and federal budget policies that are prudently designed and formulated. In order to create more jobs, it is imperative to adopt fiscal policies that encourage investment for work skills improvement and basic research while stimulating private capital formation and growth. The third is driving economic development by incentivizing investment in much-needed infrastructural projects.

7.3.2.3 Six Measures for Strengthening Regulation

(a) Issuing securities-related emergency orders to stabilize the share prices of major financial institutions. On July 15, 2008, the Securities and Exchange Commission (SEC) issued an emergency order to ban "naked" short selling in the securities of Fannie Mae, Freddie Mac, and primary dealers at commercial and investment banks. On September 17, 2008, the SEC issued new, more extensive rules against "naked" shorting of securities of all financial institutions, stating in crystal-clear terms that "the SEC has zero tolerance for abusive naked short selling." In December of the same year, the SEC required credit rating agencies to increase transparency and fully disclose credit rating details, while voicing its opposition to suspending the adoption of fair value accounting standards.

(b) Establishing the Federal Housing Finance Agency. On July 30th, 2008, President George W. Bush signed into law the Housing and Economic Recovery Act of 2008, which authorized the Treasury Department to purchase bonds issued by government-sponsored enterprises (GSEs) and establish a new regulatory body for housing financing—namely, the Federal Housing Finance Agency.

(c) Involving the Federal Deposit Insurance Corporation (FDIC) and the National Credit Union Administration (NCUA) in the fight against the financial crisis. On January 12, 2009, the FDIC released an open letter requesting the Fed, the Treasury, and other Federal Government-funded organizations to implement regulatory procedures and report systems regarding the use of federal money. This marked a high-profile participation in dealing with the financial crisis—the first ever in US history—by an American insurance company that is the last line of defense for depository security. On January 16, 2009, the FDIC, the Treasury, and the Fed issued a joint statement declaring their decision to provide rescue funds to Bank of America. Two days later, the NCUA announced its plan to provide guarantees with limited validity periods for uninsured securities issued by corporate credit unions. It should be noted that at that time, the NCUA insured the deposits of more than 92 million account holders in all federal credit unions and the overwhelming majority of state-chartered credit unions. This represented the first, openly declared measure taken by the NCUA after the financial crisis spread and deepened.

(d) Conducting "stress tests" of the banking system. In a joint statement issued on February 23, 2009, the Treasury Department, the Federal Deposit Insurance Corporation, the Office of the Comptroller of the Currency, the Office of Thrift Supervision, and the Federal Reserve Board made it clear that the US government stood firmly behind the banking system and would ensure that banks would have the capital and liquidity they needed to help put the US economy back on a growth track. Two days later, the above agencies announced that they would conduct forward-looking "stress tests" of eligible US banks holding assets of over $100 billion, with a view to estimating the range of possible future losses and the resources needed to absorb such losses. Meanwhile, systemically important financial institutions were required to file "resolution plans"—also known as "living wills"—as a timely precaution against any possible recurring financial crisis.

(e) Issuing regulations on derivatives transactions. On May 13, 2009, the Treasury Department proposed amendments to the Commodity Exchange Act and Securities Act of 1933 to strengthen government regulation of over-the-counter (OTC) derivatives markets. Key proposed changes include standardization of rules regarding OTC derivatives clearing, increased authority for the Commodity Futures Trading Commission to regulate OTC derivatives transactions, and so on.

(f) Creating the Financial Stability Oversight Council (FSOC). The FSOC, whose creation was approved by the US Congress in 2009, is assigned three tasks:

- Regulating the entire US financial system;
- Promoting and stabilizing the financial markets;
- Responding to potential risks and events that threaten the stability of the US financial system.

7.3.2.4 Economic Stimulus Packages

(a) The Bush economic stimulus package (2008). In January, 2008, the US Congress passed the Economic Stimulus Act of 2008, which was intended to boost the US economy in 2008 and to avert a recession. Upon the passing of the act, the Bush administration released its $152 billion-dollar economic stimulus package which included these key stimulus measures: tax rebates to low- and middle-income families, tax incentives to stimulate business investment, and an increase in the limits imposed on mortgages eligible for purchase by government-sponsored enterprises like Fannie Mae and Freddie Mac.

(b) The Obama economic stimulus package (2009). In February 2009, the Economic Stimulus Act of 2009 was enacted by the US Congress and signed into law by President Obama. Meanwhile, Congress also approved a $787 billion-dollar stimulus package proposed by the Obama administration, the primary objectives of which included tax cuts, extension of unemployment benefits, direct provision of cash to eligible individuals (in forms including checks, debit cards, and tax breaks), and increased spending on infrastructure and other public projects. Compared with President Bush's stimulus package authorized under the Economic Stimulus Act of 2008, President Obama's stimulus package represented a staggering increase in budgetary disbursements from US$152 billion to US$787 billion. Beyond tax rebates and incentives, the Obama stimulus package also included a mass of federal spending on infrastructure and public utilities.

(c) Raising deposit insurance limits. On May 20, 2009, President Obama signed into law the Congress-approved Helping Families Save Their Homes Act of 2009, which authorized the Federal Deposit Insurance Corporation to temporarily raise deposit insurance coverage from US$100,000 to US$250,000 per depositor.

(d) Implementing the Homeowner Affordability and Stability Plan to stabilize the housing market. On February 18th, 2009, President Obama announced the Homeowner Affordability and Stability Plan, which was primarily intended to provide financial assistance totaling US$75 billion to nine million homeowners so that they could avoid foreclosure.

(e) Creating the Public-Private Investment Program for Legacy Assets. Officially announced by the Treasury Department on March 23, 2009, the program had two parts: the Legacy loans Program that facilitated the creation of public-private investment funds for purchasing distressed loans held by banks, with the Treasury providing 50% of the equity capital for each fund; the Legal Securities Program, under which the Treasury would approve five asset managers who would set private equity funds for raising capital needed to acquire distressed securities (stocks and bonds) held by banks, with the Treasury providing 50% of the equity capital for each individual investment fund and the asset managers raising the other 50% from private and other sources. Meanwhile, the Treasury would consider the possibility of granting loans to individual private equity funds, along with favorable government support in other forms.

(f) Reforming healthcare. Verifiable statistics show that about 50% of all bankruptcies in America—both personal and corporate—are associated with inability to pay medical bills. Making up 25% of total US population, baby boomers—born between 1946 and 1964—are gradually transitioning from the workplace into retirement. It is against this backdrop that healthcare reform became one of the economic priorities of the Obama administration. In March 2010, the Patient Protection and Affordable Care Act and the Health Care and Education Reconciliation Act of 2010 were enacted by US Congress and signed into law by President Obama, which together represented the US healthcare system's most significant regulatory overhaul and coverage expansion since 1965. This healthcare reform was estimated to cost as much as US$ 940 billion for the Federal Government over a ten-year period.

7.3.2.5 Legislative Guarantee

(a) Coordinating with the Senate and House of Representatives to promote legislation for economic policy continuity. On October 3, 2008, President Bush signed into law the Emergency Economic Stabilization Act of 2008, the last piece of legislation enacted and signed during his tenure. Prior to that, several acts were signed into law for the purpose of fostering financial stability and recovering the economy.

(b) Coordinating with the Senate and House of Representatives to expand spending and pass new economic recovery acts. The financial crisis was somewhat alleviated and contained in January 2009 when Barrack Obama took the oath of office as the 44th president of the United States. The US economy, though, was not yet out of the woods, plagued by sharply slowing growth, negative GDP growth—which did not turn positive until the third quarter of 2009—and a month-by-month increase in unemployment which did not begin to turn around until March 2010 after peaking at 10.2% in October 2009. During this period, the Obama administration, by and large, continued the Bush administration's course of action in dealing with the financial crisis, whether in terms of policies or direction. Three noteworthy things occurred under Obama's first term: first, the Obama administration cut taxes by massive amounts, leading to a significant decrease in federal fiscal revenue; second, the administration continued down the path of deficit spending, seeking to stimulate the economy through expanded government spending; third, annual defense spending reached a historic high, primarily for financing the wars in Afghanistan and Iraq. It was also in this period that President Obama signed into law the American Recovery and Reinvestment Act of 2009 on February 17, 2009, which was essentially designed to stimulate the US economy by increasing federal spending on a variety of programs and providing tax incentives to individuals and companies. Disbursements were allocated for the following purposes: direct cash payments to eligible individuals; tax relief for low- and middle-income families; increased investment in infrastructure, education, healthcare, and renewable energy. The act ended up catapulting the US economy onto the path of positive growth.

(c) Making the most aggressive legislative effort since the Great Depression to reform the way financial system operates. On July 21, 2010, President Obama signed into law the Dodd-Frank Wall Street Reform and Consumer Protection Act (commonly known as Dodd-Frank), now considered the most significant piece of legislation to affect the banking and financial services industry since the Great Depression. The Dodd-Frank was introduced to initiate, in President Obama's words, "a sweeping overhaul of the United States financial regulatory system, a transformation on a scale not seen since the reforms that followed the

Great Depression." In more specific terms, it was intended to restore public faith in the US financial system by focusing on these respects: consolidation of regulatory agencies, comprehensive regulation of financial markets, consumer protection, creation of tools for financial crisis, and enhancement of international cooperation.

(d) Improving relevant legislation. From February 2007 to April 2011, the Senate and House of Representatives, through coordination and cooperation with the Bush and Obama administrations, enacted a variety of acts aimed at addressing the financial crisis, restoring investor confidence, recovering the economy, and overhauling financial regulation.

What follow are the major acts enacted by US Congress and signed into law by either President Bush or President Obama to deal with the financial crisis and recover the US economy.

A. *The Economic Stimulus Act of 2008*. In January 2008, the US Congress passed the Economic Stimulus Act of 2008, which was introduced to boost the US economy and avert a recession. This act formed the legal basis for the Bush administration to release a US$152 billion-dollar economic stimulus package that included these key stimulus measures: tax rebates to low- and middle-income families, tax incentives to stimulate business investment, and an increase in the limits imposed on mortgages eligible for purchase by government-sponsored enterprises like Fannie Mae and Freddie Mac.
B. The Housing and Economic Recovery Act of 2008. On July 30, 2008, President Bush signed into law the Congress-approved Housing and Economic Recovery Act of 2008, which was designed primarily to address the subprime mortgage crisis, provide new 30-year fixed rate mortgages, and extend lending and tax preferences to first-time homebuyers. Meanwhile, the act authorized the Treasury to purchase the obligations of government-sponsored enterprises (GSEs) and take over the two mortgage giants—Fannie Mae and Freddie Mac—through direct capital injection. It also provided legal authority for the Federal Government to create the Federal Housing Finance Agency, a new regulatory agency for housing-related finance.
C. The Emergency Economic Stabilization Act of 2008. On October 3, 2008, President Bush signed into law the Emergency Economic

Stabilization Act of 2008, the last piece of legislation enacted and signed during his tenure. Originally proposed by Treasury Secretary Henry Paulson, the act was designed primarily to stabilize the financial system and stimulate the economy. Specifically, it permitted the US Treasury to bail out—by directly supplying cash—financial institutions that had become financially distressed due to being affected by the subprime mortgage crisis. Based on this act, the Bush Administration implemented the Troubled Asset Relief Program (TARP) with an authorized budget of US$ 700 billion. The TARP program has two main parts: (1) the provision of much needed funding through the Federal Reserve to Freddie Mac and Fannie Mae; (2) authorization for the Treasury to purchase preferred shares, stocks, and warrants of major banks and large corporations including Citigroup, Bank of America, J.P. Morgan Chase, Goldman Sachs, American International Group (AIG), General Motors, Chrysler Corporation, and so on. On March 28, 2012, the Congressional Budget Office (CBO) released a report stating that actual total TARP disbursements would be reduced to US$ 431 billion.

D. The Economic Stimulus Act of 2009. In February, 2009, the US Congress enacted the Economic Stimulus Act of 2009 and approved a $787 billion-dollar stimulus package proposed by the Obama administration. Key components of the Obama stimulus package included tax cuts, extension of unemployment benefits, direct provision of cash to eligible individuals, and increased spending on infrastructure and other public facilities.

E. The American Recovery and Reinvestment Act of 2009. Signed into law by President Obama on February 17, 2009, the American Recovery and Reinvestment Act of 2009 was essentially designed to stimulate the US economy by increasing federal spending on a variety of programs and providing tax incentives to individuals and companies. Key components of the act included direct cash payments to eligible individuals, tax relief for low- and middle-income families, increased investment in infrastructure, education, healthcare, and renewable energy.

F. The Helping Families Save Their Homes Act of 2009 and the Homeless Emergency Assistance and Rapid Transition to Housing Act. These two pieces of legislation were signed into law by President Obama on May 20th, 2009, with the core objective of providing homeowners with financial assistance and legal protection when they were unable to meet their mortgage repayments or filing for bankruptcy.
G. The Dodd-Frank Wall Street Reform and Consumer Protection Act. On July 21, 2010, President Obama signed into law the Dodd-Frank Wall Street Reform and Consumer Protection Act (commonly known as the Dodd-Frank Act), which has been the most significant piece of legislation to affect the banking and financial services industry since the Great Depression. The Dodd-Frank Act was introduced to initiate, in President Obama's words, "a sweeping overhaul of the United States financial regulatory system, a transformation on a scale not seen since the reforms that followed the Great Depression." More specifically, it was intended to restore public faith in the US financial system by focusing on these respects: consolidation of regulatory agencies, comprehensive regulation of financial markets, consumer protection, creation of tools for financial crisis, and enhancement of international cooperation. Key provisions of the Dodd-Frank Act include:

- Creating the Financial Stability Oversight Council, which is tasked with identifying threats to financial stability of the United States, promoting market discipline and responding to potential risks in order to stabilize the US financial system.
- Establishing the orderly liquidation authority, a public-sector bankruptcy process for non-FDIC-insured, financially distressed institutions whose bankruptcy protection filings would have systemic impacts on the stability of the US financial system. Such potential institutions would be identified jointly by the Treasury, the FDIC, and the Federal Reserve and reported to the United States Bankruptcy Court for review.

- Abolishing the Office of Thrift Supervision and transferring its power to the Federal Reserve, state savings associations to the FDIC, and other thrifts to the Office of the Comptroller of the Currency. The Office of the Comptroller of the Currency is responsible for licensing and supervising domestic banks and depository institutions as well as branches of foreign banks in the United States.
- Beefing up regulation of the insurance industry, banks and their holding companies and depository institutions, including measures to prohibit insured depository institutions, their parent companies, and associated hedge funds and private equity funds from engaging in proprietary trading.
- Tightening up regulation of the trading of derivatives and other market instruments. Specifically, the Commodities Futures Trading Commission is given more regulatory authority on over-the-counter swaps to increase overall transparency of the derivatives market, and the Federal Reserve is provided with an enhanced role in the supervision of risk management standards for systemically important payment, clearing, and settlement activities by financial institutions.
- Establishing the Bureau of Consumer Financial Protection to educate the public on financial services and protect investors and consumers. As authorized by the Dodd-Frank Act, the Financial Stability Oversight Council and the Bureau of Consumer Financial Protection have already been created, and the power of the abolished Office of Thrift Supervision has been smoothly transferred.

H. The US Senate Permanent Subcommittee on Investigations. In April 13, 2011, the US Senate Permanent Subcommittee on Investigations released *The Financial Crisis Inquiry Report*—its final report on the causes of the financial crisis—and proposed major suggestions on preventing recurrences of financial hardships:

- Reviewing all types of structured financial products and banning abusive use of structured financing instruments.
- Limiting exceptions to proprietary trading including market making and hedging; devising strict rules in accordance with the Dodd-Frank Act to regulate and limit exceptions to proprietary trading.
- Setting powerful limitations on conflicts of interest in accordance with the Dodd-Frank Act.
- Studying the structured finance standing of banks. When monitoring and regulating banks, regulatory agencies must, in accordance with the Dodd-Frank Act, give full consideration to potential systemic financial risk derived from federal-government-insured banks designing, marketing, and investing in immeasurable, unprotected credit default swaps or other financial derivative instruments.

The release of *The Financial Crisis Inquiry Report* marked the end of the course of action taken by the US Congress and Federal Government to deal with the global financial crisis.

7.3.3 Post-Crisis Response in the United States

7.3.3.1 The US Loan-Based Consumption Pattern Remains Unchanged

The growth in consumption and demand for services constituted a key driver of economic development in the post-World War II United States. According to a report on the changes of the US economic structure from 1955 to 2009, released by the United States Department of Commerce, US personal consumption expenditures (PCE) grew by an annual average of 3.4% during that 50-odd-year period, usually accounting for 70% of annual GDP in the country. PCE represented 70.6%, 71%, and 71% of American GDP in 2010, 2011, and 2012, respectively. As reported by the US Commerce Department on August 29, 2012, the US GDP increased by 1.7% in the second quarter of the year, with 71% of the growth contributed by consumption, 13.2% by private investment, 19.6% by government spending and investment, and −3.8% by export.

(a) The US credit-based consumption pattern will remain unchanged in the foreseeable future, as determined by factors including the country's social security, credit system, government policies, demographics, and social values.

- A relatively full-fledged social security system—including education, healthcare, and retirement benefits——helps free consumers from worries about the future. American households are willing and empowered to spend in areas beyond education, thanks to the implementation of the K-12 (for kindergarten to 12th grade) public (free) education system since the end of World War II and to the accessibility to low-tuition state-run colleges and universities. The availability of various retirement savings options—as best represented by the 401 (k) plans that are supported by the Federal Government and funded by employer and employee contributions—provided economic support for retired consumers. Under the Affordable Care Act initiated by the Obama administration, all American citizens were required to have healthcare insurance coverage by the end of 2014. This has helped boost consumer confidence, putting Americans at ease about spending more money.
- Continued growth in consumption is also made possible by a well-developed financial system, a capital-market-based credit system, and strong legal protection for consumers. The highly developed US markets for stocks, bonds, and financial derivatives are instrumental for sustaining long-term consumption in the sense that they create conditions for American consumers to invest, accumulate wealth, acquire money for spending, and source needed liquidity. With support from public credit rating agencies and the Big Three credit rating agencies (Standard & Poor's, Moody's, and Fitch Group), US commercial banks are able to assess and control risks and offer lending in time, thus effectively driving consumption in housing, automobiles, and expensive household items. As authorized by the Dodd-Frank Act signed into law by President Obama in the depths of the financial crisis, the Bureau of Consumer Financial Protection has been established as an independent agency to protect and edu-

cate consumers and investors on financial products. These measures exemplify the Federal Government's long-term commitment to protect consumers and advance economic development.
- Boosting consumption has long been an economic policy priority pursued by successive US administrations. Cases in point are the Bush (2008) and Obama (2009) economic stimulus packages, both intended primarily to spur consumption by cutting taxes for families and individuals.
- The US demographics will enable healthcare services to maintain long-term growth. In the United States, approximately 78 million were born between 1946 and 1964, representing 25% of the country's population—310 million. As these so-called baby boomers begin turning age 65 and stepping into retirement, they will become a very powerful consumer segment in the next 20 to 30 years for healthcare services which account for a large proportion of consumption expenditures.
- High-tech development will underpin the continued growth of consumption in America. The constant stream of high-tech products, popular among consumers, is a main driver of growth in consumption. A case in point is Apple's iPhone, an integration of many fields into one—including technology, entertainment, art, and consumer product. On August 27th, 2012, Apple Inc. became the world's most valued company, with a US$ 67-billion market capitalization. Beyond that, it is also the largest consumer product and high-tech company in the world. Furthermore, the development of medical technologies and applications—such as regarding cardiovascular treatment, surgical instruments, early diagnosis, and treatments for infants and new biopharmaceuticals—is another factor that sustains consumption growth in the United States.
- The growth of consumption in the United States is also associated with the country's traditional consumer behaviors, habits, and values that are shaped by Western culture. The United States is, broadly speaking, a consumerist society with a favorable environment for consumption, whether in terms of cultural values, religious beliefs, moral ideals, or ways of life.

(b) Credit-based consumption will continue to move on an upward spiral, as shown by present and historical economic indicators.

- Total outstanding consumer credit continues to increase. According to the Fed's latest statistics on consumer credit, total US outstanding consumer credit (excluding home mortgages) had stood at US$2.6 trillion by June 2012, indicating a trend of uninterrupted credit growth for years—except in 2009 and 2010 due to the impacts of the financial crisis.
- Services expenditures continue to grow at a robust pace. Between 1959 and 2009, US services spending experienced a remarkable increase, especially on services relating to healthcare, finance, and insurance. Services expenditures grew by 1.3%, 1.7%, and 2.1% respectively in 2010, 2011, and the first half of 2012 (by an average of 3.4% over the past 50 years), according to the PCE (Personal Consumption Expenditures) statistics released by the US Department of Commerce. In addition, the contribution by services spending to US GDP has remained steady at around 47%, in comparison to the 70% to 71% contribution by overall consumption expenditures.
- Household savings hit a 28-year high, serving as a source of much-needed funds for sustaining consumption growth. The US household saving rate has been on a downward trajectory for 24 out of the past 28 years, reaching a record high of -0.5% in 2005 along with housing prices. It was not until after the outbreak of the financial crisis in 2008 that this downward trend was reversed. Statistics from the US Department of Commerce show that total US household savings recorded a historic high in June 2012, amounting to US$ 529.5 billion. Consumption expenditures are influenced by factors like income sources, household net worth, debt levels, and property prices. As the US economy starts to regain its footing and with property prices on an upward trend, the household saving rate is projected to maintain its growth momentum, which in turn will give a boost to consumption.

7.3.3.2 Government Takes Over Banks, Securities Agencies, and Insurance Companies, Yet with the Intention of Putting Them Back to Private Management Wherever and Whenever Appropriate

A review of the economic history of the United States reveals that the US government always decided to intervene whenever there was a financial or economic crisis in which market mechanisms had failed to work efficiently and financial institutions' self-help attempts had turned futile, causing a grave threat to the whole financial system. The primary intervention approach can be summed up as follows: The US government took over or nationalized financially distressed institutions through direct investment or direct lending and implemented proper, well-timed exit strategies to return them to private hands after the restoration of order and stability to the financial system.

Case One: Disposition of assets by the Resolution Trust Corporation (RTC). The Resolution Trust Corporation was an asset management company established by the US government in 1989 to boost financial liquidity and prevent the collapse of the US financial system following the savings and loan crisis in the 1980s. Specifically, the RTC was tasked with liquidating a tidal wave of real estate-related non-performing assets—such as mortgage-backed loans—that had previously belonged to savings and loan associations (S&Ls) already declared insolvent by the Office of Thrift Supervision in the 1980s. The RTC used equity partnerships to help liquidate real estate and financial assets, with each equity partnership involving a private-sector partner to acquire a partial interest in a portfolio of assets and control the management and sale of the assets in the portfolio. Such equity partnerships allowed the RTC to benefit from the management and liquidation efforts of their private sector partners. Eventually, the RTC managed to avert financial risks by resolving 747 failed thrift institutions with total non-performing assets of US$394 billion, though at the same time costing taxpayers US$124 billion in doing so. With order returning to the US banking sector in 1995, the RTC fulfilled its historic mission and transferred its duties to the Federal Deposit Insurance Corporation (FDIC).

Case Two: The US government's policies to "nationalize" financial institutions during the most recent financial crisis and its exit strategy. As authorized by the Emergency Economic Stabilization Act of 2008 signed into law by President Bush, the US government introduced the Troubled Asset Relief Program (TARP) on October 3, 2008, a US$ 700-billion program to address the subprime mortgage crisis. The Treasury then launched the Capital Purchase Program as part of the TARP to inject liquidity into over 700 banks, securities agencies, and insurance companies through direct purchases of their equity shares, and thus began the US government's efforts to "nationalize" financially distressed institutions during the 2008 financial crisis.

Besides exercising its rights as a shareholder, the Treasury also issued regulatory rules on senior management salary levels of institutions that had accepted government bailout funds. After the crisis was eased and stability returned to the financial system, the Treasury started to gradually recover TARP bailout funds by directly selling, auctioning, and drawing dividends from its equity positions in large banks, securities agencies, and insurances companies. Slowly but surely, the Treasury eventually exited from all of its investments in major financial institutions including Citigroup, J.P. Morgan Chase, Bank of America, Goldman Sachs, and Morgan Stanley. As of June 30, 2012, the Treasury had received US$217.9 billion from its CPP investments in direct shares of banks and securities firms, exceeding the US$ 204.9 billion it had disbursed; meanwhile, the Treasury still held stock or warrants of 309 small and community banks, but with a total value of merely US$ 10 billion.

In addition to the Capital Purchase Program, the Treasury also established the following programs under TARP:

- AIG Investment Program (formerly the Systemically Significant Failing Institutions Program) to purchase preferred shares of American International Group (AIG).
- Credit markets programs to purchase "toxic" mortgage-related securities.
- The Automotive Industry Financing Program to provide loans and inject capital to automakers and their financing arms.

Case Three: An overview of major TARP programs (Table 7.1).

Table 7.1 An overview of major TARP programs (unit: US$ 100 million)

Program name	Total amount of funds committed	Repaid TARP money	Outstanding investment (market value)	Prospective yield	Number of assisted institutions	Number of institutions from which the Treasury have exited with full recovery of investments
Capital Purchase Program	2049	2179	100	230	709	400
AIG Investment Program	1820	1520	510	210	1	–
Credit Market Programs	220	100	120	3	–	–
Automotive Industry Financing Program	800	430	370	–	–	–
Total	4889	4229	1100			

Source of data: The official website of the US Department of Treasury as of June 30, 2012

(a) Capital Purchase Program (CPP). The Capital Purchase Program was launched in October 2008 to provide capital to viable banks and securities firms throughout the United States. Under the CPP, the US Treasury Department provided, on a cumulative basis, US$204.9 billion worth of capital to 709 banks and securities firms of all sizes nationwide in exchange for preferred stock or warrants, as a way of restoring stability to the financial system. As shown in a quarterly report to Congress by the US Treasury, as of June 30, 2012, 400 banks and securities firms had repaid all the funds provided by the Treasury under the CPP; the Treasury had received—through sale, auction, and repurchases of shares and dividend payment—US$217.9 billion from its CPP investments, exceeding the $204.9 billion it had disbursed; meanwhile, the Treasury still held shares or warrants of 309 small and community banks, but with a total value of merely US$ 10 billion approximately. By the Treasury's estimates, after deductions for the cost of disposing "toxic" assets of banks, the CPP will generate a net profit of US$20 billion for American taxpayers.

(b) AIG Investment Program, a program established by the US Treasury to bail out the insurance industry and American International Group, the world's largest insurance company. Under this program, AIG received a total of approximately US$182 billion from the US government, which included US$67.9 billion that Treasury committed through TARP for the purchases of preferred stock and warrants from the insurance giant and direct loans from the Federal Reserve Bank of New York (FRBNY). As of June 30th, 2012, AIG had repaid US$152 billion (84% of the total) worth of assistance funds to both the Treasury and the FRBNY combined; the Treasury still held 53% of AIG's equity shares, with a market capitalization of about US$51 billion.

(c) Credit Market Programs, which were implemented primarily through the Treasury-spearheaded Public-Private Investment Program for Legacy Assets (PPIP). Unlike CPP that enabled the Treasury to purchase preferred stock or warrants directly from banks, PPIP was designed to facilitate purchases of legacy mortgage-backed securities (MBS) held by financial institutions by combining private equity with government equity and debt through TARP. As of June 30, 2012, the Treasury had disbursed US$22 billion under Credit Market Programs, US$10 billion of which had been repaid.

(d) The Automotive Industry Financial Program (AIFP). Under AIFP, the Treasury had disbursed a cumulative total of US$80 billion worth of bailout funds to General Motors, Chrysler, Ford, and relevant auto parts suppliers, with US$ 43 billion already recovered and US$37 billion still outstanding. It is projected that taxpayers are likely to incur a loss of US$25 billion from the implementation of AIFP.

7.3.3.3 Evolution of Financial Regulatory Legislation and Market Developments in the United States

(a) Overview of key developments and legislation in the regulation of depository institutions in a historical context

A review of the history of US depository institution regulation reveals that the depository institution regulatory system in the United States is complex and layered. The development of this regulatory system has warranted the safety and soundness of depository institutions and the banking system as a whole, thus ensuring protection of the interests of depositors and the public. In order to operate in the United States, a depository institution is required to obtain a license called "charter" from government at either the federal or state level. At the federal level, the US depository regulatory system consisted of the following five regulatory agencies prior to the enactment of the Dodd-Frank Wall Street Reform and Consumer Protection Act (Dodd-Frank Act).

- The Office of the Comptroller of the Currency (OCC);
- The Board of Governors of the Federal Reserve System (Fed);
- The Federal Deposit Insurance Corporation (FDIC);
- The Office of Thrift Supervision (OTS);
- The National Credit Union Administration (NCUA).

With the exception of the NCUA, the other four depository institution regulators have often had blurred lines of jurisdiction and responsibilities.

The development of the depository institution regulatory system in the United States is closely linked to the history of the founding of the nation. The first Treasury Secretary, Alexander Hamilton, is known for having established America's first federally chartered bank, which, sadly enough, had to close its door after US Congress refused to renew its charter. The seventh US president, Andrew Jackson, abolished the second federally chartered bank whose constitutionality, though, was confirmed by the Supreme Court of Justice. State-chartered regional banks, however, flourished across the country, despite their lack of even rudimentary internal governance and any form of government regulation. It was during this period that the State of New York started to expand its banking oversight by exercising formal government regulation and implementing reserve requirements. This situation continued all the way until the year 1861 when the American Civil War broke out. Congress passed the National Bank Act of 1863 as part of its effort to fund the Civil War debt and maintain stability in the financial system. This eventually led to the establishment of the dual banking system—still effective to date—in which state banks and national banks are chartered and supervised at different levels. In the post-Civil War period, Congress passed the Federal Reserve Act of 1913, which resulted in the creation of the Federal Reserve System—the US central bank responsible for executing monetary policy and conducting oversight. During the Great Depression in the 1930s, Congress enacted the Glass-Steagall Act as part of the Banking Act of 1933. The Glass-Steagall Act separated commercial and investment banking activities. Following the end of World War II, Congress enacted the Bank Holding Company Act of 1956 as an attempt to prohibit the acquisition of multiple commercial banks under a single holding company structure. The macroeconomic conditions in the 1970s and 1980s, coupled with deregulation, resulted in severe losses on the part of many deposit-accepting and loan-making thrift institutions across the United States. It was in response to this thrift crisis that Congress enacted the Financial Institutions Reform, Recovery and Enforcement Act of 1989. In 1999, Congress passed the Gramm-Leach-Bliley Act, also known as the Financial Modernization Act of 1999, to remove the Glass-Steagall Act's barriers that prohibited any one institution from becoming a combination of an investment bank, a commercial bank, and an insurance company.

(b) Following the Great Depression, Congress enacted a series of legislative acts to beef up regulation on the financial market, which, as best represented by the Glass-Steagall Act, played a crucial role in promoting the stability and development of the US financial system in the following 60 years.

As affiliations between banks, securities firms, and insurance companies were allowed in the 1920s when the US economy experienced a post-World War I rebound, commercial banks poured a tidal wave of cash—deposited by savers—into the stock market operated by investment banks. This predatory practice became one of the direct causes of the 1929 Stock Market Crash and the subsequent Great Depression. The Dow Jones Industrial Average plummeted by 11%, 12.8%, and 11.7% respectively on October 24, 28, and 29 in 1929, and thus began the worst economic catastrophe in US modern history. During the depths of the Great Depression in 1933, the United States recorded a whopping 30% decline of its GDP and an official unemployment rate as high as 25%. It took a good 25 years for the Dow Jones Industrial Average to recover and surpass its pre-collapse high in November 1954.

Following the Great Depression, Congress enacted a series of legislative acts that had significant implications for commercial banking and securities business, most notably the Banking Act of 1933 (more commonly known as the Glass-Steagall Act) and the Securities Act of 1933. The Glass-Steagall Act had two main effects: the creation of the Federal Deposit Insurance Corporation (FDIC) to protect the interests of depositors in commercial banks and the mandatory separation of commercial banking from investment banking. Meanwhile, the Glass-Steagall Act also prohibited the combination of banking, securities, and insurance services under any single financial institution. In the 60 years that followed, the Glass-Steagall Act played a crucial role in maintaining the stability and facilitating the development of the US financial system.

(c) After a long period of financial steadiness, the US government relaxed financial market regulation in response to the changed financial landscape in the 1980s and 1990s. The Gramm-Leach-Bliley Act, enacted in 1999, marked the start of "mixed operation" in the US financial industry, a financial business model that has continued to this day.

During the 1980s when the Reagan administration deregulated the banking industry, significant changes started to take place in the financial service landscape, as indicated by increasingly diverse needs of consumers and investors and by the ever-growing business activities between commercial banks, securities firms, and insurance companies. Against this backdrop, certain financial regulatory provisions were considered irrelevant and obstructive to the development of financial services and the expansion of service providers. For this reason, the US government and legislative branch agencies took steps to amend the Glass-Steagall Act. In 1998, the US government greenlighted the merger of Citicorp with the insurance company Travelers Group to form the conglomerate Citigroup. The Federal Reserve gave Citigroup a temporary waiver in September 1998, because the merger violated the Glass-Steagall Act (specifically the provision that prohibited the combination of banking, securities, and insurances services under one institution) and the Bank Holding Company Act of 1956 that banned affiliations between banks and insurance companies.

In December 1999, President Bill Clinton signed into law the Gramm-Leach Bliley Act (GLB), also called the Financial Services Modernization Act of 1999, to repeal the Glass–Steagall Act's prohibitions on affiliations and management interlocks between banks, securities firms, and insurance companies, thus making it possible for qualifying institutions to participate in commercial banking, securities underwriting and dealing, and insurance underwriting all under one holding company structure.

(d) Objectives and measures of the US government regarding short-term, intermediate-term, and long-term financial regulation

Following the outburst of the financial crisis, there was much rethinking and soul-searching on the part of the US government about the financial regulatory system, which culminated in the proposal and formulation of new measures for regulating banking, securities, futures, and insurance. These new measures were crystalized in the *Blueprint for a Modernized Financial Regulatory Structure* (hereinafter referred to as *The Blueprint*) which was drafted under the leadership of the then US Treasury Secretary Hank Paulson and submitted to Congress in March 2008. Certain contents of *The Blueprint* were later incorporated into the Dodd-Frank Act.

1. Measures for improving short-term regulation

The US Congress works to improve short-term regulation on three fronts: adjusting the financial regulatory structure, create a new federal-level regulatory authority, and strengthen the Federal Reserve's role as a liquidity provider.

The first approach is to reinforce the purposes and functions of the President's Working Group on Financial Markets (PWG), a committee which was created under President Ronald Reagan in 1988 and chaired by the Treasury Secretary to facilitate inter-agency coordination and communication with respect to addressing financial market issues. Specific measures include:

- Incorporating the heads of the Office of the Comptroller of the Currency (OCC), the Federal Deposit Insurance Corporation (FDIC), and the Office of Thrift Supervision (OTS) as new members into the PWG, which previously consisted of the heads of the Treasury Department, the Federal Reserve System, the Securities and Exchange Commission, and the Commodity Futures Trading Commission;
- Reinforcing the PWG as an ongoing financial policy coordination and communication mechanism with respect to mitigating financial market risks, enhancing capital market stability, and promoting consumer and investor protection;
- Establishing an effective mechanism to enable the PWG to issue reports or other documents to the US president.

The second short-term approach is to create the Mortgage Origination Commission (MOC) as a new federal regulatory authority and charge it with setting recommended minimum licensing standards for mortgage brokers, regulating mortgage market participants, and enforcing relevant federal regulatory laws.

The final short-term approach is to strengthen the actions taken by the Federal Reserve during the crisis to inject liquidity into the financial system, including the use of the discount window as a monetary tool for lending to non-depository institutions. Meanwhile, the Federal Reserve must coordinate with the PWG to protect the financial market from potential negative impacts caused by lending to non-depository institutions.

2. Measures for improving intermediate-term regulation

The key objective is to modernize the regulatory structure and make it more applicable to modern financial services sectors (i.e., banking, insurance, securities, and futures) by (1) eliminating the overlaps and duplication in the federal regulatory system and (2) transitioning the federal thrift charter to the national bank charter. Specific measures include:

- Merging the Office of Thrift Supervision with the Office of the Comptroller of the Currency within a two-year period and transitioning the federal thrift charter to the national banking charter, thus removing the need for separate federal regulation of thrifts.
- Strengthening federal regulation of state-level banking by appropriately improving the roles of the Federal Reserve and the Federal Deposit Insurance Corporation (FDIC) in the supervision of state-chartered banks, with the Federal Reserve and the FDIC conducting study and tests on such banks and coming up with regulatory recommendations.
- Creating a mandatory federal charter for certain payment and settlement systems, with the Federal Reserve required to charter, regulate, and supervise any systemically important payment or settlement system.
- Building a federal insurance regulatory system to preempt the existing state-based system and creating an office of national insurance.

- Unifying oversight and regulation of the futures and securities industries through the following specific measures: establishing a self-regulatory regime for securities and futures regulation, merging the Commodity Futures Trading Commission into the Securities and Exchange Commission, and adopting core principles for clearing and exchanges agencies to meet the need for modern market development and to increase the competitiveness of US securities firms in the international market. Meanwhile, the Securities and Exchange Commission is advised to offer recommendations to Congress on expanding the Investment Company Act to permit a new "global" investment company.

3. Measures for improving and optimizing long-term regulation

The overarching objective is to establish a modernized regulatory structure through the following measures:

- Creating a market stability regulator and charging it with managing overall conditions that could impact financial market stability; empowering the Federal Reserve with broader authority regarding market regulation and financial stability maintenance, in addition to its traditional role as a monetary policy implementer and a liquidity provider for the financial system.
- Creating a prudential financial regulator and tasking it with supervising and regulating financial institutions with explicit government guarantees associated with their business operations; establishing a federal insurance guarantee corporation as an insurer for institutions regulated by the prudential financial regulator.
- Creating a business conduct regulator that is responsible for business conduct regulation across all types of financial firms.
- Creating a corporate finance regulator and tasking it with regulating all publicly traded and securities, with detailed responsibilities covering corporate disclosures, corporate governance, accounting and auditing oversight and other similar matters. The Securities and Exchange Commission will continue to perform its functions under this framework.

(e) Improving financial regulation through the enactment of the Dodd-Frank Act

After delving into the causes and characteristics of the 2008 financial crisis, the US government undertook a series of actions to reform and strengthen financial regulation. These actions eventually resulted in the enactment of the Dodd-Frank Wall Street Reform and Consumer Protection Act (commonly known as the Dodd-Frank Act).

In addition to what is mentioned about the Dodd-Frank Act in Section 3 under the rubric "legislative guarantee" for tackling the 2008 financial crisis, this historically significant legislative piece also contains provisions designed to institute the most sweeping overhaul of financial regulation since the subsequent reform that came with the Great Depression in the 1930s, an overhaul that covered the structure of government regulatory agencies, systemic risk prevention, financial segments and products, consumer protection, risk aversion, crisis management, and international cooperation.

- Creating the Financial Stability Oversight Council as a new federal regulator to supervise and regulate the whole US financial system, promote stability in financial markets, identify and prevent systemic threats, and engage in dealing with emerging risks and events that threaten financial system stability.
- Improving the Federal Reserve's abilities to govern itself as well as its monitoring, auditing, and reporting systems; empowering the Federal Reserve with the authority to establish prudential standards for the institutions it supervises.
- Improving financial regulatory standards by introducing the so-called Volcker Rule, which prohibits a bank from owning more than 3% in a hedge fund or private equity fund of the total ownership interest and limits a bank's total investments in such funds to 3% of its Tier 1 capital. Under the Dodd-Frank Act, a financial company is prohibited from combining with another company if the resulting company's liabilities would exceed 10% of the aggregate consolidated liabilities of all financial companies.

- Improving the asset-backed securitization process by requiring securitizers to retain no less than 5% of the credit risk for an asset that is not a qualified residential mortgage.
- Enhancing corporate governance and executive compensation by requiring companies to provide shareholders with a non-binding vote on the compensation of named executive officers at least once every three years and by requiring the decoupling of executive compensation from performance-related incentive mechanisms.

Expanding the scope of the Federal Deposit Insurance Corporation's regulatory power. Under the Dodd-Frank Act, the FDIC is empowered with the responsibility for the orderly liquidation of all systemically important financial institutions. As regards non-FDIC-insured institutions, orderly liquidation processes are established to make clear the losses and responsibilities that should be incurred respectively by shareholders, creditors, management, and potentially involved federal agencies in case of a default.

Reducing competition and overlaps between banking and thrift regulators for higher regulatory efficiency and avoiding duplicated regulation by abolishing the Office of Thrift Supervision and transferring its power over the appropriate holding companies to the Federal Reserve System, state savings associations to the FDIC, and other thrifts to the office of the Comptroller of the Currency.

Establishing the Bureau of Consumer Financial Protection to protect and educate investors and consumers on financial products and services; strengthening the Securities and Exchange Commission's role in supervising and regulating securities firms, listed companies, and credit rating agencies by increasing the SEC's budget and creating two new offices and one new committee under the SEC's jurisdiction, namely the Office of Investor Advocate, the Office of Credit Rating, and the Investor Advisory Committee.

Creating the Federal Insurance Office within the Treasury Department and tasking it with monitoring at the federal level all aspects of the insurance industry and bringing a national voice to the insurance regulatory system that was originally based on state-level regulation.

Giving the Commodity Futures Trading Commission more regulatory power regarding the transactions of securities-based swaps and other derivatives for realizing full oversight of the financial markets and higher transparency in the derivatives market.

Providing the Federal Reserve with an "enhanced role in the supervision of risk management standards for systemically important payment, clearing and settlement activities by financial institutions."

Establishing a private equity fund registration system, in which hedge funds that exceed US$15 billion asset management are required to register under the SEC.

Beefing up regulation of the home mortgage market by establishing national underwriting standards for residential loans, standardizing lending procedures, and preventing mortgage-induced systemic risk.

The financial regulatory reform advocated by the Obama administration was met with challenges and setbacks in the Republican-controlled Congress. The Dodd-Frank Act, in and of itself, also has some deficiencies and questionable aspects. For example, the act makes no specific reference whatsoever to the controversial debate over whether or not to limit the practice of combining banking, securities, and insurance services under any single financial institution; instead, it merely attempts to manage the internal conflict of interests within financial institutions. Thus, it is projectable that the future landscape of the US financial services industry will continue to be dominated by the model of multiple banks, securities firms, and insurance companies operating as independent institutions under one single holding conglomerate.

The Dodd-Frank Act, notwithstanding its apparent deficiencies and shortcomings, will remain a major influencing factor of the development of financial markets for a long period of time to come, in the sense that it has restructured competent federal regulatory agencies and created new agencies to close regulatory gaps and loopholes, thus highly instrumental for strengthening regulation of the financial services industry.

7.4 China Must Anchor Financial Development in Financial Stability

The primary cause of the 2008 international financial crisis can be summed up as follows: large financial holding companies, banks, securities firms, and insurance companies in the United States sank into financial distress—with some of them even forced to the point of collapsing or being acquired—on a scale and scope that produced a substantial, sweeping ripple effect across the global financial landscape.

1. Under the influence of the Federal Reserve's long-standing quantitative easing program, commercial banks and home mortgage institutions implemented excessively easy credit policies with general disregard for risk control.
2. The US financial market was plagued by the rampancy of mortgage-backed bonds and other related derivatives that were based on home assets and bank loans. These derivative products, complex in structures, were traded by securities firms with reckless abandon and without transparency, which resulted in the emergence of bubbles in their pricing and transactional prices. The successive collapse of Lehman Brothers and Bear Stearns—two important Wall Street market makers and subprime mortgage bond dealers—led to the escalation of the financial crisis.
3. US institutions that provided a mixed combination of financial services failed to resolve and avert the conflict of interest between banks (as loan providers), securities firms (as loan securitizers), and insurance companies (as bond purchasers or bond insurers) in the area of subprime mortgage lending.
4. Major buyers of subprime mortgage bonds failed to control investment risk, holding bonds too large in value relative to the size of their total assets. Such buyers included Fannie Mae, Freddie Mac, and insurance companies like American International Group (AIG). After reaching its peak in 2006, the US housing bubble burst and ignited a panic sell-off among property investors, causing subprime mortgage bond prices to take a nosedive and immediately pushing large mortgage bond holders to the brink of insolvency.

5. US credit rating agencies contributed to the bubble of subprime mortgage bonds by giving them high credit ratings without fully and accurately alerting the public on potential risks.
6. The US government's financial deregulation policy and the failure of regulators to fulfill their share of regulatory responsibilities.
7. The evolution and self-adjustment of the financial markets, among other factors.

Mistakes from the 2008 international financial crisis must not be repeated in the future, such as the absence of macro-prudential management, overlooking the systemic risk of shadow banking, inadequate regulation on systemically important financial institutions, lack of arrangements for risk management and orderly liquidation, laxity in financial consumer protection, and so on. And lessons should be learned, particularly proper balance to be needed for national economic and financial development, a rational combination of fiscal, monetary, exchange-rate, and regulatory policies to be in place when it comes to macroeconomic management, dealing with financial risks sooner rather than later by means of strong government intervention wherever and whenever necessary, strengthening the overhaul and regulation of systemically important financial institutions and shadow banks, steering financial institutions toward servicing the real economy and to beef up protection of financial consumers, and so on.

Feasible precautions should be taken against the recurrence of international financial crises, such as establishing a crisis alert mechanism focused on the interaction between macroeconomic policies along with a counter-cyclical financial macro-prudential framework, promoting macroeconomic restructuring at the national level with priority placed on stimulating economic recovery for the short term and optimizing industrial structure and building a full-fledged corporate governance framework for the long term, stabilizing the financial markets by strengthening regulation and formulating effective regulatory measures with respect to systemically important financial institutions, managing international capital flows, taking timely, effective contingency measures, such as establishing an orderly disposal mechanism in the event of potential financial crises, and so on.

Given the above, it is imperative that China anchor financial development in financial stability, promoting rule-based competition and seeking development amid stability. The current priority for China must be to strengthen the positioning of its financial markets while enhancing financial legislation and regulation.

First, great importance must be attached to steering the financial industry toward servicing the real economy. The prerequisite for achieving financial stability is to ensure that the real economy is well served by financial institutions. Sound and solid real economic fundamentals constitute the deepest foundation for financial stability. In recent years, China's real economy has quickened its pace of transformation and upgradation, thus affording limitless possibilities for financial innovation. International finance, FinTech, industrial finance, rural finance, and livelihood finance are converging effectively to drive the socioeconomic transformation and upgradation in China. Against this backdrop, it is of critical importance to give the financial industry a bigger role in expediting China's transformation of economic development patterns by redressing the mismatches between finance and the real economy, such as the financing difficulties facing medium-, small-, and micro-sized enterprises, underdevelopment of rural financial services, inadequate support from the financial industry for high-tech industrialization, industrial-chain integration and value-chain upgradation, financial imbalances among regions, and so on. Concrete steps must be taken to realize the virtuous development of the real economy by enabling it to be better serviced by the financial industry.

Second, more emphasis must be put on consolidating the legal basis for financial stability. A full-fledged legal system is the prerequisite for the fundamental, long-term stability of finance. Efforts should be exerted to explore every possibility of financial innovation, but in ways that suit China's specific national conditions and are compliant with and reflective of the legislative spirit behind finance-related laws. Currently, China is intensifying its rule-making and institutional building efforts with respect to finance, such as stepping up regulation and standardization of financial institutions, clamping down on illicit financial activities, and establishing a credit inquiry system, all with a view to providing solid institutional guarantee for financial experimentation.

Third, more priority must be given to improving the financial regulatory structure. A full-fledged regulatory organizational structure, coupled with a long-term regulatory mechanism, forms the basic guarantee for properly managing and diffusing financial risks. When it comes to conducting financial reform and innovation, China must lay stress on perfecting its financial regulatory structure, so that financial innovation is well predicated on comprehensive, standardized, rational regulation and oversight. Specifically, China can, on the basis of a national financial coordination mechanism and auxiliary regulatory bodies, set up mechanisms for task coordination, information sharing, and joint disposal with respect to financial stability, so as to achieve cross-departmental management of overlapping financial activities, major financial risks, and fundamental problems threatening financial stability. Equally important is the need to reinforce regulatory awareness and duties, establish regulatory bodies with relatively strong capabilities in crisis and risk management, and step up regulation and oversight of quasi-financial institutions and over-the-counter markets. A multi-dimensional system must be built to monitor, assess, and warn of financial risks, so as to make sure that financial risks are detected in time and nipped in the bud.

Fourth, greater attention must be paid to enhance the self-management capacity of financial market entities. Enhancing the self-management capacity of China's financial institutions, systemically important ones in particular, is conducive to stimulating the innovative vitality of financial entities and critical for promoting financial stability in China. Deepening the reform of financial institutions—such as by conducting "stress tests" and requiring "living wills"—must be placed at the top of the priority list of overall financial reform and innovation. This requires China to work on three fronts:

- Empowering systemically important financial institutions to develop industry-leading competitiveness and risk management capabilities by enhancing corporate governance, innovating operational models, and implementing business differentiation strategies.
- Cultivating innovative financial institutions that can contribute to refining labor specialization and strengthening financial markets' overall innovative capabilities and resilience to risks.

- Reducing inappropriate government intervention in financial institutions and enabling them to grow and expand amid competition as market-based entities in the real sense.

Fifth, great stress must be laid on developing marketized mechanisms for responding to and managing financial risks. Such marketized mechanisms include risk sharing mechanisms between shareholders and creditors, executive accountability systems, deposit insurance systems, programs for the recovery and disposal of systemically important financial institutions, government assistance management and exit mechanisms, and so on. These mechanisms combine to become a flexible, resilient web-like network for risk absorption and mitigation, capable of guarding against the proliferation and amplification of financial risks. Such a network forms the basis for reducing the costs and improving the efficiency of risk management and diffusion. The establishment of a set of highly efficient and marketized mechanisms for risk diffusion makes it possible to nip in the bud any risk derived from financial reform and innovation. In order to promote steady financial reform and innovation, it is important for China to explore the possibility of setting up marketized risk response and diffusion mechanisms that are suited to China's actual conditions and engage government, the central bank, and regulatory departments at all levels.

Sixth, the protection of small and medium investors must receive a higher priority. Protecting the interest of small and medium investors is one of the basic requisites for keeping financial markets stable and sustainable. It also holds the key to preventing and resolving financial risks. When it comes to advancing financial reform and innovation, it is imperative to strike a balance between promoting the development of the financial industry and protecting small and medium investors; it is prohibited to create false prosperity at the expense of small and medium investors' interest. China must explore the possibility of devising government- and regulator-led supervisory measures for protecting investors of new financial products and services. China must also seek the possibility of setting up specialized rights protection organizations for financial consumers. Equally important is the need to strengthen self-discipline in the financial industry and enhance mechanisms for compliant, supervision, and financial dispute arbitration, so that channels remain open for financial consumers to have their disputes settled. Meanwhile, industry-wide reviews and discussions must be encouraged to increase the standardization and transparency of financial products and services.

In conclusion, it is imperative for China to conscientiously review and make good sense of financial fragility, its mutually constraining relationship with financial liberalization and the very pernicious impacts of financial risks and crises on a nation. With this awareness in mind, China needs to take a multi-pronged approach toward the prevention, management, and diffusion of financial risks.

8

Innovation and Improvement of the International Financial Architecture—China's Plan for Engagement in International Finance

As elaborated in Chap. 1, a modern financial architecture must encompass six key building blocks: a modern financial market system, a modern financial organizational system, a modern financial legal system, a modern financial regulatory system, a modern financial environment system, and modern financial infrastructures. In this chapter, given the actual developments of finance in the world, it is best that we analyze, ponder, and examine the present and future of the international financial architecture as well as the necessity of restructuring it by focusing on these three respects: the structure of international financial institutions, international financial infrastructures, and international financial regulation and management.

8.1 The Structure of International Financial Institutions

Broadly speaking, financial institutions are grouped into three categories: commercial, regulatory, and policy institutions. As things stand today, the existing international financial institutions, however, can be referred to more as operational or operational coordinating institutions than as commercial, regulatory, or policy institutions.

(a) The Bank for International Settlements (BIS)

The Bank for International Settlements (BIS) is a syndicate consisting of central banks from the UK, France, Germany, Italy, Belgium, and Japan, and of J.P. Morgan and Citigroup to represent the interests of the US banking community. It was established under the law of Switzerland in May 1930, and its headquarters are based in Basel, Switzerland.

The BIS was originally intended to facilitate the payments of reparations imposed on Germany by the Treaty of Versailles after World War I and to deal with related settlement matters. After World War II, the BIS acted as a clearing institution for members of the Organization for Economic Co-operation and Development (OECD), and the bank's mission also changed with the change of its role, which was to foster cooperation between central banks, facilitate international financial operations, and serve as an agent or trustee in connection with international financial settlements. The BIS is neither an intergovernmental institution for financial decision making nor a development assistance institution. It has become, in effect, a bank for central banks.

The BIS receives its funding primarily from three sources. The first is share capital paid by its central bank members. The bank was founded with authorized capital (also called registered capital) of 500 million gold francs in 1930, which increased to 1.5 billion gold francs in 1969. After that, the bank floated its shares several times. As it stands today, 80% of the bank's shares are owned by central bank members and the remaining 20% by private holders. The second is borrowing. The BIS can borrow from its central bank members to replenish its pool of capital. The third is deposits. The BIS accepts gold deposits from central banks and deposits from commercial banks.

The BIS's scope of business includes: (1) dealing with international financial settlements; (2) serving as an agent or trustee in connection with banking activities; (3) hosting on a regular basis international central bankers' conferences to discuss about international financial cooperation, carry out research on issues of relevance for monetary and financial stability, provide financial services to central banks, and facilitate the implementation of all types of international financial agreements.

The BIS was born with 500 million gold francs in seed capital that was divided into 200,000 shares, with each share worth 2500 gold francs. These shares were subscribed for equally by six central banks and the American banking group. In December 1969, the BIS amended its constituent charter and changed its mission into fostering cooperation among central banks in international financial settlements, facilitating international financial operations, and serving as an agent or trustee in connection with international financial settlements. The bank's capital was increased to 1.5 billion gold francs accordingly and divided into 600,000 shares, 2500 gold francs for each share. A total of 80% of the shares were owned by its central bank members, while the remaining 20% were sold through central banks to private investors who, nevertheless, were not entitled to attend the shareholders' meeting. It had 32 members including 26 central banks from Europe, 5 central banks from Canada, Australia, Japan, Turkey, and South Africa respectively and J.P. Morgan acting in the interest of the United States. In September 1996, the BIS decided to induct into its membership nine new members, which were either central banks or institutions exercising central banking functions from the People's Republic of China, India, the Republic of Korea, Singapore, Brazil, Mexico, Russia, Saudi Arabia, and Hong Kong. This represented the first attempt of the BIS to welcome new members into its membership within a 25-year period. As it stands today, the BIS's membership consists of 45 members, a marked increase from 7 members at the time of its founding.

IMF was created in Washington, D.C., on December 27, 1945, under the *International Monetary Fund Agreement* which was signed at the Bretton Woods Conference in July, 1944. Established concurrently, the IMF and the World Bank are on a par with each other as the world's two predominant financial institutions. Headquartered in Washington, D.C., the IMF is working to oversee the exchange rate arrangements and trade between countries, provide technical and financial assistance to its members, and facilitate the smooth operation of the global financial system.

The mandate of the IMF is to promote international monetary cooperation and facilitate consultation and collaboration on international monetary issues; to ensure the expansion and balanced development of international trade, thus promoting and supporting employment, actual income growth and the development of productive resources in its member countries; to stabilize international exchange rates by maintaining orderly exchange rate arrangements and avoiding competitive exchange rate devaluation between its members.

The primary functions of the IMF are: (1) to formulate and oversee exchange rate policies between its members as well as rules with respect to current account payments and currency convertibility; (2) to provide emergency liquidity assistance to members with balance of payments problems whenever necessary, thus protecting other members from potentially damaging effects; (3) to provide a forum for member countries to conduct international monetary cooperation and consultation; (4) to promote international cooperation in connection with financial and monetary matters; (5) to accelerate the pace of international economic integration; (6) to maintain orderly international exchange rates; (7) to assist member countries in establishing regular multilateral payment systems.

The organization is made up of 189 countries, with the Board of Governors as its highest decision-making body. The Board of Governors consists of one governor and one alternate governor for each member country. Each member country appoints its two governors, usually the minister of finance or the head of the central bank. The Board of Governors meets once a year, customarily in September, with each individual governor exercising the voting power of his or her representing country. A member country's voting power is largely determined by its IMF quota or, to put it in another way, the size of its subscription to the organization.

The funding of the IMF comes from the members' subscriptions to the IMF capital. In 1969, the IMF created special drawing rights (SDRs). Also called "Paper Gold," SDRs constitute a world reserve asset and a unit of account for the IMF. They are allocated by the IMF to member countries for them to use the fund's resources. Specifically, when a member country is running an international current account deficit, it can transfer its allocated SDRs to other IMF-designated member countries in exchange for foreign currency reserves that it needs to pay for its current account deficit or IMF loans. SDRs can also serve as an international reserve asset the same way as gold and other freely convertible currencies do. Technically, the SDRs are not a currency per se, but a unit of account, and thus have to be exchanged into a currency before use. To put it in another way, the SDRs cannot be used directly to pay for trading or non-trading transactions. The SDRs are so named because they are a supplement to the IMF's ordinary drawing rights.

On November 30, 2015, the IMF decided to include the Chinese renminbi (RMB) into its SDR basket valuation formula. As a result, the SDR basket weights were readjusted as follows: US dollar, 41.73%; Euro, 30.93%; Chinese renminbi, 10.92%; Japanese yen, 8.33%; Pound sterling, 8.09%. On January 27, 2016, the IMF announced that the 2010 IMF Quota and Governance Reform officially became effective, making China the third-largest shareholder of the organization. Subsequently, China's quota share in the IMF soared from 3.996% to 6.394%, enabling the country to leap from the sixth-largest to the third-largest shareholder in the club after the United States and Japan. On March 4th, 2016, the IMF announced that it would separately identify RMB-denominated assets in its official foreign reserve database as of October 1, 2016, with a view to reflecting its members' holdings of RMB-denominated foreign exchange reserves.

The IMF, notwithstanding its positive role, has its own institutional flaws, including: (1) structure-wise, the IMF is primarily controlled by the United States and the European Union; (2) according to how the IMF's quota shares and voting rights are distributed, the United States has veto power over major decisions within the organization; (3) the IMF has a track record of going out of its way to defend the US dollar's position as the dominant international reserve currency; (4) the IMF is not adequate in its abilities to adjust balances of payments, thus resulting in a severely imbalanced balance of payments globally.

The World Bank Group is a family of five multilateral institutions engaged in various economic development activities, namely the International Bank for Reconstruction and Development (IBRD), the International Development Association (IDA), the International Finance

Corporation (IFC), the Multilateral Investment Guarantee Agency (MIGA), and the International Center for Settlement of Investment Disputes (ICSID). Created in 1945, the World Bank Group started its business in June 1946. Headquartered in Washington, D.C., the group has more than 10,000 employees in more than 120 offices worldwide. By custom, the Bank President has always been a US citizen nominated by the president of the United States, serving a five-year, renewable term.

The five institutions in the family of the World Bank Group are as follows:

(a) The International Bank for Reconstruction and Development (IBRD). Established in 1945, the IBRD provides loans to middle-income countries and low-income countries with good credit ratings.
(b) The International Finance Corporation (IFC). Created in 1956, the IFC is the world's largest development institution that focuses exclusively on the private sector. It offers investment, advisory, and asset management services for both enterprises and governments to help developing countries achieve sustainable growth.
(c) The International Development Association (IDA). Established in 1960, the IDA offers concessional loans (also called interest-free loans) and grants to the world's poorest developing countries.
(d) The Multilateral Investment Guarantee Agency (MIGA). The MIGA was established in 1988 to promote foreign direct investment in developing countries for economic growth, poverty reduction, and livelihood improvement. It fulfills its mission by providing political risk insurance and credit enhancement guarantees to investors and lenders.
(e) The International Center for Settlement of Investment Disputes (ICSID). The ICSID is an international arbitration institution established in 1966 to resolve legal disputes and facilitate conciliation between international investors.

One thing to note is that people usually speak of the World Bank Group in narrow terms, erroneously equating it with the World Bank, which only consists of the IBRD and the IDA.

The mandate of the World Bank is: to help reconstruct and rejuvenate its members by investing in production activities and to encourage the development of resources in underdeveloped countries; to promote private sector investment by providing guarantees or participating in private lending or other facilities for private investment. When a member country finds itself unable to acquire private investment under reasonable conditions, it can use the bank's own capital or raised capital to compensate for the lack of private investment; to encourage international investment, assist member countries in improving productivity, promote the balanced development of international trade between member countries, and enhance international balances of payments; to coordinate with other international lenders when providing loan guarantees. The functions of the World Bank are focused on providing financial products and services, sharing innovative knowledge, lending, non-lending assistance, multilateral cooperation, and coordinating positions of its members. The sources of capital resources for the World Bank include: the members' subscriptions to the bank's capital; loans from international financial markets; issuance of bonds and interest income on lending.

The World Bank was created under the shareholding principle. The Bank's initial authorized capital was US$10 billion, which was divided in 100,000 shares, with each share worth US$100000. Every member country is required to subscribe for the Bank's shares, and the number of shares to be subscribed is determined through consultation between the subscribing member and the Bank and subject to approval by the Board of Governors. Generally speaking, the number of shares to be subscribed by a member country of the Bank is commensurate with its economic power and the size of its subscription to the IMF.

Important matters of the World Bank are put to a vote by member countries, with each member having voting power that is positively correlated with the number of shares it has subscribed for. Each new Bank member country is allotted 250 votes, plus one additional vote for each share it holds in the Bank's capital stock. Given that it holds most shares in the Bank's capital stock, the United States has the most voting power with 226,178 votes, or 17.37% of the Bank's total votes. Thus, it is fair to say that the United States has a very important say over the Bank's business and major lending projects. After the World Bank completed its second-phase voting power reform in 2010, the five largest shareholders of the IBRD are as follows: the US (15.85%), Japan (6.84%), China (4.42%), Germany (4.00%), France (3.75%), and the UK (3.75%). China has become the third largest shareholder of the World Bank, with its percentage in the Bank's total voting power increased from 2.77% to 4.42%.

The relationship between the World Bank and the IMF. A country has to be a member of the IMF to become a member of the World Bank, but an IMF member does not necessarily need to join the World Bank. The IMF and World Bank collaborate regularly and at many levels to assist member countries. Mainly responsible for matters of relevance to international monetary business, the IMF works to eliminate foreign exchange restrictions, promote foreign exchange stability, and facilitate the expansion of international trade by providing short-term foreign currency loans to member countries with balance of payments problems. The World Bank promotes long-term economic recovery and development by providing medium- and long-term loans to member countries.

Much of the international criticism of the World Bank centers around it being influenced by some countries—in particular the United States—and thus adopting policies that tilt in their favor. Major regional international financial institutions include the Inter-American Development Bank (IADB), the European Investment Bank, the Asian Development Bank, the European Bank for Reconstruction and Development, the African Development Bank, the Caribbean Development Bank, and the Arab Monetary Fund. The Inter-American Development Bank (IADB), founded on December 30, 1959, is the earliest and largest regional multilateral development bank in the world, with its headquarters based in Washington, D.C. The mandate of the IADB is to pool together the strengths of its member states and promote economic and social development projects in Latin America and the Caribbean by providing financing and technical assistance, thus enabling them to make individual and collective contribution to the acceleration of economic development and social progress. Though as a specialized organization for Latin American and Caribbean countries, the IADB also opens its membership to countries from other regions. Non-Latin-American members, however, are not allowed to use the bank's funds and can only participate in biddings organized by the bank.

The Asian Development Bank (ADB) is a regional development bank established on November 24th, 1966, with its headquarters based in Metro Manila, Philippines. The bank defines itself as a social development organization dedicated to reducing poverty in Asia and the Pacific through inclusive economic growth, environmentally sustainable growth, and regional integration. In order to realize its vision of a poverty-free Asian and Pacific region, the ADB provides assistance to its developing members, which takes four forms: lending, equity investment, technical assistance, and co-financing guarantee. The bank supports the development of its members in infrastructure, energy, environmental protection, education, and health care services through policy dialogues, technical assistance, and investments in the form of loans, grants, and guarantees.

The African Development Bank (AFDB) is a regional multilateral development bank established in 1964 and headquartered in Abidjan, the economic center of Côte d'Ivoire. As the largest intergovernmental development-oriented financial institution in Africa, the AFDB works to promote the socio-economic advancement of its African members. The Arab Monetary Fund (AMF) is a regional Arab organization, a working sub-organization of the Arab League. It was founded in April 1977 and is based in Abu Dhabi, the capital of the United Arab Emirates. It is a regional multilateral financial institution dedicated to correct and balance the payments of Arab, Islamic countries and promote the integration of the Arab economies. The Arab Monetary Fund's main purposes are to provide financial assistance to member countries with balance of payments difficulties, offer preferential loans to member countries with fiscal deficit, enable all members to achieve balanced socio-economic development, increase the sources of fiscal revenue for Arab countries, and realize Arab economic integration.

The Asian Infrastructure Investment Bank (AIIB). The AIIB is a multilateral intergovernmental development bank that aims to support the building of infrastructure in the Asia-Pacific region. The purposes of the AIIB are to promote the interconnectivity of infrastructure development and economic integration in the Asia-Pacific and strengthen China's cooperation with other countries and regions in Asia. Headquartered in

Beijing, the AIIB constitutes the first multilateral financial institution ever created under China's proposal. The initial authorized capital of the AIIB is US$100 billion. The bank was officially inaugurated on December 25th, 2015. The board of governors of the bank convened its inaugural meeting in Beijing between January 16th and 18th, 2016, in which the bank was declared open for business. The bank's governance structure is composed of the Board of Governors, the Board of Directors, and the Senior Management Team. As the bank's top-level and highest decision-making body, the Board of Governors consists of one governor and one alternate governor appointed by each member country. The Board of Directors consists of 12 governors, nine from members within the Asia-Pacific region and three from members outside the region. The senior management team includes the president, the five vice presidents, and the general counsel.

The main functions of the AIIB include: (1) to promote investment in the region of public and private capital for development purposes, in particular for development of infrastructure and other productive sectors; (2) to utilize the resources at its disposal for financing such development in the region, including those projects and programs which will contribute most effectively to the harmonious economic growth of the region as a whole and having special regard to the needs of less developed members in the region; (3) to encourage private investment in projects, enterprises, and activities contributing to economic development in the region, in particular in infrastructure and other productive sectors, and to supplement private investment when private capital is not available on reasonable terms and conditions; (4) to undertake such other activities and provide such other services as may further these functions.

The establishment of the AIIB is significant, not just for China and Asia but for the world at large. As far as China is concerned, the establishment of the AIIB has ushered China into a "new era." China has become the third largest outbound investor in the world; its outbound investment reached a record high in 2012, amounting to US$ 87.8 billion, a year-by-year increase of 17.6%. According to the statistics released by the Ministry of Commerce, the National Statistics Bureau, and the State Foreign Exchange Administration in September 12, 2019, China's direct foreign investment amounted to US$ 143 billion, totaling US$ 1.98

trillion, 66.3 times that of 2002, through over 30 years of development and accumulation. China has formed a full-fledged industrial chain in infrastructural equipment manufacturing and has evolved into a global leader in the construction of infrastructural facilities like highways, bridges, tunnels, and rail lines. Under such circumstances, it is only natural that Chinese companies involved in infrastructural development are looking to go global at a faster pace. They, however, are facing difficulties on several fronts, including the inability of Asian economies to tap into their large reservoirs of savings, a lack of effective mechanisms for multilateral cooperation, and a shortage of investment necessary to translate capital into infrastructural projects. The AIIB can, to a great extent, help to clear these bottlenecks for China and Chinese companies.

From the perspective of the whole of Asia, the establishment of the AIIB can help address the infrastructural backwardness of the continent. Home to 60% of the world's population, Asia accounts for one third of global economic output and is the most economically vibrant and promising region in the world. Due to insufficient infrastructure funds, some Asian countries, however, have long been plagued by a severe lack of infrastructures—including rail lines, highways, bridges, ports, airports, and telecommunications facilities. This, to some extent, has become a salient impediment to the economic development of the region.

From the global perspective, the establishment of the AIIB signals the staggering rise of emerging economies in Asia. The 2008 financial crisis has plunged developed countries into a protracted economic slump. Emerging economies, as represented by China, have moved out of the shadow of the financial crisis, becoming not only new drivers of the global economy but also major actors in global governance. Thus, the reform of unfair and irrational international financial mechanisms must be placed on top of the world's agenda in order for emerging countries to play a bigger, better role in global economic and financial governance.

The New Development Bank (NDB), formerly referred to as the BRICS Development Bank, is a multilateral development bank proposed in 2012 and declared open for business on July 21, 2015. The bank is headquartered in Shanghai, China. The international financial market experienced volatility of capital flows in the wake of the 2008 international financial crisis, primarily as a result of the changes in financial policies in the United States. This produced significant impacts on the stability of the value of currencies in emerging markets. The Chinese renminbi fluctuated in a narrow range, but its counterparts in other major emerging economies suffered massive devaluation, which eventually led to hovering inflation.

Given the lack of timeliness and intensity regarding IMF assistance, the BRICS countries planned to build a reserve currency pool as a shared financial safety net to avoid currency instability in the event of future financial crises. The goal of the pool is to give BRICS member states opportunity to provide each other financial assistance in case of problems with their balance of payments.

It was against this backdrop that BRICS countries, led by China, proposed the idea of setting up the New Development Bank and the BRICS Contingency Reserve Arrangement. The initial authorized capital of the New Development Bank is US$100 billion. The initial subscribed capital of the bank was equally distributed among the founding members. The BRICS Contingency Reserve Arrangement (CRA) is a mechanism for the provision of support to BRICS countries in response to actual or potential short-term balance of payments pressures. It is an assistance mechanism rather than a profit-making mechanism. The capital of the CRA is US$100 billion and is used to assist BRICS countries in dealing with financial contingencies. Contributions to the fund are as follows: China, US$41 billion; Russia, US$18 billion; Brazil, US$18 billion; India, US$18 billion; South Africa, US$5 billion.

The New Development Bank (NDB) is intended primarily to support the building of infrastructure in the BRICS countries and other developing countries through "loans, guarantees, equity participation and other financial instruments." Given the huge gap of infrastructure development in Brazil, South Africa, Russia, and India, there is a remarkable need for these countries to work together in infrastructure financing, especially when they find themselves financially squeezed. The NDB provides financial support not only to the five BRICS members, but also to all developing countries. BRICS members, however, enjoy priority when it comes to getting loans from the bank. The NDB has opened up new possibilities for China's cooperation with other BRICS countries. As an exemplary of financial cooperation among BRICS members, the NDB will continue to explore new areas of BRICS cooperation. Meanwhile, the NDB also represents new steps by BRICS countries toward international financial cooperation.

A review of history reveals a clear evolutionary timeline and structure of the international financial institutions system. Three observations can be made. First, the existing international financial institutions system is still built, by and large, on the framework established after World War II. Second, the United States plays a predominant role in the formation of the system. Third, practically all of such international financial institutions are products of post-World War II reconstruction efforts, except the European Bank for Reconstruction and Development (EBRD), created in 1991, the Asian Infrastructure Investment Bank (AIIB), and the New Development Bank, both created in 2015. On the one hand, these international financial institutions continue to play a positive role in promoting the development of global and regional economies; on the other hand, as these institutions have been and will continue to be dominated by a small fraction of countries, the economic needs and suggestions of most developing countries often go unanswered and unheeded. Consequently, the voices for reforming and improving the international financial institutions system are growing stronger with each passing day.

8.2 International Financial Infrastructure

Why is there the need to analyze "international financial infrastructures?" This is because they are both a prerequisite for the effective operation of the international financial system and a critical factor for realizing safe trading, risk hedging, and information acquisition in international finance.

Trading in international financial markets is divided into two categories: on-exchange trading and over-the-counter (OTC) trading (also called off-exchange trading). Relevant procedures of all transactions—whether conducted on exchange or over the counter—are transmitted to post-trade infrastructures, otherwise known as financial market infrastructures (FMIs). This explains the importance of analyzing financial infrastructures.

In a narrow sense, international financial infrastructures refer to critically important institutions (typically central banks) responsible for providing clearing and settlement of monetary and other financial transactions. In a broad sense, international financial infrastructures include legal procedures, accounting and auditing systems, credit ratings and financial standards, trading rules, and other services critical to the smooth, effective functioning of international financial markets. The basic framework consists of important payment systems, trust systems, clearing systems, counterparties, and trading databases.

8.2.1 Payment and Clearing Systems (On-Exchange Trading)

A payment and clearing system, also called a payment system, refers to a type of financial arrangements for the liquidation of financial claims and obligations and the transfer of funds. It usually consists of intermediaries that provide payment and clearing services and special technical methods for transferring payment instructions and for clearing funds. An international payment and clearing system comprises of five basic elements, that is, a payer, a payer's deposit bank, a clearing house, a payee's deposit bank, and a payee.

The Committee on Payment and Settlement Systems (CPSS) is a forum housed within the Bank for International Settlements (BIS) that allows central banks to monitor and analyze developments in payment, clearing, and settlement systems. The overarching principle for international clearing or cross-border payment is when a payment is made for floating commercial paper—whether in the importer's currency, the exporter's currency, or a third-party's currency—both the drawer and drawee can be any individual or company anywhere in the world, but the payer or whoever assumes the payer's role must be a bank affiliated with the paying currency's clearing center. One can complete a cross-border payment by opening a foreign currency deposit account in the currency's issuing and clearing center.

In reality, international payment and clearing systems can be grouped into three categories according to operator identities: (1) those owned and operated by central banks; (2) those owned and operated by private clearing houses; (3) intra-bank payment systems owned and operated by banks. They can be divided into two categories if grouped according to service objects and the value per payment: high-value payment systems and bulk electronic payment systems. If grouped according to areas of services, they fall into two categories, namely, domestic payment systems and international payment systems.

As of today, the US dollar still remains the dominant means of clearing payments in the international financial system. Broadly speaking, the US payment and clearing network consists of the two payment systems, namely Fedwire and CHIPS. Fedwire is a real-time gross settlement funds and securities transfer system operated by the United States Federal Reserve Banks. It allows financial institutions to send and receive funds in US dollar anywhere in the country through accounts at their local Federal Reserve Banks. The Fedwire system has two components: Fedwire Funds Transfer Service and Fedwire Book-Entry Securities Service. There are three things to note about Fedwire. Fedwire is used primarily to provide interbank overnight loans, settle commercial payments, settle positions between banks, buy and sell securities. Fedwire payment messages are sent over a communications network that links the 12 Federal Reserve Banks and the financial institutions holding accounts at the Federal Reserve System. Payment messages from financial institutions are transmitted to the host computer systems of local Reserve Banks to be processed. Over 70% of participants—accounting for 99% of the Fedwire business—in the Fedwire system are linked electronically to the Federal Reserve System.

Created in 1970, the Clearing House Interbank Payment System (CHIPS) is one of the largest private payment and clearing systems in the world. Owned and operated by the New York Clearing House Association, CHIPS is primarily used to make large-value domestic and international USD payments. As of today, CHIPS settles well over US$1.9 trillion a day in more than 340,000 interbank payments in around 95% of international USD transactions. There are four other things to note about CHIPS: (1) Participant users: CHIPS currently has 47 member participants that have set up deposit accounts at Federal Reserve Banks and are allowed to directly use the CHIPS system to transfer funds; (2)

Non-participant users: A non-participant wishing to make international payments using CHIPS is required to employ one of the CHIPS participants to act as its correspondent or agent; (3) CHIPS participants may be New York-based commercial banks, Edge Act corporations, investment companies, and foreign banks with a branch or an agency in New York City; and (4) CHIPS participants are also required to file copies of their annual financial statements with, and are subject to a periodic credit review by, the CHIPCo board.

As the world's largest privately operated payment system, CHIPS must deal with risks associated with payment and clearing activities, including credit risk (the potential that a bank borrower or counterparty will fail to meet its obligations as per agreed terms), operational risk (the prospect of a payment instruction to a receiver being overruled), liquidity risk (the potential of a payment instruction failing to be executed due to a lack of funds), and other types of risk with respect to international clearing. As such, CHIPS and other private bulk electronic payment systems are required by the Federal Reserve to ensure the smooth running of clearing procedures.

Major international payment and clearing systems outside of the United States include TARGET2, CIPS, SIC, CHAPS, BOJ-NET, CHATS, and so on.

The Trans-European Automated Real-time Gross Express Transfer System (TARGET2) is a real-time gross settlement (RTGS) system that exemplifies the integration of European payment systems after the launch of the Euro single currency. Officially incepted on January 1, 1999, TARGET2 links the RTGS systems in all 24 participating EU member states and operates for 11 hours every business day from 07:00 to 18:00 (Frankfurt time). Of course, besides TARGET2, there exist five other payment and clearing systems in Europe to clear cross-border transfers between commercial banks in the Eurozone and their counterparts around the world.

The Cross-border Interbank Payment System or CIPS is a payment system which offers clearing and settlement services in cross-border RMB payments and trade. Officially incepted on October 8th, 2015, CIPS constitutes a modernized payment system that has integrated existing channels and resources for RMB cross-border payments, intended primarily to improve the efficiency and security in settling RMB cross-border transactions and meet the growing demand for RMB-denominated transactions in the world's major time zones. Given that renminbi has become the fourth largest payment currency and the second largest trading currency worldwide, there is an objective imperative to enhance the RMB global clearing services system by building an independent RMB cross-border payment system. CIPS is designed to be developed into two phases. In Phase One, CIPS adopts a real-time gross settlement mechanism to facilitate processing of cross-border RMB business and supports settlement of cross-border trade in goods and services, cross-border direct investment, and financing activities. In Phase Two, CIPS will adopt a mixed settlement model—which will be more efficient in the use of liquidity—to boost efficiency in settling and clearing RMB cross-border and offshore transactions. In this way, CIPS will be able to provide safe, stable, and efficient support for the cross-border use of RMB in various areas, including the settlement of RMB-denominated cross-border trade and investment, the settlement of domestic money market transactions, and the simultaneous reception and payment of renminbi and other currencies. The first batch of direct participants in CIPS includes 19 banks. In addition, 38 domestic banks and 138 overseas banks located in Asia, Europe, Oceania, and Africa have participated in the system as indirect participants.

Swiss Interbank Clearing (SIC) is a real-time gross settlement (RTGS) system designed to execute interbank payments in Swiss francs finally and irrevocably 24 hours a day with funds held at the Swiss National Bank (SNB). SIC is the only electronic central payment system in Switzerland. It is a gross payment system, which means that all payments are settled individually in the participants' accounts. SIC is both a large-value payment system and a retail payment system, with no value limits. Since 1987, the SIC system has been operated by SIX Interbank Clearing AG on behalf of the Swiss National Bank.

The Clearing House Automated Payment System or CHAPS is a British payment system that is currently used by 20 direct-participant banks (including the Bank of England) to transfer cleared sterling funds. Other non-participant commercial banks can also transfer sterling funds through CHPAS via a direct-participant bank. Non-participant banks are required to open an account at a direct-participant bank for balance transfers. The final balances among direct-participant banks are transferred via their accounts at the Bank of England. CHAPS is not a centrally managed system, with all participants required to act in accordance with agreed terms. All direct participants are also required to keep their transfer channels open during prescribed opening time. Once an electronic payment is made and the funds are received by the CHAPS channels, the issuing bank must pay to the designated direct-participant bank even if the payment instruction is immediately confirmed wrong.

The Bank of Japan Financial Network System (BOJ-NET), launched into operation in October 1988, is a real-time gross settlement system managed by the Bank of Japan. It is a completely computerized nationwide system, primarily used by financial institutions including the Bank of Japan for payments for money market transactions and government bond transactions. Financial institutions are required to open an account at the Bank of Japan in order to directly use the BOJ-NET system. BOJ-NET participants include banks, securities firms, short-term loan agents, and foreign banks and securities firms with offices in Japan. The system processes inter-institutional transfers of funds in connection with money market transactions, securities transactions, and the transfer of funds within the same financial institution, settle positions in private payment and clearing systems, and facilitate fund transfers between financial institutions and the Bank of Japan (including treasury funds transfer).

The Clearing House Automated Transfer System or CHATS is a real-time gross settlement (RTGS) system for the transfer of funds in Hong Kong. With 13 participants including Bank of China (Hong Kong) limited, the system can be used to achieve fast and easy transfers of funds in four currencies: Hong Kong dollar, US dollar, Euro, and RMB.

8.2.2 Central Counterparty Clearing and Transaction Register (OTC Transactions)

Central counterparty clearing (CCP), also referred to as a central counterparty, is a central clearing institution for over-the-counter (OTC) transactions of financial derivatives. As things stand today, there are two parallel systems for clearing and settling financial derivative transactions: bilateral clearing and central counterparty clearing. Transaction registers (TRs) are used to provide information to regulators, market actors, and the general public, thus increasing the transparency of OTC derivatives markets.

What follow are two international organizations that provide central counterparty clearing services and transaction registers. The Society for Worldwide Interbank Financial Telecommunications (SWIFT) is an international non-profit, interbank cooperative founded in 1973 and headquartered in Brussels, Belgium. SWIFT runs its secure messaging network from three data centers—one in New York, United States, one in Amsterdam, the Netherlands, and one in a secret location known only by a restricted number of employees for security reasons. SWIFT consists of national data concentration centers that are connected to each other via leased telephone lines. A key mandate of SWIFT is to provide fast, accurate, and excellent services to financial institutions worldwide.

As of today, the vast majority of banks in most countries and territories have been linked to the SWIFT network. The use of the SWIFT network has resulted in a huge increase of the speed at which banks worldwide settle and clear payment transactions, because it enables them to send and receive information in a secure, reliable, fast, standardized, and automated environment. It was in 1987 that non-bank financial institutions—including stock brokers, investment firms, securities firms, and stock exchanges—started to use the SWIFT network. As of 2010, the SWIFT network covered more than 8000 financial institutions in 206 countries and territories, providing secure financial message transmission services and interface services. It has also linked real-time gross settlement systems in over 80 countries and territories.

Broadly speaking, SWIFT provides four types of services: (1) interfaces; (2) financial information transmission; (3) transaction processing, which means processing transactions for foreign exchange brokerages, currency markets, and financial derivatives certification organizations through SWIFT's IP network infrastructure known as SWIFTNet; (4) analytical services and tools, which in specific terms include financial data transmission, file transmission, Straight Through Process (STP), netting settlement, netting delivery, operational information services, software services, certification technology services, client training, round-the-clock technical support, and so on. Since its operation, SWIFT has been providing a full-fledged set of efficient, reliable, low-cost services, thus playing a positive role in boosting global trade, facilitating the circulation of currencies worldwide, expediting international financial settlement, and promoting financial modernization and standardization internationally.

The Committee on Payment and Settlement Systems (CPSS)—now known as the Committee on Payments and Market Infrastructures (CPMI)—is hosted by the Bank for International Settlements (BIS) in Basel. By providing a platform of communication, the CPSS enables its member central banks to study, monitor and analyze developments in payment, clearing and settlement systems and cross-border multi-currency settlement mechanisms. The CPSS is committed to the reform and development of payment and settlement systems. It also works to build stable, efficient payment and settlement systems and strengthen global financial market infrastructures.

The CPSS undertakes specific studies and publishes reports on its findings, which relate to high-value fund transfer systems, securities settlement systems, foreign exchange trading settlement arrangements, OTC derivatives clearing arrangements, bulk electronic payment systems, among others. For example, it has published a succession of programmatic documents, most notably including the *Core Principles for Systemically Important Payment Systems*, the *Recommendations for Securities Settlement Systems*, the *Recommendations for Central Counter Parties*, the *Central Bank Oversight of Payment and Settlement Systems*, and the *General Guidance for National Payment System Development*. These documents have been highly valued by the central banks and supervisory authorities of CPSS members, widely recognized as guiding materials for the regulation of payment and settlement systems and securities trading settlement systems. The publication of these CPSS documents has gone a long way toward promoting the development of payment and settlement systems in many countries and territories all over the world.

Currently, the CPSS is exploring the possibility of (1) introducing central counter-party mechanisms into over-the-counter (OTC) markets, in particular derivative instruments trading markets, and (2) establishing mechanisms for central counterparty clearing, data storage, data processing and data monitoring. These measures, if well designed, will have profound and far-reaching implications for the future developments of international payment and settlement systems.

Prior to the eruption of the 2008 international financial crisis, institutional arrangements such as central counterparties (CCP) and transaction registers (TR) were widely overlooked. This was especially true where the disclosure of information about financial derivatives trading was concerned. In the wake of the crisis, the international community began to attach great importance to post-crisis reconstruction of rules, institutions, and payment system services (i.e., DVP-Delivery Versus Payment) regarding OTC markets, central counterparties, and transaction registers. The G20's Financial Stability Board (FSB) started to establish transaction registers and central counterparties for OTC derivatives trading in as early as April 2010. The FSB also requested the CPSS and IOSCO to jointly create a steering committee in charge of guiding researches on international principles for financial market infrastructures (FMIs), including with respect to promoting compliant alternatives of cross-border trading, expanding the scope of central clearing and mandatory reporting, strengthening the risk resilience of central counterparties, and increasing the availability and accessibility of transaction data.

On April 16, 2012, the CPSS and the Technical Committee of the IOSCO jointly published the *CPSS-IOSCO Principles for Financial Market Infrastructures*, which sets out 24 principles to be followed in supervising five types of financial market infrastructures (FMIs)—namely systemically important payment systems, central depositories, securities settlement systems, central counterparties, and trade repositories. The CPSS and IOSCO also published the *Principles for Financial Market Infrastructures: Disclosure Framework and Assessment Methodology* to promote the observance by FMIs of the principles and responsibilities set forth in the PEMIs. Meanwhile, the United States and major developed economies in Europe have either formulated new or amended existing domestic laws and regulations that govern the supervision of central counterparties (CCP) and transaction registers (TR) in OTC derivative markets. How well financial market infrastructures are designed and operated is critically important for the promotion and maintenance of financial stability.

8.2.3 Credit Rating and Financial Standards

8.2.3.1 The World's Big Three Credit Rating Agencies

A credit rating agency is a private intermediary agency established according to law to assess the financial strength of entities, either governments or private enterprises. As an important intermediary organization in financial markets, it reviews and rates the creditworthiness of securities issuers and securities credits (including international and local bonds), typically consisting of experts in economic, legal, and financial realms. The world's Big Three credit rating agencies, also universally recognized to be the most authoritative internationally, are Standard & Poor's (S&P), Moody's, and Fitch Group. S&P and Moody's are based in the United States, while Fitch Ratings is dual-headquartered in New York City and London and is controlled by Hearst.

Fitch Ratings Inc. is the only European-based credit rating agency among the "Big Three," smaller in size than the other two and with dual headquarters in New York and London. The agency has approximately 2000 credit rating professionals who work for its more than 50 subsidiaries and joint ventures worldwide. The agency's vast client network covers over 80 countries and territories. At its core, Fitch Ratings provides forward-looking opinions on the creditworthiness of financial institutions, corporations, national governments, local governments, and structured finance products. As of today, the agency has completed credit ratings for over 1600 banks and non-bank institutions, over 1000 corporations, around 1400 local governments, and 78% of structured finance products worldwide, along with 70 sovereign debt ratings.

A long-term credit rating issued by Fitch Ratings can be taken as a measure of a debtor's ability to pay off its debts—either denominated in the debtor's domestic currency or a foreign currency. Fitch Ratings issues two types of long-term credit ratings: investment-grade and speculative-grade. Its investment-grade ratings range from AAA to BBB, and its speculative-grade ratings include ratings of BB, B, CCC, CC, C, RD, and D. There are 11 categories in total, with AAA as the highest rating to indicate the lowest default risk, and D as the lowest rating to indicate that an entity or the government of a sovereign state has defaulted on obligations and will generally default on most or all obligations.

Fitch's short-term ratings mostly indicate the potential level of default within a 13-month period. Short-term ratings focus more on the liquidity that a debt issuer needs in order to meet its obligations when they become due. Fitch's short-term ratings are assigned on an alphabetic scale from F1 to D, including those of F1, F2, F3, B, C, RD, and D. Fitch uses the intermediate modifiers "+" and "−" to denote relative status within the categories from AA to CCC when it comes to long-term ratings. As regards short-term ratings, Fitch designates a plus sign to the F1 category (i.e., F1+). Fitch also offers outlooks at three levels—positive, stable, and negative—to indicate possible changes of a credit rating within the next one or two years. A positive or negative outlook respectively signals that the credit rating in the medium to long term might be raised or lowered, while a stable outlook indicates that the rating most probably will stay at the same level.

Standard & Poor's Financial Services LLC (S&P) is headquartered in New York City, United States. S&P issues credit ratings for the debt securities of public and private companies in over 100 countries and territories, with a total debt value of approximately US$32 trillion. It provides 79 major stock market indices worldwide. A case in point is the S&P Global 1200 Index, a free-float weighted stock market index of global equities. The index covers 31 countries and approximately 70% of global stock market capitalization. As it stands today, the agency has about 8500 employees working in 23 countries.

S&P provides high-quality market intelligence in the form of credit ratings, index services, investment research, risk assessment, and data services. S&P's long-term credit ratings are divided into two grades: investment-grade and speculative-grade. Investment-grade ratings indicate high creditworthiness and investment value, while speculative-grade ratings denote a low level of creditworthiness and a high risk of default. Investment-grade ratings are on a scale ranging from AAA to BBB, representing the range from the highest to lowest quality. The speculative grade covers ratings of BB, B, CCC, CC, C, and D. These long-term ratings range from AAA to D in a descending order, with AAA as the highest rating to indicate the highest credit quality, and D as the lowest to indicate default on obligations. Intermediate ratings are offered at each level between AA and CCC (e.g., BBB+, BBB, and BBB–). In addition, S&P also offers outlook ratings to assess the potential direction of a long-term credit rating over the intermediate term (typically six months to two years), which are divided into five levels: positive (likely to be upgraded), negative (likely to be downgraded), stable (remaining unchanged), uncertain (likely to be either upgraded or downgraded), and meaningless.

The company rates short-term issues on a scale from A-1 to D. Within the A-1 category it can be designated with a plus sign (+). This indicates that the issuer's commitment to meet its obligation is very strong. The company also offers guidance—termed a "credit watch"—to assess the potential direction of a short-term credit rating, at three levels: positive (likely to be upgraded), negative (likely to be downgraded), and uncertain (likely to be either upgraded or downgraded). Moody's Corporation, often referred to as Moody's, is an American business and financial services company headquartered in Manhattan, New York City. Moody's has approximately 4500 employees working in its headquarters and subsidiaries across 26 countries and regions, including some 800 analysts and over 1700 assistant analysts. Credit ratings provided by Moody's include national sovereign ratings, US public finance ratings, bank ratings, corporate finance ratings, insurance financial strength ratings, bond fund ratings, and ratings of structured finance products. Moody's is by and large similar to Standard & Poor's in terms of business, rating grades, and standards.

Moody's long-term obligation ratings are opinions of the relative credit risks of fixed income obligations with an original maturity of one year or more. They address the possibility that a financial obligation will not be honored as promised and reflect the likelihood of default and any financial loss suffered in the event of default. Moody's short-term ratings are opinions of the ability of issuers to honor short-term financial obligations which generally have an original maturity not exceeding 13 months.

The scale for Moody's long-term ratings ranges from Aaa to C, with nine grades (Aaa, Aa, A, Baa, Ba, B, Caa, Ca, C) in total. As the highest rating, Aaa indicates the highest credit quality and the lowest credit risk. C is the lowest rating assigned by Moody's to a bond to indicate default and low likelihood of recovering principal or interest. To each of its ratings from Aa through Caa, Moody's appends numerical modifiers 1, 2, and 3; the lower the number, the higher-end the rating. It is generally held that Moody's investment-grade ratings range from Aaa to Baa, and the speculative grade ratings start from Ba1 all the way down to C.

Moody's short-term ratings range from "Prime-1 (P-1)," which represents a superior ability for repayment of senior short-term debt obligations, to "Prime-3 (P-3)," which represents an acceptable ability for repayment of such obligations. Issuers rated "Not Prime" do not fall within any of the Prime rating categories. Moody's also puts on its credit watch list short-term obligations that are likely to be subject to a change of rating. They will not be removed from the list until a rating is assigned to them. In addition, Moody's also offers outlook ratings to assess the potential direction of a long-term credit rating over the intermediate term, which are divided into four levels: positive (likely to be upgraded), negative (likely to be downgraded), stable (remaining unchanged), and developing (contingent upon an event).

8.2.3.2 The International Big Four Accounting Firms

Deloitte, Ernst & Young (EY), KPMG, and PricewaterhouseCoopers (PwC) are the four biggest professional services networks in the world, offering audit, assurance services, taxation, management consulting, advisory, actuarial, corporate finance, and legal services.

PWC was created on July 1, 1998, when Coopers & Lybrand merged with Price Waterhouse. Headquartered in London, UK, this multinational professional services network has 1183 operations and 8979 partners worldwide and employs 42,954 people. PWC is committed to working with its clients to deliver solutions that help them take on the challenges of the ever-changing business environment. Its major international clients include: ExxonMobil, IBM, the Nippon Telegraph and Telephone Corporation (NTT), Johnson & Johnson, AT&T, BT Group, Dell, Ford, Chevrolet, Compaq, Nokia, and so on.

Seated in Amstelveen, the Netherlands, KPMG has 6561 partners and employs 59,663 people working in its 844 operations worldwide. KPMG provides three lines of services: audit, tax, and advisory. Its major international clients include General Electric, Royal Dutch Shell, Pfizer, Nestlé S.A., Mercedes-Benz, PepsiCo., Citibank, and so on. DTT commonly refers to a subsidiary of Deloitte Touche Tohmatsu or the Swiss brand under which independent firms throughout the world collaborate to provide excellent client services. Globally, this multinational professional services network has 695 operations, 5145 partners, and 52,520 professionals. It is headquartered in London, U K, committed to providing expert services and advice to its vast client base, with its lines of services centered on audit, tax, consulting, and financial advisory. The company's major international clients include Microsoft, General Motors, Vodafone, and Chrysler.

EY was formed by a merger of Ernst & Whinney (founded in Cleveland, United States in 1903) and Arthur Young & Co. (founded in New York City in 1906) in 1989. It became known as Ernst & Young until 2013 when it underwent a rebranding to EY. Headquartered in London, UK, this multinational professional services firm has 674 operations, some 6000 partners, and around 57,000 professional staffers worldwide. EY provides assurance (including financial audit), tax, consulting, and advisory services to companies. Its major international clients include: 3i Group, Aviva plc, Aon Hewitt, ING Group, Rabobank, Piper Jaffray Companies, Canadian Imperial Bank of Commerce (CIBC), Manulife Financial Corporation, MAN Group, VTB Bank, Toronto–Dominion Bank, UBS Group AG, Bank of America, SunTrust Banks, Regions Financial Corporation, Unum Group (formerly known as UnumProvident), National Australia Bank, Babcock & Brown Capital, Chubb Limited, Renaissance Institutional Equities Fund (RIEF), Bank of Cyprus, and Capital One Financial Corporation.

8.2.3.3 Financial Standards

Financial standards are standardized norms and universal languages that must be observed collectively by those involved in international finance.

They are used to define and delimit financial activities and can serve as a frame of reference against which to gauge financial behaviors. Examples of financial standards include accounting norms and principles, Basel Committee on Banking Supervision Basel III, risk management standards, statistical standards, and so on.

As things stand today, financial standards are concentrated in the Financial Sector Assessment Program (FSAP), a joint IMF and World Bank effort introduced in May 1999. The international standards used in the FSAP program include: (1) the *Core Principles for Effective Banking Supervision* issued by the Basel Committee on Banking Supervision; (2) the *Objectives and Principles for Securities Regulation* issued by the International Organization of Securities Commissions (IOSCO); (3) the *Insurance Core Principles (ICPs)* issued by the International Association of Insurance Supervisors (IAIS); (4) the *Core Principles for Systemically Important Payment Systems (CPSIPS)* introduced by the Committee on Payment and Settlement Systems (CPSS); (5) the *Recommendations for Securities Settlement Systems* jointly introduced by IOSCO and CPSS.

From what is illustrated above, it can be seen that financial infrastructures constitute the hardware facilities and institutional arrangements that underpin the functioning of finance. "Financial infrastructure," however, is an all-encompassing term that includes but is not limited to the following: on-exchange payment and clearing systems where central banks play a predominant role, payment and settlement systems for OTC derivatives transactions (primarily represented by central counterparty clearing and transaction registers), financial safety nets in connection with corporate governance, credit norms, accounting, auditing, legal environment, investor protection, financial regulation, and supervision and countermeasures against money laundering. These elements converge to form financial market infrastructures that are critically important for the economic development, social stability, and financial safety of individual countries and the world at large. A review of many financial examples across the world—both encouraging and cautionary—reveals that the level of financial infrastructures has a close, strong bearing on how economically developed, technologically advanced, and financially evolved a country is. Generally speaking, the more developed and full-fledged financial infrastructures a country has, the steadier and more coordinated economic growth it enjoys, together with larger and more efficient accumulation, agglomeration, and flows of and fusion between industrial capital and financial capital. On the contrary, the less developed and full-fledged financial infrastructure a country has, the more vulnerable and susceptible it becomes to financial crisis.

8.3 Coordination of International Financial Regulation

The above texts have given us a general picture of the present international financial institutions system and financial infrastructure system.

On the one hand, the trend of financial internationalization is gaining momentum with each passing day. On the other hand, the ever-advancing financial internationalization processes are posing challenges to international financial regulation, as indicated as follows: (1) there are ever-deepening contradictions between the internationalization of financial institutions and services and the localization of financial regulation, which have resulted in the presence of regulatory vacuums; (2) given the lack of financial infrastructures, there exists asymmetry of information between regulators and regulated institutions, which has led to a higher difficulty in achieving effective regulation; (3) the innovation in international financial services, as evidenced in particular by the ever emergence of financial derivative products, is breaking regulatory frameworks and generating new objects of regulation; (4) there exist ever-widening contradictions between the transnational conglomeration of financial institutions and cross-sectoral integration of financial services and the decentralization of international financial regulation.

Meanwhile, the contradictions between the internationalization of financial development and the localization of financial regulation can result in two possible outcomes in connection with regulatory disequilibrium between countries: one is regulatory competition—a race between countries to deregulate in order to attract financial resources; the other is financial arbitrage, meaning that regulated financial institutions seek to gain profits by exploiting regulatory differences between countries. Both of these possible outcomes will directly impact the effectiveness of international financial regulation, though in different ways. With financial development comes financial risk. This is as true internationally as nationally. As such, it is an objective imperative to strengthen coordination of financial regulation at the international level.

8.3.1 International Organizations for Financial Regulatory Coordination

International financial supervisory organizations with no legally binding powers on member countries include the following: (1) The Basel Committee on Banking Supervision (BCBS), formerly known as the Basel Committee on Banking Regulations and Supervisory Practices, is a committee of banking supervisory authorities that was established in 1974 by the central bank governors of the Group of Ten countries—Belgium, Canada, France, Germany, Italy, Japan, the Netherlands, Sweden, Switzerland, the UK, and the United States. As an international committee formed to develop standards for banking regulation, the BCBS consists of senior representatives of bank supervisory authorities and central banks. The Committee's Secretariat is located at the Bank for International Settlements (BIS) in Basel, Switzerland. The Committee has nearly 30 technical working groups and task forces working to meet goals and carry out plans devised at its regular meetings, which are held four times a year.

On the one hand, the Basel Committee formulates broad supervisory standards and guidelines and recommends statements of best practices in banking supervision, known as Basel Accords (i.e., the *Core Principles for Effective Banking Supervision* and the *International Convergence of Capital Measurement and Capital Standards*), with a view to compensating for the deficiencies of individual countries' commercial banking regulatory regimes and reducing the risks and costs of potential bank defaults. The Basel Committee exemplifies a primary form of coordinated international regulation on commercial banking. It has played a critical role in stabilizing the international financial order. On the other hand, the Basel Committee per se has no statutory power whatsoever for transnational regulation; nor do the conclusions it draws or the regulatory standards and guidelines it formulates possess any legal effect for compliance or enforcement purposes. For this reason, what the BCBS can do in reality is to encourage convergence toward common approaches and standards under the principles of "unavoidability of supervision for foreign banking business" and "moderate supervision."

(2) The International Organization of Securities Commissions, also known as IOSCO, is an association of organizations that regulate the world's securities and futures markets. The IOSCO was officially born in 1983 from the transformation of its predecessor the "Inter-American Regional Association" (created in 1974) into a truly global cooperative. Headquartered in Madrid, Spain, the IOSCO has 193 members, including 110 ordinary members, 11 associate members, and 72 affiliate members. The mandate of the IOSCO is to promote the healthy development of global securities markets through information sharing; to ensure fair and efficient securities markets by coordinating its members in formulating common norms and establishing effective mechanisms for regulation on the international securities industry; to promote safe transactions by unifying its members in the effort against illicit cross-border transactions. IOSCO members meet once a year on an annual conference focused on coordinating and promoting the implementation of relevant regulatory norms for the steady, healthy development of global securities markets.

(3) Founded in 1994, the International Association of Insurance Supervisors (IAIS) is a voluntary membership organization of insurance supervisors and regulators from over 190 jurisdictions in more than 140 countries. In 1998, this internationally important body moved its headquarters from Washington, D.C., United States to Basel, Switzerland. Under the direction of its Members, the IAIS conducts activities through a Committee system designed to achieve its mandate and objectives, which include developing and renewing supervisory material (principles, standards, and guidance) for effective supervision of insurance-related activities, providing insurance-related training and supporting insurance supervision, and organizing joint meetings for insurance supervisors.

In addition, the IAIS holds annual conferences to bring supervisors, business representatives, and experts together for joint discussions on issues with respect to the development of the insurance industry and insurance-related laws and regulations. Such issues include formulating solvency and accounting standards, enhancing the sharing of supervision-related information to play a bigger role in international forums, promoting and monitoring the implementation of international rules in connection with insurance supervision, and strengthening communication and connections with other international financial regulatory bodies.

The BCBS, the IOSCO, and the IAIS constitute the "Big Three" international financial supervisory bodies, all universally recognized as playing a positive role in promoting the stability and orderly development of international finance. Given their lack of legally binding powers on member countries, however, cooperation among their member countries can only be conducted on the basis of "gentlemen's agreements."

Supervisory organizations that are based on international or regional laws and have legally binding powers on member countries include the following: (1) The European System of Financial Supervision (ESFS), as already introduced in Sect. 2.3 of Chap. 2 in this book. In September 2010, the European Parliament approved a package of proposals to reform the EU's financial supervisory architecture. This package envisaged the creation of a new supervisory framework consisting of a European Systemic Risk Board (ESRB) and three new European Supervisory Authorities (ESAs) for exercising prudential regulation and supervision at both macro and micro levels. This new supervisory framework, now known as the European System of Financial Supervision (ESFS), entails legally binding obligations for all EU member states. As things stand today, financial supervisory instructions for the EU are formulated and provided by the following bodies: the European Central Bank (ECB), the European Banking Authority (EBA), the European Insurance and Occupational Pensions Authority (EIOPA), and the European Securities and Markets Authority (ESMA). Based on regional laws, the European System of Financial Supervision (ESFS) serves to promote transnational financial regulation and supervision among EU members.

(2) The Financial Stability Board (FSB). The predecessor of the FSB was the Financial Stability Forum (FSF), which was founded by the finance ministers and central bank governors of G7 countries in 1999 to promote international financial stability. At the 2009 G20 London Summit, held on April 2, 2009, it was decided that the membership of

the FSF would be expanded to include emerging economies such as China, as a way to meet the ever-pressing needs of boosting global economic growth and fostering international financial stability. Consequently, the FSB was established as a successor to the FSF to incorporate members of the G20 who had not been FSF members. As of today, the FSB membership includes all G20 member countries and a number of international bodies, most notably the European Commission (EC), the Bank for International Settlements (BIS), the European Central Bank (ECB), the European Council (EC), the International Monetary Fund (IMF), the Organization for Economic Co-operation and Development (OECD), the World Bank (WB), the Basel Committee on Banking Supervision (BCBS), the International Accounting Standards Board (IASB), the International Organization of Securities Commissions (IOSCO), the International Association of Insurance Supervisors (IAIS), the Committee on Payment and Settlement Systems (CPSS), the Committee on the Global Financial System (CGFS), and other international standard setting bodies (SSBs). Hosted and funded by the Bank for International Settlements, the board is based in Basel, Switzerland.

The FSB is mandated by G20 to address the problem of financial fragility by formulating and implementing regulatory and other policies that are conducive to promoting international financial stability. (a) Financial regulation. The FSB works to design a set of mechanisms to ensure that there won't be competitive deregulation by state actors when it comes to the formulation and enforcement of regulatory standards. Progress in this respect has been reported at the 2013 G20 summit in Pittsburg, United States. (b) Banking capital adequacy. At the end of 2009, the Basel Committee on Banking Supervision proposed a whole set of regulations for strengthening the capital adequacy and liquidity of banks. The FSB helped bring these regulations into effect in the second half of 2010. (c) Securitization. In September 2009, the International Organization of Securities Commissions (IOSCO), as an FSB member, issued *Final Regulatory Recommendations on Securitization and CDS (credit default swap) Market*, which eventually came into effect. In addition, the FSB also deals with matters in connection with the governance structure of financial institutions, executive remuneration and capital, the coordination between remuneration structure and risk, information disclosure, and regulation of systemically important financial institutions. In accordance with its new charter and work-procedure guiding documents, the FSB has officially developed the Legal Entity Identifier as part of its efforts to address problems associated with global financial fragility, promote international financial reforms, and improve international financial regulatory coordination. As such, it is fair to say that the FSB has become a crucial driver for international financial regulation and reform.

8.3.2 Forms of International Financial Regulatory Coordination

As things stand today, international financial regulatory coordination exists primarily in four forms, as shown by the real development of international finance.

(1) Bilateral memorandums of understanding (MoU). A memorandum of understanding is signed between two countries to define and make clear their responsibilities and obligations on a specific area of financial regulation where they have reached consensus through in-depth discussions. Today, bilateral regulatory coordination between countries is mostly achieved by signing MoUs.
(2) Multilateral forums. A multilateral forum is held to launch discussions on a specific regulatory issue and sign a regulatory statement or document, which though has no legal effect in most instances.
(3) Coordination based on unified regulatory standards. A case in point is the Basel Accords, which are unified banking regulations set by the Basel Committee on Bank Supervision (BCBS) and observed by its members.
(4) Unified regulation. This refers to transnational financial regulation uniformly exercised by a regulatory body. As it stands today, such a regulatory model has yet to take shape in the international financial regulatory architecture. The nearest thing we have today is the European Union's regulatory architecture, which merely amounts to the embryonic form of a unified regulatory model.

8.3.3 Specifics of International Financial Regulatory Coordination

Specifics of international financial regulatory coordination include the following: (1) Establishing mechanisms for regulatory information sharing. At present, international mechanisms for financial information sharing mainly take two forms: bilateral cooperation and communication mechanisms and multilateral cooperation and communication mechanisms. The Financial Stability Board (FSB) is taking steps to develop information sharing mechanisms in greater depth and breadth.

(2) Strengthening regulation on transnational financial institutions. The most typical example in this regard is the Basel Accords, which incorporated principles for regulating foreign subsidiaries of commercial banks in 1975, principles for cross-border banking regulation and supervision in 1996, among others. International regulations like the Basel Accords point the way toward improved regulation on transnational financial institutions.

(3) Implementing consolidated supervision over transnational financial institutions. The creation of the consolidated supervision approach must be attributed to the Basel Committee on Banking Supervision (BCBS). In 1979, the BCBS proposed the consolidated supervision principle, which means that parent banks and parent supervisory authorities monitor the risk exposure of the banks or banking groups for which they are responsible, as well as the adequacy of their capital, on the basis of the totality of their business wherever conducted. Consolidated supervision goes well beyond the scope of accounting reports, as it includes not only consolidated reporting (the production of financial reports on a consolidated basis) but also information contained in consolidated financial reports. Consolidated supervision has become a mechanism for coordinating international financial regulation and supervision.

(4) Creating internationally unified regulatory standards, which are mostly found in the regulations set by the "Big Three" international financial regulatory coordinators: the Basel Committee on Banking Supervision (BCBS), the International Organization of Securities Commissions (IOSCO), and the International Association of Insurance

Supervisors (IAIS). Some of the most striking examples include the *Core Principles for Effective Banking Supervision* issued by the BCBS, the *Objectives and Principles for Securities Regulation* by the IOSCO, the *Insurance Core Principles (ICPs)* by the IAIS, the Core Principles for Systemically Important Payment Systems by the Committee on Payment and Settlement Systems (CPSS), among others. Regulations like these are standardized norms and universal languages that must be observed collectively by those involved in international finance can be used to define and delimit financial activities. What is especially noteworthy—and probably the most successful set of financial standards—is the Basel Accords for regulating banking capital.

(5) Intensifying regulation on financial conglomerates. This is important for addressing problems that arise from the combination of banking, securities, and insurance services under a single financial institution—especially systemically important ones that have grown and developed out of financial conglomeration. The BCBS, the IOSCO, and the IAIS have, in effect, been exploring ways to improve regulation on financial conglomerates. Such efforts began in as early as the year 1993 when a "Tripartite Group" was formed under the auspices of the BCBS, IOSCO, and the IAIS to address a range of issues relating to the supervision of financial conglomerates by coordinating between banking, securities, and insurance regulators.

(6) Promoting regional integration of financial regulation. The most notable endeavor in this regard was made by the European Union following the outburst of the 2008 international financial crisis. Specifically, the EU went all out to achieve effective combination of macro-prudential and micro-prudential financial regulation. This endeavor by the EU also serves as a model for the FSB to emulate in furthering the development of international financial regulation.

International financial regulatory coordination, in sum, finds its concrete expression in the above-mentioned six respects.

8.3.4 The Outlook for International Financial Regulatory Coordination

On the one hand, obstacles do exist in this area, as indicated in prior texts. (1) There is no mechanism to regularize and guarantee bilateral regulatory coordination. Memorandums of understanding on bilateral regulation either become formalistic or produce sporadic exchanges of information at best. (2) Multilateral regulatory coordination too often stops at the level of conceptual exploration and has no legally binding power per se. (3) The European Union has realized partially unified regulation, but the real, substantive regulatory power is still distributed across the regulatory authorities of individual members. (4) The regulatory standards issued by the "Big Three" international regulatory coordinators—the BCBS, the IOSCO, and the IAIS—cannot reflect and meet the diverse development needs of individual countries. The differences between countries—which exist in development levels, ideas, interests, legal systems, regulation, and standards—also constitute major obstacles to realizing the international unification of financial regulation.

On the other hand, modern international finance is moving toward coordinated and standardized regulation, as evidenced by the ever-increasing role of the G20's Financial Stability Board (FSB). Meanwhile, the trend of unification is also growing in strength and depth with respect to information technology, organizational structures, and regulatory rules and standards. Thus, it is a compelling imperative to promote and intensify the coordination of international financial regulation in the light of the growing trend toward technological, organizational, institutional, and supervisory unification in international financial markets.

The current problems hindering the coordination of international financial regulation come from two sources: (1) regulatory malfunctions and (2) regulatory voids in international finance. Financial internationalization and integration are key to resolving these problems. In specific terms, the international community needs to work toward: (1) global integration of the rules of financial games; (2) global integration of market participants; (3) global integration of financial tools; (4) global integration of financial markets; (5) diversification of traded currencies; (6)

convergence of interest rates; (7) globalization of financial risks. Meanwhile, while pursuing financial internationalization and integration, countries around the world must face up squarely to and delve collectively into issues regarding international financial stability and regulatory effectiveness, and at the same time work out a blueprint to reform and renew the international financial regulatory regime.

8.4 China Should Proactively Participate in the Building of International Financial Architecture

As stated above, the modern financial architecture, or the modern international financial architecture, consists of six key building blocks: a modern financial market system, a modern financial organizational system, a modern financial legal system, a modern financial regulatory system, a modern financial environment system, and modern financial infrastructures. The priorities for reforming and perfecting the modern international financial architecture must be on improving and enriching various modern financial systems and supplementary elements.

Six observations can be made based on the aforementioned analysis of the status quo of international finance. First, the global financial landscape is still dominated by three international financial institutions, namely the International Monetary Fund (IMF), the World Bank (WB), and the Bank for International Settlements (BIS). Second, two organizations play a predominant role in international payment and clearing: the Bank for International Settlements (BIS), which houses the Committee on Payment and Settlement Systems (CPSS), and the Society for Worldwide Interbank Financial Telecommunication (SWIFT). Third, as regards credit rating, the "Big Three" structure remains unchanged, meaning that Standard & Poor's, Moody's, and Fitch Group continue to be the world's three dominant credit rating agencies. Fourth, the international architecture of financial regulatory coordination is underpinned by the Basel Committee on Banking Supervision (BCBS), the International Organization of Securities Commissions (IOSCO), the International

Association of Insurance Supervisors (IAIS), and the Financial Stability Board (FSB) created at the 2009 G20 London summit. Fifth, international financial regulatory coordination is still dominated by two models: bilateral coordination and multilateral coordination, though the emergence of the G20's FSB as an organization with certain legally binding powers has added a new alternative. Finally, international financial regulatory coordination is primarily focused on matters with respect to financial information, financial institutions, consolidated supervision, and financial standards. It is important for countries across the world to put innovation and improvement of international financial systems on their national agendas for financial stability, effective supervision, and risk prevention.

The real-life patterns of international financial regulatory coordination and cooperation can be summed up as follows: in terms of geographical sphere, financial regulatory coordination and cooperation is both global and regional; as regards specifics of coordination and cooperation, there are two types of coordination and cooperation: comprehensive and targeted; there are three pathways for financial regulatory coordination and cooperation: agreement-based, rule-based, and institution-based; when it comes to frequency, there is both regular and provisional coordination and cooperation; with respect to entities, there is inter-institutional and inter-governmental coordination and cooperation. Given what is stated above, it is important for China to proactively participate in the reform, innovation, and development of international financial architecture by working on three fronts: steering financial institutions toward servicing the real economy, shaping modern financial systems, and building a new international financial order.

8.4.1 Building New Engines of Global Economic Development

In 1948, the Estonian international economist Ragnar Nurkse metaphorically referred to trade as the "engine of growth" for the twentieth century in his attempt to rationalize "import substitution"—a trade policy aimed at promoting economic growth by restricting imports that competed with domestic products in developing countries. Battered by the aftershocks of the 2008 financial crisis, global trade recorded annual growth of less than 4% between 2012 and 2014. Under such circumstances, some officials in the World Bank suggested revisiting and reinstating the "trade as the engine of growth" hypothesis. This author holds the view that the model of factor-driven growth—using production factors such as resources, land, and labor to boost economic growth—has been exhausted to its limit and has become unsustainable in many economies, particularly in those that are rich in oil, natural gas, minerals, and agricultural produce. In the light of this new development, it is imperative to propel investment, innovation, and rules to become new engines of growth in the process of building modern market systems and modern financial systems for the twenty-first century. This is particularly important for economies around the world if they want to successfully evolve from being factor-driven to investment-driven and finally to innovation-driven. This is equally important for the development of the global real economy, for international financial governance and for the establishment of a new international financial architecture.

(a) Promoting investment as a new engine for global growth

Investment-driven growth is sustainable for the long term, because it is conducive to deeper market development, increased capital, technological revolution, and job creation for countries around the world. Efforts on the following six fronts are critically important for realizing investment-driven growth. Advancing a new type of industrialization by focusing on three areas:

- Supporting and steering the transformation and upgradation of traditional industries. By supporting and steering enterprises to renovate and revamp their production technologies, countries all over the world can release the gushing vitality of their large stocks of assets and optimize and enhance industrial quality and efficiency, thus boosting demand and driving economic growth.
- Supporting and nurturing the development of strategic emerging industries and high-tech industries. Countries around the world must give priority to supporting and incentivizing the efforts of enterprises in the research, development, innovation, transfer, and industrializa-

tion of core and key technologies, so that superior industries and leading industries can be nurtured to shape full-fledged industrial chains and modern services networks.
- Boosting the core competitiveness of enterprises. This can be achieved by promoting the mergers, acquisitions, reorganizations, consolidations, and recapitalizations of enterprises based on market competition. Increasing core competitiveness is key to realizing effective investment and accelerating the shift from old growth drivers to new ones.

(b) Expediting the modernization of agriculture by focusing on five areas.

- Given that agricultural modernization encompasses both large-scale land operation and the "modernization of farmers," it is necessary to guide and lift farmers out of folly and backwardness to become new, modernized farmers that are "well-informed culturally, well-trained technically, and well-versed managerially."
- In terms of organization, it is imperative to matchmake agricultural cooperatives or disparate farmers with the market, so as to achieve alignment in the pre-production, production, and post-production processes that cover the purchase of capital goods and the storage, processing, transportation, and sale of agricultural produce.
- Promoting moderately large-scale farming.
- Advancing moderate urbanization.
- Developing vocational agricultural education.

The realization of worldwide agricultural modernization can help create a stable social environment for industrialization and urbanization, thus leading to lower social costs and greater economic prosperity.

(c) Promoting a new type of urbanization. In developed countries, cities and towns account for over 80% of national population. Given the ever-advancing trend of urban-rural integration and with the gradual formation of cities-focused urban systems, economies around the world will be vitalized with new growth impetus, which comes from the following sources: the planning and development of people-centered urbanization;

the construction of "sponge cities," "sponge communities," underground corridors, and flood control and drainage facilities; the construction of urban-rural integrated infrastructures for the supply of water, electricity, transportation, and natural gas; the development of facilities for the delivery of public services relating to education, healthcare, culture, and sport; the development of leisure tourism, commercial logistics, information industries, and public transport.

(d) Promoting infrastructure modernization. This means the modernization of infrastructural facilities relating to energy, transportation, environmental protection, information and irrigation, and water conservancy. Investment in infrastructure modernization offers much leeway for maneuvering and promises immense potential economic benefits for countries around the world.

(e) Increasing spending on high-tech R&D projects. Examples in this regard include: the NNNI initiative (the National Network for Manufacturing Innovation) in the United States, which is funded by a one-time investment of $1 billion in Phase I and intended to build 45 institutions for manufacturing innovation (IMIs) within a 10-year period; the Knowledge Transfer Partnership (KTP) program in the UK; the "Industrie 4.0" (Industry 4.0) strategic initiative in Germany, which revolves around CPS (cyber physical system)-based intelligent manufacturing technologies. Programs such as these can integrate individual, corporate, and organizational resources for innovation, set the pace and trend for industrial research and development, and boost industrial transformation and upgradation. Investment in the development of Big Data, cloud computing, the Internet of Things (IoT), NBIC technologies, biotechnologies, information technologies, and artificial intelligence will create new economic growth points.

(f) Enhancing the supplementary role of finance. This means steering financial institutions toward servicing the real economy and enabling the integration of finance, technology, and industry. Countries around the world need to reform, innovate, and modernize their financial systems in order to promote investment as a new engine of economic growth.

8.4.2 Promoting Innovation as a New Engine of Global Growth

There is a need to reform, innovate, and enhance the public mechanisms or public goods that (1) are the products of historical competition, coordination, and cooperation between states and (2) are intended for global economic and financial governance.

(1) Pushing forward the conceptual innovation of ideological public goods. As stated in prior texts, a modern market system or modern financial system, if it is to be complete, must consist of elements in six respects. Some countries have put excessive emphasis on the importance of competition at the level of market elements and market organizations while overlooking the necessity of building sound, full-fledged market infrastructures like legal regulatory systems and market credit systems. This kind of thinking will result in a deviation from the market principle of "equity, justice and openness." Governments around the world must take actions to adjust the allocation of industrial resources, the supply of social public goods, and the development of urban resources in ways that encourage and incentivize competition. National governments must play an important role in regulating and coordinating the economic and financial growth worldwide.

(2) Advancing technological innovation of material public goods. Currently, the most distinctive feature of high-tech development lies in the fusion of information technologies with industrialization, urbanization, agricultural modernization, and infrastructure modernization, as encapsulated by the Chinese catchphrase "Internet Plus." When intelligent technologies are applied to the provision of public services to a city's and even a country's residents—such as in public transport, urban management, education, healthcare, culture, commerce, administration, environmental protection, energy, and security—a combination of tangible and intangible elements can be achieved to create a safe, efficient, convenient, and green urban environment that not only benefits the residents but also is conducive to expediting the transformation of industrialization, the restructuring of urbanization, and the upgradation of

internationalization for countries around the world. Moreover, this can also boost the rise of emerging economies.

(3) Pushing forward managerial innovation of organizational public goods. Managing the world is like managing a country or a city. Traditionally, cities have been planned and sprawled the same way as making a pancake. A city thus developed and organized is susceptible to problems like traffic congestion and blockage, air pollution, traffic light malfunction, and low operational efficiency, notwithstanding the presence of a multi-layer ring road network. Clustered development is the future for modern cities. Just as the Internet needs to reshape spatial orders in order to develop and the development of global supply chains can easily make "national boundaries" irrelevant, the clustered structure of cities is conducive to addressing problems that arise from sprawled urban development or centralized city management. This is as true for the organization of cities as it is for the organization of global economic and financial orders. This means that the world must transition from the single-center model to the clustered, pluralistic development model when it comes to the management and organization of economic and financial orders. Meanwhile, this new model must be matched with new rules and necessary infrastructure investment.

(4) Promoting rule-related innovation of institutional public goods. The development of a country involves conceptual planning, urban-rural planning, and land planning and requires a series of rigorous, well-organized measures relating to strategic planning, structural positioning, implementation standards, policy assessment, and legal guarantee. Global economic governance should be underpinned by the Charter of the United Nations, the Organization of Economic Cooperation and Development, the World Trade Organization, and other rules-based mechanisms. On the basis of these mechanisms, global financial governance must also be supported with fiscal, monetary, exchange-rate and regulatory policies and reform measures from individual countries around the world, in order that a new global economic and financial governance architecture can take shape, one that features joint consultation, joint development, sharing, and sustainable growth.

8.4.3 Promoting Global Rules as a New Engine of Growth

China advocates the establishment of a world economy characterized by "four Is"—innovative, invigorated, interconnected, and inclusive. To this end, China proposes the need to enhance the global economic and financial governance architecture.

(1) The rules for the security order of the international community—peace and stability. This has become a unanimous consensus among members of the international community. In this connection, it is imperative to strengthen international security cooperation, safeguard the purposes and principles of the UN Charter and establish a peaceful, stable, just, and rational security order in the international community.

(2) The rules for international economic and financial competition—fairness and efficiency. Fairness and efficiency are also the basic norms governing corporate competition for the allocation of industrial and financial resources around the world. A case in point is the 2016 G20 Summit held in Hangzhou, China, which set forth the guiding principles of fostering "open and transparent global trade and investment," promoting "fair and open competition," and creating "a sound business environment." What these guiding principles emphasize is the need to strengthen fair market competition, effective market regulation, the rule of law and actions against financial crimes. This is a striking example of the necessity for countries to abide by the rules of fairness and efficiency when striving for economic and financial development.

(3) The rules for common governance of the international system—cooperation for win-win outcomes. This is also the basic norm governing intergovernmental coordination and cooperation on the international stage. A new type of urbanization, smart city development, and infrastructure investment (primarily focused on energy, transportation, environmental protection, information, and water conservancy) are set to become new engines of economic and financial growth for countries around the world, bringing with them immense benefits in the form of increased capital, job creation, technological revolution, deeper market development, economic sustainability, social welfare betterment,

environmental improvement, national strength enhancement, and so on. Given the differences among countries in terms of development stages, policy designs, implementation structures and institutional arrangements, however, the international community must work toward a kind of intergovernmental coordination and cooperation that enables countries to jointly enhance the global economic and financial governance structure and jointly innovate the modes of financial growth. To put it in another way, cooperation for win-win outcomes must be made the basic principle for global economic and financial governance. A new global economic and financial architecture—one that is innovative, open, interconnected, and inclusive and has at its core the principle of cooperation for win-win outcomes—will be able to continually innovate the modes of growth, thus delivering tangible benefits to countries around the world.

8.4.4 Promoting the International Financial Architecture (Order) as a New Engine of Growth

Promoting the reform, innovation, enhancement, and development of the international financial architecture and orders must be placed on the policy agendas of individual countries around the world, following the establishment of investment and innovation as new growth engines for the global real economy and following the creation of the rules for the security order of the international community, for international financial and economic competition, and for common governance of the international system. There exist in the world two lines of thinking regarding how to reach this desired destination: (1) the reinvent-the-wheel mentality, which seeks to build a new international financial architecture and a new set of international financial orders to replace the old ones; (2) the reform-and-innovation mentality, which seeks to transition from the traditional model of single-center, sprawled development to the innovative model of pluralistically structured, clustered development. It is our view that we should repudiate the "reinvent-the-wheel" mentality when endeavoring to reshape the international financial architecture and orders. Thus, countries all over the world must strive to reform, innovate, enhance, and better the international financial architecture and orders based on existing international financial institutions, financial infrastructure, and financial regulatory coordinators, for the overarching objective of ensuring global financial stability, effective regulation, and risk prevention.

(a) Advancing the conceptual innovation of international finance

A review of the practices and development of international finance shows that conceptual innovation of international finance requires us to at least reemphasize or further clarify three financial concepts.

- Concept one: Financial institutions must work toward servicing the real economy. This is critically important because otherwise, finance would stray away from the real economy and become like "water without a source and a tree without roots," easily susceptible and vulnerable to financial fragility, financial risks, and financial crises.
- Concept two: The international financial architecture should be built and developed in a way that includes the six key building blocks of modern financial systems. This requires countries all over the world to commonly develop not only an international financial market system and organizational system but also an international financial legal system and regulatory system. This also requires countries all over the world to work in concert toward enhancing and perfecting the international financial environment and infrastructure. Any deviation or deficiency in this connection would cause impediments to the improvement and perfection of the international financial architecture and orders.
- Concept Three: The "Big Finance" concept needs to be firmly established. This means that countries around the world must effectively link and integrate their monetary policies with fiscal, exchange-rate, regulatory, and industrial policies to realize policy coordination and interaction. This enables a country to bring their monetary policy tools to bear for achieving desired policy objectives and outcomes. This also enables a country to realize economic and financial stability, coordination, and sustainable development. This "Big Finance" concept should be established as a guide for economic and financial coor-

dination and cooperation on the global scale, because it can benefit the world the same way as it benefits a country.

(b) Advancing the institutional innovation of international finance

The following should be done in relation to monetary and exchange rate systems: (1) Deepening the reform of the SDRs (special drawing rights). The Belgian-American economist Robert Triffin raised three propositions regarding how to develop and improve the international financial system: (a) transforming the International Monetary Fund (IMF) into a real global central bank; (b) converting the financial contributions of IMF members into reserve asset currencies and national currencies for countries all over the world; (c) determining the rights to borrow from the IMF based on a majority voting system. The unsaid but implied message in Prof. Triffin's propositions is that there is a need to break or tackle the dominance of the US dollar in the current international monetary system. Here, let us, for the time being, not venture into a discussion on the feasibility of Prof. Triffin's propositions, but the propositions themselves are thought-provoking for us as we ponder the innovation of the international monetary system. Three possible steps can be taken to innovate the international monetary system: (1) creating conditions for a multiple reserve currency system to emerge by enabling the SDRs to replace the US dollar as the dominant reserve currency basket; (2) adopting a fixed exchange rate for the SDR reserve currencies to stabilize the international monetary system; (3) establishing common SDRs-centered principles to govern the issuance of currencies in the international monetary system. These three steps, which focus on deepening the reform of the SDRs, can objectively drive the reform of the international monetary and exchange rate systems.

(1) Converting temporary swap agreements into standing arrangements. On October 31, 2013, the world's six major central banks—the US Federal Reserve, the European Central Bank, the Swiss National Bank, the Bank of England, the Bank of Canada, and the Bank of Japan—issued a press release to announce that they would convert existing temporary bilateral liquidity swap agreements into long-term standing arrangements. The latest swap arrangements allow any signature bank to provide liquidity in the form of any of the other five major currencies

within its jurisdiction. It is fair to say that this move by the six major central banks has, in essence, pointed to the necessity and urgency of reforming the US dollar-dominated international monetary system. It also reveals the basic framework for the international monetary system going forward: a long-term, multilateral, multi-currency, stable currency swap network between the world's major central banks. This is a question that deserves in-depth reflection in order for us to innovate and develop the international monetary system in the light of the system's actual conditions.

(2) Robert Mundell's "Three Islands of Stability" monetary reform proposition. Robert Mundell—a world-renowned financial economist and the 1999 Nobel Prize winner in economics—put forth four propositions regarding the reform of the international monetary system: (a) The Eurozone should strive not only for financial integration, but also for political integration. (b) The exchange rate between US dollar and euro should be stabilized and fixed between 1:1.2 and 1:1.4. (c) As the yuan (RMB) gradually moves toward free convertibility, it should be incorporated steadfastly into the US dollar-Euro fixed exchange rate regime to create a "supranational currency area"—a trinity of currencies consisting of the US dollar, the euro, and the yuan. This is known as Professor Robert Mundell's "Three Islands of Stability" hypothesis. (d) A world currency standard should be created to replace the dollar standard. Prof. Mundell called this world currency standard "INTOR," a name he coined by combining a contraction of "international" with the French word for gold, "OR". An analysis of Prof. Mundell's "Three Islands of Stability" hypothesis reveals that INTOR does not mean a uniformly issued world currency, but rather a multi-currency stable mechanism or, in other words, an alliance of currencies. Prof. Mundell envisioned INTOR to be a "world currency" standard that would encompass the US dollar, the euro, and the yuan at a fixed exchange rate and would be tied to gold, with other currencies allowed to float against it. Based on Robert Mundell's "Three Islands of Stability" hypothesis, it is reasonable to propose establishing a new, multipolar international monetary system that consists of multiple reserve currencies. Such a system is conducive to maintaining the stable operation of the international financial architecture.

Hereby, reform and innovation of the international financial regulatory system mean the following: anchoring the international financial regulatory system on the basis of stable financial development, effective financial regulation, and effectual prevention and diffusion of financial risks and crises through (1) strict separation of functional regulation and behavioral regulation and (2) effective combination of macro-prudential regulation with micro-prudential regulation in international finance. Functional financial regulation means regulation on matters in connection with "indirect financing" in banking and insurance sectors. Behavioral financial regulation means regulation on matters with respect to "direct financing" in securities and capital markets and by investment banks. Macro-prudential regulation means that after setting nominal anchors for monetary policy—which are basic norms by which central banks abide in their determination of monetary policy goals (i.e., to control the overall supply of money, to control inflation or deflation, to control exchange rate fluctuations, etc.)—central banks adopt a series of measures—different from those adopted by banking or insurance regulators—to analyze, address and diffuse a variety of financial risks including macro financial risks, asset risks, overall credit risks, and systemic risks. In contrast, micro-prudential regulation seeks to enhance the safety and soundness of individual financial institutions by analyzing, supervising, and monitoring their capital adequacy, liquidity, and NPL (non-performing loan) ratios. Thus, every country can improve the effectiveness of its financial regulation by effectively combining macro-prudential regulation with micro-prudential regulation. As elaborately illustrated in Chap. 2 of this book, the combination of macro- and micro-prudential regulation is conducive to the reform, innovation, and healthy development of the international financial regulatory system.

Based on the analysis conducted in this chapter, the reform and innovation of international financial standards should be focused on unifying and improving the international standards with respect to financial infrastructures, financial disclosure and assessment, and financial laws and regulations—no further elaboration will be made here. The objective in this connection is to enable international financial rules and standards to become new engines of growth and play a positive role in global financial architecture governance. It is fair to say that reform and innovation of international financial standards is one of the three critical points of departure for innovating the international financial architecture, with the other two being reform and innovation of international monetary and exchange-rate systems and of international financial regulatory systems. Institutional reform and innovation in these three areas will serve as a driver for future reform and development of the international financial architecture.

(c) Advancing the organizational innovation of international finance

First, it is imperative to facilitate the rise of multilateral international financial institutions. Striking examples of efforts in this direction are the Asian Infrastructure Investment Bank (AIIB) and the New Development Bank (NDB), both created in 2015. Most of the existing international financial institutional systems are products of the post-World War II era, primarily designed for unilateral purposes and thus unable to meet the needs of emerging economic and financial powers.

Second, it is imperative to enhance the legally binding powers of the "Big Three" international financial regulators. As elaborated in prior texts, documents, and papers issued by the world's three major financial regulators—most notably the *Core Principles for Effective Banking Supervision* by the BCBS, the *Objectives and Principles for Securities Regulation* by the IOSCO, the *Insurance Core Principles (ICPs)* by the IAIS—have played a positive role respectively in their targeted financial sectors. The BCBS, the IOSCO, the IAIS, and their likes—which advance cooperation among members through "gentlemen's agreements"—are well-positioned to play bigger roles in promoting financial stability and coordination and preventing the occurrence and spread of financial risks and crises, provided that they are given legally binding powers or that the legally binding powers they possess are strengthened.

Third, it is imperative to enable the G20's Financial Stability Board (FSB) to play a better, bigger role in coordinating international financial regulation. What follows is a Graph 8.1 that indicates how major international financial regulatory bodies coordinate and cooperate with one another.

Three observations can be made by looking at the graph:

8 Innovation and Improvement of the International Financial...

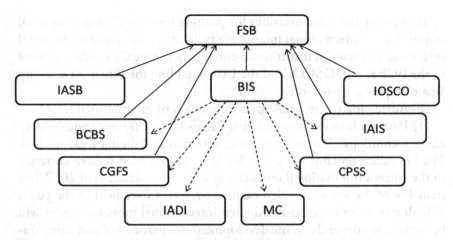

Graph 8.1 The relations among the Financial Stability Board (FSB), the Bank for International Settlement (BIS), and international financial standard-making bodies. FSB: The Financial Stability Board; BIS: The Bank for International Settlement; IASB: The International Accounting Standards Board; BCBS: The Basel Committee on Banking Supervision; CGFS: The Committee on the Global Financial System; IADI: The International Association of Deposit Insurers; MC: Market Commissions; CPSS: The Committee on Payment and Settlement Systems; IAIS: The International Association of Insurance Supervisors; IOSCO: The International Organization of Securities Commissions

- The G20's FSB is underpinned by a number of national financial authorities and central banks.
- The G20's FSB is at the core of the organizational structure of the international financial regulatory system.
- The G20's FSB is an international financial regulator that has legally binding powers—derived from international laws—on its member countries.

The G20's FSB will be able to play a bigger role in promoting the sound and steady development of the international financial architecture, so long as it remains committed to reform and innovation and never relents in its efforts to enhance its institutional mechanisms and law enforcement capabilities and perfect international financial regulatory rules and standards.

To sum up, the three measures for pushing forward the organizational innovation of international finance are facilitating the rise of multilateral international financial institutions; enhancing the legally binding powers of the BCBS, the IOSCO, and the IAIS; enabling the Financial Stability Board to play a bigger role.

(d) Advancing the technological innovation of international finance

(1) Pushing forward innovation in "artificial intelligence" and "blockchain technology" for the creation of international digital legal tenders. The US dollar remains the unchallenged, predominant reserve currency in the current international monetary system. In contrast, as of 2017, less than 1% of the world's foreign exchange reserves were held in the yuan. Whether or not the dollar-dominated international monetary order will be overturned depends on the development orientations of and comparative positions among the US dollar, the euro, and the yuan. Three possibilities may arise in this connection: (a) the emergence of a supranational single currency; (b) the evolution of the SDRs (special drawing rights) into a world currency; (c) the rise of a new globally accepted digital currency as a supranational currency. The odds for the first possibility to become a reality border on impossible, given the absence of a "world government" in real life to make it happen. As regards the second possibility, the likelihood is very slim for it to be actualized, because once becoming a world currency, the SDRs will diminish the interests of monetary sovereign states on the world stage. Then we are left with the third possibility—creating a world digital legal tender by harnessing and combining the wonder of "AI" and "blockchain technology." It is possible for a world digital legal tender to topple the dollar-dominated international monetary order, provided that relevant technologies are developed to maturity and that central banks around the world make continuous efforts to promote the operation of digital legal tenders. It is also possible for the existing international monetary system to be turned on its head by the emergence, spread, and expansion of mutually competing cryptocurrencies, as best represented by Bitcoin. Thus, when it comes to breaking the dominance of the US dollar in the international monetary system, a plausible option is to enable the creation of a world digital legal tender by advancing the technological innovation of international finance.

(2) Perfecting international payment and clearing systems (on-exchange trading). This has two layers of meaning. Firstly, the technologies that underpin the international payment and clearing systems undergo constant transformation, innovation, and improvement at both intrastate and interstate levels, thus growing in speed, convenience, and effectiveness and becoming more standardized, regulated, and stable. Secondly, mobile money services are rising around the world, exhibiting ever-expanding penetration and ever-diminishing differences across borders with each passing day. As one of the electronic forms of digital legal tenders, mobile money allows people to receive, store, and spend money outside the traditional banking system by use of nothing more than a mobile phone. Financial payment innovations like this that harness the power of information and communication technologies and transcend banks' physical networks, should they develop in certain depth, breadth, scale, and complexity, will likely constitute a challenge to the payment and clearing systems of countries around the world. This calls for more support for and enhancement of on-exchange payment and clearing systems.

(3) Establishing OTC international central counterparties and transaction registers. This project requires not only the achievement of transaction reporting and central clearing of international financial derivatives transactions, but also the improvement of mechanisms relating to data storage, processing, and monitoring. It also encompasses the establishment, development, and strengthening of OTC infrastructures and relevant rules and regulations.

To sum up, the three measures for pushing forward the technological innovation of international finance are pushing forward innovation in "artificial intelligence" and "blockchain technology" for the creation of international digital legal tenders, perfecting international on-exchange payment and clearing systems (on-exchange trading), and establishing OTC international central counterparties and transaction registers.

Some people once made the proposition of creating a world financial organization to facilitate international coordination and cooperation with respect to the reform and innovation of international financial systems and orders and ultimately to realize a long-term, multilateral, multi-currency, and stable international financial architecture, on the grounds that there is WTO for international coordination and cooperation in trade and the World Health Organization for international coordination and cooperation in health issues. Let us not, for the time being, delve into a debate over the feasibility of this proposition. One thing is for sure, however, the modern international financial architecture and orders will become more stable, sound, and full-fledged as long as countries around the world—China included—remain unswerving in their commitment to pushing forward the conceptual, institutional, organizational, and technological innovation of international finance and steering financial institutions toward servicing the real economy.

References

Chen, Yunxian et al. *Studies on Capital Regulation in the Securities Industry*[M]. Beijing: China Financial Publishing House. 2011.
Chen, Yunxian et al. *Studies on Risk Management and Economic Capital Measurement of Securities Companies*[M]. Beijing: China Financial Publishing House. 2013.
Chen, Yunxian et al. *The Theory on Risks and Returns Matching and Operation for Investment Banking*[M]. Beijing: China Financial Publishing House. 2012.
Chen, Yunxian, Gu, Wenjing. *Messoeconomics*[M]. American Academic Press. 2018.
Chen, Yunxian, Gu, Wenjing. *Regional Government Competition*[M]. Oxford: Routledge. 2019.
Chen, Yunxian, Qiu, Jianwei. *Government Foresighted Leading*[M]. Oxford: Routledge. 2017.
Chen, Yunxian. City Management—Managing Cities as a Resource[J]. *Foshan Daily*. April 2004.
Chen, Yunxian. *Evolution of Financial Crisis Management and Regulation in the U.S.* [M]. Beijing: China Financial Publishing House. 2013a.
Chen, Yunxian. *Explorations in Chinese Financial Reform and Development*[M]. Beijing: China Financial Publishing House. 2017.
Chen, Yunxian. *Explorations in Fiscal and Financial Theories and Practices*[M]. Beijing: China Financial Publishing House. 1999.

Chen, Yunxian. *Exploratory Studies in the U.S. Financial System*[M]. Beijing: China Financial Publishing House. 2001a.
Chen, Yunxian. *Foresighted Leading*[M]. Germany: Springer. 2013b.
Chen, Yunxian. *The Theory on Investment Banking*[M]. Beijing: Peking University Press. 1995.
Chen, Yunxian. *The Theory on Response to Risks and Return*[M]. Beijing: Peking University Press. 1998.
Chen, Yunxian. The Theory on Risks and Returns: The Core of Investment Banking Management [J]. *Securities Market Herald*. April 2001b.
Chen, Yunxian. *The Theory on Securities Investment*[M]. Beijing: Peking University Press. 1991.
Chernow, Ron. *Alexander Hamilton*[M]. Penguin Books. 2005.
Grimsey, Darrin et al. *PPP Revolution*[M], translated by Jumbo Consulting. Beijing: China Renmin University Press. 2016.
Gu, Yan. Bitcoin Blackmailing Virus Coming [J]. *China Strategic Emerging Industry* (Volume 21). 2017: 91–91
Huang, Da. *Finance*[M]. Beijing: China Renmin University Press. 2013.
Keynes, John M. *The Economic Consequences of the Peace*[M], translated by Zhang Jun and Jia Xiaoyi. Huaxia Publishing House. 2008.
Keynes, John M. *The General Theory of Employment, Interest, and Money*[M], translated by Lu Menglong. China Social Science Press. 2009.
Kindleberger, Charles P. *Manias, Panics, and Crashes: A History of Financial Crises* (2007) Wiley: Palgrave Macmillan
Legal Affairs Department. *Law of the People's Republic of China on Commercial Banks* (1995). People's Bank of China. (2003). Beijing: Law Press
Li, Yining, Lin, Yifu, Zheng, Yongnian et al. *Understanding "Belt and Road"* [M]. Beijing: CITIC Press Group. 2017.
Ma, Mei, Zhu, Xiaoming, Zhou, Jinhuang. Payment Revolution: Third Party Payment of the Internet Age [J]. *China Science and Technology Information* (Issue z1). 2014: 178–178.
Marx, Karl. *Capital*[M]. Translated by the Central Compilation and Translation Bureau. People's Publishing House. 2004.
Smith, Adam. *An Inquiry into the Nature and Causes of the Wealth of Nations*[M], translated by Guo Dali and Wang Yanan. The Commercial Press. 1972.
Smith, Adam. *The Theory of Moral Sentiments*[M], translated by Fan Bing. Shanxi Economic Publishing House. 2010.
U.S. Department of the Treasury. Blueprint for a Modern Financial Regulatory Structure (2008).

Wang, Xin, Guo, Dongsheng. Indian note-banning movement creates a "cashless society": Impacts of Note Banning in India and its Inspirations [J]. *China Finance* (Issue 2). 2018:79–80.

Xi, Jinping. Some Opinions on Serving the Real Economy, Preventing and Controlling Financial Risks, and Deepening Financial Reform. National Financial Work Conference. Beijing, July 2017

Zhang, Lusheng. Sweden to become the first cashless country. [J]. *Grand Garden of Science*. 2015 (5): 6–7